Learn AWS Serverless Computing

A beginner's guide to using AWS Lambda, Amazon API
Gateway, and services from Amazon Web Services

Scott Patterson

BIRMINGHAM - MUMBAI

Learn AWS Serverless Computing

Commissioning Editor: Vijin Boricha
Acquisition Editor: Meeta Rajani
Content Development Editor: Alokita Amanna
Senior Editor: Rahul Dsouza
Technical Editor: Dinesh Pawar
Copy Editor: Safis Editing
Project Coordinator: Anish Daniel
Proofreader: Safis Editing
Indexer: Tejal Daruwale Soni
Production Designer: Arvindkumar Gupta

First published: December 2019

Production reference: 1231219

Published by Packt Publishing Ltd.
Livery Place
35 Livery Street
Birmingham
B3 2PB, UK.

ISBN 978-1-78995-835-5

www.packt.com

Packt.com

Subscribe to our online digital library for full access to over 7,000 books and videos, as well as industry leading tools to help you plan your personal development and advance your career. For more information, please visit our website.

Why subscribe?

- Spend less time learning and more time coding with practical eBooks and Videos from over 4,000 industry professionals

- Improve your learning with Skill Plans built especially for you

- Get a free eBook or video every month

- Fully searchable for easy access to vital information

- Copy and paste, print, and bookmark content

Did you know that Packt offers eBook versions of every book published, with PDF and ePub files available? You can upgrade to the eBook version at www.packt.com and as a print book customer, you are entitled to a discount on the eBook copy. Get in touch with us at customercare@packtpub.com for more details.

At www.packt.com, you can also read a collection of free technical articles, sign up for a range of free newsletters, and receive exclusive discounts and offers on Packt books and eBooks.

Contributors

About the author

Scott Patterson is a cloud architecture lead, a product owner, and a proud technology geek. With a healthy obsession of all things AWS, Scott gets most excited about the things you can build with serverless patterns and modern cloud-native architectures. He has empowered many organizations to rethink, rearchitect, and accelerate the release of their products by using these very patterns.

Scott is also a huge advocate for AWS within the developer community, being a co-founder of the AWS User Group in Wellington he runs events and conferences throughout New Zealand.

Outside of work, Scott lives a high-adrenaline life where he enjoys paragliding from mountains, building cars, and racing motorcycles.

I would like to thank the people who have encouraged and supported me, especially my friends for being so understanding!

Also, a big thank you to Simon Coward and Will Scalioni for your expertise and guidance on event-driven applications and data processing.

About the reviewers

Sebastian Krueger serves as the cloud engineering leader for Deloitte New Zealand. Sebastian brings a proven track record in leading the delivery of advanced AWS solutions. As a leader and technologist, he enjoys building high-performing teams that deliver outstanding client results, with a focus on cloud solutions, supported by all nine AWS certifications. Prior to joining Deloitte New Zealand as a partner, Sebastian was the executive director and cofounder of API Talent. In March 2018, API Talent was acquired by Deloitte New Zealand. He is also an inaugural member of the Global AWS APN Ambassador program.

Mike Lewis currently works in the Cloud Enablement practice at Slalom Consulting in Atlanta, Georgia, specializing in AWS and DevSecOps. A computer science major and a U.S. naval submarine veteran with over 25 years' experience in the computer industry, he has been at the forefront of emerging technologies, from the boom of the internet to the latest trends in serverless and cloud computing. He and his wife Julie reside in Georgia with their three wonderful children.

Packt is searching for authors like you

If you're interested in becoming an author for Packt, please visit authors.packtpub.com and apply today. We have worked with thousands of developers and tech professionals, just like you, to help them share their insight with the global tech community. You can make a general application, apply for a specific hot topic that we are recruiting an author for, or submit your own idea.

Table of Contents

Preface   1

Section 1: Why We're Here

Chapter 1: The Evolution of Compute   7
  Understanding enterprise data centers   8
    The physical data center   8
    Colocating our gear   9
    Cloud born   9
  Exploring the units of compute   10
    Physical servers – scale at the physical server layer   10
    Virtual machines – density efficiencies achieved by virtualizing the hardware   11
    Containers – better density with faster start times   12
    Functions – best density by abstracting the runtime   13
  Understanding software architectures   15
    Monolith – single code base   16
    N-tier – achieve individual scale   17
    Microservices – do one thing and do it well   18
    Nanoservices with serverless   19
  Predicting what comes next   22
  Summary   22
  Questions   23
  Further reading   24

Chapter 2: Event-Driven Applications   25
  Understanding modern applications   25
    Event-command   26
    Event-driven or event-first   27
  Evolution of integration patterns   30
    Enterprise Application Integration   30
    ESB   31
    Serverless integration   33
  Automation with serverless   35
    Scripts on a server   35
    Configuration management   36
    Automation as a Service   36
  Summary   37
  Questions   38
  Further reading   39

Section 2: Getting Started with AWS Lambda Functions

Chapter 3: The Foundations of a Function in AWS   43
  Technical requirements   44
  Learning about AWS Lambda   44
    Fundamentals of a function   44
      Invoking a function   45
      Pricing model   46
      Ephemeral state   46
      High availability   47
      Service limits   47
    Use cases   47
  Setting up security   48
    Execution policies   49
    Function policies   51
  Invoking Lambda functions   52
    Invocation types   52
    Event sources   55
    Execution environment   56
    Environment variables   56
  Anatomy of a Lambda function   58
    Handler function   58
    Event, content, and context objects   59
  The programming model   61
    Runtimes   61
    Writing, building, and packaging   62
    Deployment   66
    Testing, monitoring, and debugging   70
  Writing your first Lambda function   76
    Hello, world! in the console   76
    Hello, world! using the command line   81
  Summary   83
  Questions   84
  Further reading   85

Chapter 4: Adding Amazon API Gateway   87
  Technical requirements   87
  Introducing Amazon API Gateway   88
    Serverless APIs   88
    Deployment options   92
    WebSockets   93
    Use cases   95
  Securing an API   98
    IAM permissions and policies   98

Authentication with Cognito   99
Lambda authorizers   103
Certificates   105
Building, deploying, and managing APIs   107
Building APIs   107
Deploying APIs   111
Throttling and quota management   114
Monitoring and logging   115
Building a Lambda-backed API   117
Hello world using the console   118
Hello world via the CLI   125
Summary   128
Questions   128
Further reading   129

Chapter 5: Leveraging AWS Services   131
Technical requirements   132
Using Amazon S3 with Lambda   132
Revision   132
S3 as an event source   133
Interacting using the SDK   136
Using Amazon DynamoDB with Lambda   138
The basics   138
Triggering a Lambda function   140
Interacting using the SDK   144
Using AWS Step Functions as an Orchestrator   147
State machines with Lambda   148
Integrating with other services   151
Step Functions Local   152
Summary   153
Questions   153
Further reading   154

Chapter 6: Going Deeper with Lambda   155
Technical requirements   155
Bringing your own runtime to Lambda   156
Runtime API and bootstrapping   156
Putting it all together   158
Enabling code reuse through layers   160
Understanding Lambda layers   161
Using a Lambda layer   163
Sharing a Lambda layer across multiple AWS accounts   167
Use cases for Lambda layers   168
Operationalizing   168
Using environment variables   168

Secrets management 170
Concurrency and error handling 172
Observability 174
Development practices 177
Structuring a function 178
Handler function 179
Controller 179
Service 180
Reuse and optimization 180
Using the ecosystem 183
Summary 184
Questions 184
Further reading 185

Section 3: Development Patterns

Chapter 7: Serverless Framework 189
Technical requirements 189
Understanding the need for a framework 189
Developer focus 190
Managing a serverless project 193
Exploring the core concepts of the Serverless Framework 193
Services 194
Functions 195
Events 195
Resources and plugins 197
Layers 198
Deploying your first service 199
Installation and the CLI 199
Hello World API in 5 minutes 202
Understanding the deployment 205
The dashboard 207
Serverless offline (run it locally) 210
Testing and debugging 214
Unit testing lambda functions 214
Integration testing 217
Logging and monitoring 219
Summary 220
Questions 220
Further reading 221

Chapter 8: CI/CD with the Serverless Framework 223
Technical requirements 223
Using serverless development pipelines 224
Patterns 224
Continuous integration 225

Continuous delivery   225
Continuous deployment   226
Using serverless stages   228
Understanding deployment patterns   229
Deploying all at once   229
Blue/green environment switching   230
Canary or traffic shifting   232
Introducing AWS services   233
AWS CodePipeline   234
AWS CodeBuild   234
AWS CodeCommit   236
Building a pipeline   237
Creating the pipeline in production   237
A pipeline that deploys itself   247
Summary   250
Questions   250
Further reading   252

Section 4: Architectures and Use Cases

Chapter 9: Data Processing   255
Technical requirements   256
Getting across the processing types   256
Batch   256
Micro-batch   257
Streaming   257
Building a batch data processing workload   258
Where do I start?   258
The ETL blueprint   259
Data storage using S3   260
Data cataloging – Glue   261
Custom classifiers   261
Databases   264
Crawlers   266
Data transformation – Glue   272
Creating a Glue job   273
Running a Glue job   282
Data analytics and transformation   284
Querying data in S3 with Athena   285
Summary   289
Questions   289
Further reading   291

Chapter 10: AWS Automation   293
Technical requirements   293
Embedded security   293

Enforcement via tagging   294
Automatic detection and remediation with AWS Config   297
Implementing continuous compliance   298
Running scheduled tasks   302
Replacing server-based local schedulers   302
Auditing and reporting   305
Summary   307
Questions   307
Further reading   308

Chapter 11: Creating Chatbots   309
Technical requirements   309
Building a chatbot with Amazon Lex   310
Understanding the language model   310
Intents   310
Utterances   311
Slots   311
Prompts   312
Fulfillment   313
Building and testing your bot   316
Building a Slackbot using Serverless Framework   321
Understanding the architecture   322
Deploying a Slackbot   323
Registering a new Slack app   323
Crafting the bot's brain   325
Connecting our bot to Slack   326
Summary   330
Questions   330
Further reading   331

Chapter 12: Hosting Single-Page Web Applications   333
Technical requirements   333
Understanding serverless SPAs on AWS   334
The architecture   334
The components   336
Amazon S3   337
Amazon CloudFront   338
Backend services   339
Building SPAs with Serverless Framework   340
Summary   341
Questions   341
Further reading   342

Chapter 13: GraphQL APIs   343
Technical requirements   343
Introduction to GraphQL   344

Core concepts   344
Building GraphQL APIs   347
Lambda-backed endpoint   347
Using an AWS-managed service   348
Summary   350
Questions   351
Further reading   352
Appendix A: Assessment   353
Chapter 1: The Evolution of Compute   353
Chapter 2: Event-Driven Applications   353
Chapter 3: The Foundations of a Function in AWS   353
Chapter 4: Adding Amazon API Gateway   354
Chapter 5: Leveraging AWS Services   354
Chapter 6: Going Deeper with Lambda   354
Chapter 7: Serverless Framework   354
Chapter 8: CI/CD with the Serverless Framework   355
Chapter 9: Data Processing   355
Chapter 10: AWS Automation   355
Chapter 11: Creating Chatbots   356
Chapter 12: Hosting Single-Page Web Applications   356
Chapter 13: GraphQL APIs   356
Other Books You May Enjoy   357
Index   361

Preface

Serverless technology is the latest paradigm in cloud computing that enables builders to create applications that are highly scalable, performant, and cost effective without having to manage or maintain servers.

This book will start with the history of how serverless technologies have become popular, and focus in on event-driven applications using AWS Lambda. You will step through combining Lambda with Amazon API Gateway, Amazon DynamoDB, and other popular services from Amazon Web Services. Moving on, this guide will show you how to write, run, and test Lambda functions using examples in Node.js, Java, Python, and C#. Next, you will develop and deploy AWS Lambda functions efficiently within the Serverless Framework in keeping with DevOps practices. Lastly, you will gain some tips and best practices in terms of leveraging serverless services so as to implement new architecture patterns and use cases.

By the end of this book, you will be well versed in building, securing, and running applications and APIs without managing any servers.

Who this book is for

This book is for cloud solution architects and developers who want to build scalable systems and deploy serverless applications in AWS. Some basic understanding or experience of building solutions in AWS is required to derive the most benefit from the examples.

What this book covers

Chapter 1, *The Evolution of Compute*, explores the drivers and benefits behind moving from deploying hardware in physical data centers to scalable services in the cloud. At a high level, we cover the progression of hardware, compute, and software architectures.

Chapter 2, *Event-Driven Applications*, introduces the event-first mindset used to establish modern integration patterns. This chapter also highlights some of the challenges faced, including scale, distributed transactions, and failures.

Chapter 3, *The Foundations of a Function in AWS*, covers the core foundations of a Lambda function, including security constructs and the programming model. You then break down a function to understand its anatomy before following an example to build and deploy your first function.

Chapter 4, *Adding Amazon API Gateway*, introduces an API management solution that is used to build more control and governance in connection with developing and publishing RESTful APIs. You will need to understand the concepts and then create your own API backed by a Lambda function.

Chapter 5, *Leveraging AWS Services*, explores how to use other AWS services as event sources for AWS Lambda, and then how to use the SDK to interact with the services during a function execution. Services covered include Amazon S3, Amazon DynamoDB, and AWS Step Functions.

Chapter 6, *Going Deeper with Lambda*, unlocks the more advanced areas of AWS Lambda to make best use of resources. You will learn how to structure a function for maximum code reuse, thereby making development and executions more efficient.

Chapter 7, *Serverless Framework*, introduces an application framework focused on providing the best developer experience available. You will cover the core concepts and start building and deploying your first service using the framework.

Chapter 8, *CI/CD with the Serverless Framework*, adds good development practices to Serverless Framework workflows by teaching you about the patterns and AWS services involved with continuous integration and continuous deployment.

Chapter 9, *Data Processing*, covers the different types of data processing and then dives into a real-world example using serverless AWS services.

Chapter 10, *AWS Automation*, explores some of the operational and security tasks involved with AWS ecosystems, including an introduction to continuous compliance and resource tagging.

Chapter 11, *Creating Chatbots*, explores how to create a chatbot with native AWS services, and then covers how to wrap a different type of chatbot into a project in the Serverless Framework.

Chapter 12, *Hosting Single-Page Web Applications*, walks through the steps involved in hosting a single-page web application on AWS using multiple services.

Chapter 13, *GraphQL APIs*, explains how GraphQL APIs are a relatively new way of building and querying APIs, and that they map particularly well to the serverless model. This chapter introduces the concepts of GraphQL APIs and what GraphQL APIs are used for, before going through some details on how to create GraphQL components, first with Lambda, and then using AWS AppSync.

To get the most out of this book

To get the most out of this book, you should have experience using AWS; knowledge of public cloud architecture patterns; an understanding of Infrastructure as a Service, Platform as a Service, and Software as a Service; experience of developing using a common development language such as Node.js or Python; and you should also have your own AWS account to follow along with the examples.

Download the color images

We also provide a PDF file that has color images of the screenshots/diagrams used in this book. You can download it here: http://www.packtpub.com/sites/default/files/downloads/9781789958355_ColorImages.pdf

Conventions used

There are a number of text conventions used throughout this book.

CodeInText: Indicates code words in text, database table names, folder names, filenames, file extensions, pathnames, dummy URLs, user input, and Twitter handles. Here is an example: "Save that file as message_vendor.py, in a folder called python."

A block of code is set as follows:

```
def hello_handler(event, context):
    if not event:
        return {
            "body": "Hello, world!"
        }
```

Any command-line input or output is written as follows:

```
docker pull amazonlinux
docker run -it -v ~/Desktop/lolcode-lambda:/root amazonlinux /bin/bash
```

Bold: Indicates a new term, an important word, or words that you see on screen. For example, words in menus or dialog boxes appear in the text like this. Here is an example: "Let's click on **Integration Request** and see what's available."

 Warnings or important notes appear like this.

 Tips and tricks appear like this.

Get in touch

Feedback from our readers is always welcome.

General feedback: If you have questions about any aspect of this book, mention the book title in the subject of your message and email us at customercare@packtpub.com.

Errata: Although we have taken every care to ensure the accuracy of our content, mistakes do happen. If you have found a mistake in this book, we would be grateful if you would report this to us. Please visit www.packtpub.com/support/errata, selecting your book, clicking on the Errata Submission Form link, and entering the details.

Piracy: If you come across any illegal copies of our works in any form on the internet, we would be grateful if you would provide us with the location address or website name. Please contact us at copyright@packt.com with a link to the material.

If you are interested in becoming an author: If there is a topic that you have expertise in, and you are interested in either writing or contributing to a book, please visit authors.packtpub.com.

Reviews

Please leave a review. Once you have read and used this book, why not leave a review on the site that you purchased it from? Potential readers can then see and use your unbiased opinion to make purchase decisions, we at Packt can understand what you think about our products, and our authors can see your feedback on their book. Thank you!

For more information about Packt, please visit packt.com.

Section 1: Why We're Here

The objective of *Section 1* is to give context to where Functions as a Service (FaaS) resides in the compute abstraction spectrum and introduce AWS Lambda.

This section comprises the following chapters:

- Chapter 1, *The Evolution of Compute*
- Chapter 2, *Event-Driven Applications*

The Evolution of Compute
1

You're here to learn a new skill, to expand your understanding of new ways of compute, and to follow along with the examples in this book to gain practical experience. Before we begin, it would be helpful to know a bit of the history and context behind why serverless exists. This chapter will explain the progression of thinking from the humble data center through to the new goalposts of serverless.

We'll learn how the placement of physical hardware has evolved from the perspective of the infrastructure engineer and developer, and how the different stages have allowed us to achieve new layers of compute abstraction. The evolution of these factors has also driven new ways of structuring software, and we will explore some of the reasons behind this.

The following topics will be covered in this chapter:

- Understanding enterprise data centers
- Exploring the units of compute
- Understanding software architectures
- Predicting what comes next

We will delve in these topics one by one and learn how each aspect functions.

Understanding enterprise data centers

How we view a data center has changed with the introduction of new technologies and software development methods. We will begin with a recap of the characteristics of a fully self-managed data center and go on to explain how our views have changed over time:

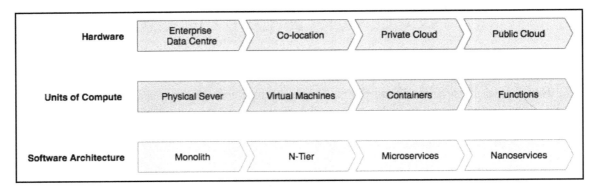

Evolutionary changes in hardware, compute, and software architectures

It's worth noting that, in all the examples in this book, there is still an underlying data center that has to be managed, but now we're talking about shifting that responsibility of management. In the preceding diagram, each stream of evolution is not tightly linked. For example, monoliths can still be run on private or public clouds. In this section, we will cover the evolution of hardware over time and focus in on the following topics:

- The physical data center
- Colocating our gear
- Cloud born

The physical data center

Your typical data center consists of a room with some metal racks arranged into rows with corridors between the rows. Each rack is filled with servers, networking gear, and maybe storage. The room must be kept at a consistent temperature and humidity to maintain the efficiency and reliability of the hardware components within the servers and other pieces of kit. The machines and equipment in the room also need power to run—lots of power.

Often three phases of power are needed to power back up batteries (in an uninterruptible power supply) in case of a brief power interruption, and then one or more backup power generators are used in the event of sustained mains power loss.

All of these components that make up a data center require special technical engineers to install and maintain them. All of these components also have dependencies for installing the application that runs the business code.

Once the servers are racked and plumbed into power and networking, you still need to install and configure them, as well as the operating system and the latest patches. The administration and maintenance of these things doesn't stop once the application is deployed either, so this would require dedicated operations staff.

Wouldn't it be good if we didn't have to be concerned about challenges such as finding available thermal space or adding redundant power sources? The drive to gain efficiencies in the way we do business has led to the emergence of new models, such as the next one.

Colocating our gear

Thankfully, if we already have our own servers that we need to run, we can use what's called a colocated space. This is when an organization running a data center has spare space (space meaning rack space, thermal space, power space, and networking space) and will rent it to you for a fee. You still maintain total control over your own server hardware.

The good thing about renting space in a data center is that we can reduce the number of specialist engineers that are needed to manage the hosting. We still need hardware and storage engineers, but we don't have to worry about making sure the air conditioning is operational, keeping track of the leasing and maintenance contracts, or depreciating the non-server assets over a given period of time.

Colocating can also go a step further where, instead of providing your own servers, you can rent the actual bare metal as well. This can save the burden on the finance team that's related to tracking IT assets.

Cloud born

Most consumers of server resources are not in the business of building data centers and aren't looking to scale the business or create this capability. They are concerned about building their application into a product that has business value. This group of builders needs a system that abstracts the details of the physical hardware and insulates the consumer from the failure of that hardware. They can't wait around to procure more hardware to scale if their product suddenly becomes popular.

A lot of these drivers (and there are plenty of others) are the reason that the cloud as we know it today was conceptualized.

Exploring the units of compute

In the previous section, we were reminded of the progression of building data centers to consuming cloud resources. We can also relate this shift to how we provision, deploy, and scale our compute resources. Let's have a look at how our thinking has moved from deploying physical servers to scaling our applications and to scaling at an application function level:

- **Physical servers**: Scale at the physical server layer
- **Virtual machines**: Density efficiencies achieved by virtualizing the hardware
- **Containers**: Better density with faster start times
- **Functions**: Best density by abstracting the runtime

Physical servers – scale at the physical server layer

When designing for scale in a physical server world, we needed to predict when our peak load may exceed our current capacity. This is the point at which one or more of our servers are fully utilized and become a bottleneck for the application or service. If we had enough foresight, we could order a new server kit and get it racked and bring it into service before it's needed. Unfortunately, this isn't how internet-scale works.

The lead time and work behind getting that new gear into service could include the following processes:

- Securing a capital expenditure budget from finance or the **Project Management Office (PMO)**
- Procuring hardware from a vendor
- Capacity planning to confirm that there is space for the new hardware
- Updates to the colocation agreement with the hosting provider
- Scheduling engineers to travel to the site
- Licensing considerations for new software being installed

The unit of scale here is an entire server, and, as you can see from the preceding list, there is a considerable list of work ahead of you before you make the decision to scale. Compounding this problem is the fact that once you have scaled, there's no scaling back. The new hardware will live in service for years and now your baseline operational costs have increased for the duration.

Virtual machines – density efficiencies achieved by virtualizing the hardware

The drawback of scaling by physical nodes is that we always have to spec out the gear for a peak load. This means that, during low load times, the server isn't doing a lot of work and we have spare capacity.

If we could run more workloads on this single server, we could achieve more efficient use of the hardware. This is what we mean when we talk about density – the number of workloads that we can cram into a server, virtual machine, or operating system. Here we introduce the hypervisor. A hypervisor is a layer of software that abstracts the server's operating system and applications from the underlying hardware.

By running a hypervisor on the host server, we can share hardware resources between more than one virtual operating system running simultaneously on the host. We call these guest machines or, more commonly, **virtual machines** (**VMs**). Each VM can operate independently from the other, allowing multiple tenants to use the same physical host.

The following is a diagram showing how the layers can be visualized. A hypervisor sits between the host operating system and the virtual machines and allows a layer of translation so that the guest operating systems can communicate with the underlying hardware:

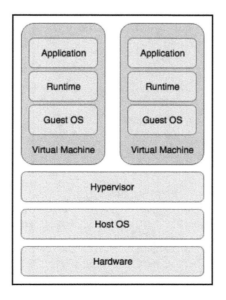

Multiple virtual machines running on an abstracted hardware layer (IaaS)

Now, our unit of scale is the virtual machine. Virtual machines are configured and deployed in minutes using the hypervisor management software or through the APIs that are provided. The life cycle of a VM is typically weeks or months, though it can sometimes be years.

When we add virtual machines to a physical server, we also have to take into consideration that the underlying CPU and memory resources are finite.

With virtual machines, we still have to run and maintain entire operating systems. The next evolution of compute utilizes the hardware more efficiently.

Containers – better density with faster start times

Of course, a virtual machine can still sit under-utilized or even idle when the demand is low. If you've ever worked in a role managing a fleet of servers, you would have noticed the dramatic under-utilization of compute during low demand periods. Ideally, we don't want the overhead of deploying and configuring a full operating system every time we need to run a workload.

To achieve this, we can make use of containerization technologies such as Docker. Docker allows applications running on an operating system to be isolated from each other by running inside a container. Each container holds only the application and associated dependencies (binaries and libraries):

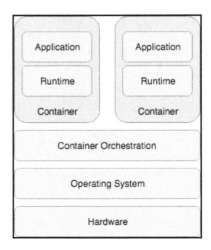

Containers sharing an operating system, orchestrated by a control plane (PaaS)

For every operating system running on a physical server, we can run many container workloads in that same OS. Containers are more efficient to run, partly because they share the resources of a single operating system. Because each container doesn't have to run its own full operating system environment, you can achieve a better density of containers over virtual machines. This means we can make better use of the hardware resources that are available.

 By using containers to isolate workloads, we can increase the density of the workloads running in an operating system by factors into the tens or even hundreds.

It may take minutes to deploy and configure a VM, but it takes seconds to initialize a container. This makes it much more efficient to be able to add capacity during a scale event, which is done by spinning up more containers. It also means you can achieve better granularity of scale, so you're not deploying more capacity than you need at the time. Our unit of scale here is down to the application level. Typically, the life cycle of a container runs for minutes or hours. A request or system may only use part of an application to achieve a result.

The next evolution of compute breaks up the applications into functions so that we can achieve further efficiencies of infrastructure use.

Functions – best density by abstracting the runtime

Finally, the next evolutionary stage in our units of compute is functions. While containerization technologies such as Docker are commonplace in cloud-native applications, we can take another step further by dividing our applications into discrete functions. **Function as a Service** (**FaaS**) is another level of abstraction and is where we get to choose the runtime to execute our code on, some execution parameters such as memory allocation, and that's about it. The hardware, operating system, and runtime are all managed for you.

Martin Fowler at `https://martinfowler.com/articles/serverless.html` says, *"Fundamentally, FaaS is about running backend code without managing your own server systems or your own long-lived server applications."*:

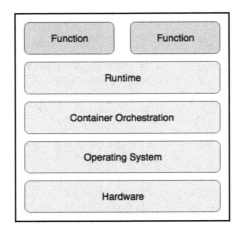

Functions running on an abstracted runtime (FaaS)

 AWS was the first to release their FaaS service, called AWS Lambda in 2014, and a lot of this book is focused around this service as a core building block for applications.

There are many reasons and benefits behind running serverless compute, as follows:

- You don't pay for idle resources. This means you only pay when your code is running.
- The scale is instantaneous and continuous—you can run multiple instances of the same code in a parallel.
- A sequential batch process running on a server has a ceiling of the maximum throughput of that server's resources. With serverless, this process could be executed in parallel, saving the cost of processing time while getting the results sooner. Our unit of scale here is at the function level, so we can scale relative to the size of the workload.

One of the biggest shifts that is most pertinent to me is that serverless means developers can focus more on building the code that directly relates to outcomes for the business. Developers don't have to grind their gears understanding how to harden their operating system, how to maintain configurations across platforms, or how to tune an application server to get the most performance out of their runtimes.

The tasks of system administration and operations have also changed significantly. With the complexities of the platform abstracted away, the traditional tasks to do with making sure the underlying infrastructure is available has shifted. Instead, serverless operations are more focused on proactive tasks such as monitoring service latency or observing transactions to ensure they are being completed using meaningful data.

 I believe that the future of modern organizations lies in the minds and capabilities of visionary developers, and serverless compute reduces the complexities of turning their ideas into reality.

Functions can be deployed in milliseconds and typically live for seconds. Long-running processes may not be the best fit for a serverless workload, but we'll get to this later. Next, let's learn how our evolutions in hardware abstraction have influenced software architectures.

Understanding software architectures

The evolution of compute has also opened new possibilities regarding how we structure and architect our applications. Mark Richards talks about *"Ingredients that go into an evolutionary cauldron – agility, velocity, and modularity"* (source: keynote talk, *Fundamentals of software architecture* at O'Reilly Software Architecture Conference in London 2016). By this, he means that, when we are talking about the topic of software architecture, we need the ability to change and evolve the way we do things in order to keep up with the ever-increasing expectations we have of new technologies. Instead of investing in complex analysis and planning, organizations should invest in making sure their software solutions include the essential evolutionary ingredients so they can change and evolve at an acceptable pace when they need to.

With the progress that's being made in serverless compute technologies today, we can unlock new levels of these key ingredients. In the upcoming sections, we are going to explore the various evolutionary steps in software architect at a high level, as follows:

- Monolith—single code base
- N-tier—achieve individual scale
- Microservices—do one thing and do it well
- Nanoservices with serverless

Monolith – single code base

In the earlier days, we used to create software that was single-tiered. The frontend and backend code was combined, and often the database was also running on the same machine. At the time, this was the best method for delivering new services to users. When user demand was high, it was necessary to scale the entire application and not just the parts that were being used the most. If this is sounding similar to the evolution of compute, you're right on the mark. The ability to distribute and independently scale our compute providers has directly influenced how software is architected, developed, and tested.

Let's dig into some of the challenges with building a solely-monolithic application:

- Picture a team of 100 developers who all have the code checked out to their local dev environments. The team has multiple managers, ranging from change and release managers to human wellness and business owners.
- There may also be another team responsible for testing the application once a major release becomes ready.
- There's another team for operating the application once the features go live in production. All of these groups of people must coordinate and agree, often through a ticket management system, on a whole host of issues and decisions.
- The time that's spent by developers organizing environments, lining up testers, and dealing with management noise greatly encroaches on the time that's available for writing actual business logic in code.
- Adding to that, once the code is in production, it's very hard to make changes or add features.
- The application has to be fully built again by passing multiple testing environment stages that may or may not be fully integrated. Then, they need to be scheduled for release during the next version.

If a monolith is kept relatively small, there is no issue with scaling that. However, if you increase the complexity, you're in for a whole set of challenges. This usually leads to an n-tier model, where we can scale individual components of the application.

N-tier – achieve individual scale

With the introduction of virtual machines also came software-defined networking. This gave us more flexibility in how we can build, configure, and scale networks. With the network also being virtual, we weren't bound by the requirement to have certain types of workloads on specific servers. Our public and private resources could now reside on the same physical server because of the hardware abstraction that was introduced by the hypervisor.

This means we can build more secure applications by separating the tiers of workloads. Our load balancing or web layer can be separated from the backend application server logic and data stores by a network barrier. We can hide the databases behind a network boundary that further protects from intrusion. Running the tiers on different virtual machines also means the code and configuration can be deployed independently (provided backward-compatibility is maintained).

Teams can now be responsible for their siloed areas of responsibility:

- DBAs can maintain the databases.
- Developers can deploy to the web or presentation tier.
- Engineers can tune the balancing tier.

This sounds ideal in theory, but we still have the challenge of people working in silos. A developer has to request for a network engineer to open ports, or ask for a certain feature in a database to be enabled. The idea of ownership is still very much entrenched in the areas of responsibility, which can give rise to a culture of blame. Have you ever heard someone say *works for me*, or *not my issue*?

In terms of hardware utilization, the biggest impact here is that we can now scale by workload type. If the user demand was running a task that was creating a high load on the processing tier, we can add more compute nodes (virtual machines) to this tier, independently of the web tier. This is called scaling horizontally.

Amazon EC2 and Autoscale Groups is a great way to do this automatically in response to a certain metric threshold—for example, the number of user sessions or the utilization of a CPU. For on-demand EC2 instances, AWS charges for the amount of time that an instance is running.

The added benefit of autoscaling groups is that we can be elastic with our compute—we can scale it down when servers are underutilized, saving costs.

Of course, once our application grows significantly, we may have multiple developers working on different parts of the application. Each feature may evolve differently and may deal with data in different ways. Microservices can help break an application into domains where each can use their own implementation strategy and database.

Microservices – do one thing and do it well

Around the time Docker started becoming popular, software architecture was also evolving. The **Service-Orientated Architecture (SOA)** pattern was a common way of layering applications into services separated by a bus or other messaging system to allow each service to communicate with each other. The microservices approach follows the same principle of a loosely-coupled application and takes it a step further in terms of granularity.

Microservices focus more on decoupling an application, and the communication mechanism is lightweight and typically HTTP. The mantra of a microservice is that it should do one thing and do it well. Large complex applications can be broken down into components with a bounded context, meaning that developers think about building within a domain instead of a generic service. Think about the example of a new customer signup service using REST rather than an abstract data service:

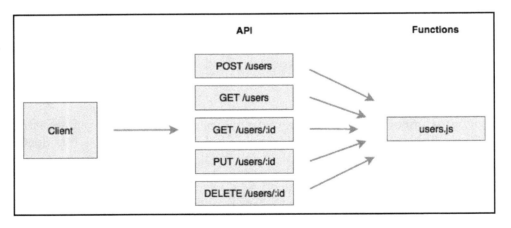

Microrservice with one function performing all the operations

 An added benefit is that they can also be deployed independently from other microservices.

Deploying independently means that development teams have the freedom to choose the runtime, define their own software life cycles, and choose which platform to run on. Naturally, containerization matches up on a lot of parallels. Containers make it easier to break the monolith into smaller applications that can be modular. Since we're now scaling at the microservice level, we can add more compute capacity by starting up more containers.

The DevOps revolution helped with the adoption of microservice application architectures as well. The benefits behind both industry trends included agility, deployability, scalability, and availability among others. Microservices allowed us to truly own what we built because we were already responsible for configuring and deploying all the tiers. When we apply microservices principles to the function level, we get nanoservices. Let's explore these.

Nanoservices with serverless

These days, with the use of serverless technology, we aim to deploy smaller pieces of code much faster. We're still developing within a domain, but we no longer have to worry about the details of our runtime. We're not focusing on building infrastructure, platform services, or application servers – we can use the runtime to write code that maps directly to business value.

A key reason for a serverless development model is that it lowers the Time to Value. The time it takes to define a problem, build the business logic, and deliver the value to a user has dramatically reduced. A factor that contributes to this is that developer productivity is not constrained by other dependencies, such as provisioning infrastructure. Furthermore, each developer can produce a higher value output because the code they are writing actually does useful things. Developers can ship releases sooner—a few days from dev to production—meaning the overall development costs are less as well.

Microservices can become more modular again with the introduction of nanoservices. While a microservice may accept multiple commands, for example, get user, create user, modify user attribute—a nanoservice will do exactly one thing, for example, get user. The lines between micro and nano are often blurred, and it raises a challenge as to how small or big we actually make that nanoservice.

A nanoservice still works within a particular domain to solve a problem, but the scope of functionality is narrower. Many nanoservices can make up one microservice, with each nanoservice knowing where to find the source data and how to structure the data for a meaningful response. Each nanoservice also manages its own error handling. For example, when paired with a RESTful API, this would mean being able to return a 5xx HTTP response. A 5xx response is an HTTP status code.

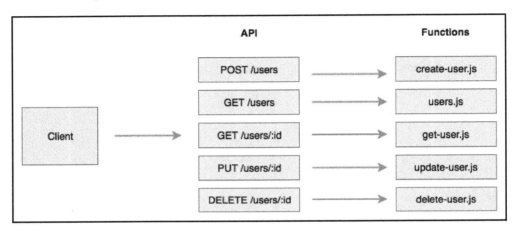

Nanoservice with one function for each API operation

Nanoservices can be helpful because they allow us to go deeper into the parts of the application that we are getting the most use out of. Reporting for cost control can be fine-grained and can also help a Product Owner prioritize the optimization of a particular function.

 One key principle of a nanoservice is that it must be more useful that the overhead it incurs.

While the code within a function can be more simple, having many more functions increases the complexity of deployment, versioning, and maintaining a registry of functionality. As we'll find out later in this book, there is an application framework called the **serverless framework** that is very useful for managing these challenges. Something else that was released recently is the AWS Serverless Application Repository, which is a registry of useful domain logic (nanoservices) that developers can use as building blocks in their own functional applications.

In terms of communication overheads between nanoservices, it's advisable to minimize the number of synchronous callouts that a nanoservice does; otherwise, the service may be waiting a while for all the pieces of information it needs before the service can assemble a response.

 In that case, a *fire-and-forget* invocation style where functions are called asynchronously may be more suitable or rethinking where the source data resides.

A nanoservice should be reusable but doesn't necessarily have to be usable as a complete service on its own. What it should follow is the Unix principles of small, composable applications that can be used as building blocks for larger applications. Think about the sed or grep Unix commands. These smaller utilities are useful by themselves, but can also be used to make up larger applications. An example of this is that you may have a microservice that is responsible for managing everything to do with room bookings in a hotel. A nanoservice may break this into specific discrete tasks to do with bookings, such as creating a new booking, finding a specific attribute, or performing a specific system integration. Each nanoservice can be used to make up the room booking workflow, and can also be used by other applications where useful.

Developing applications that are made up of nanoservices makes it easier to make changes to functions with a smaller potential impact. With serverless technologies such as AWS Lambda, it's also possible to deploy these changes without an outage to the service, provided the new change is still compatible with its consumers.

As we mentioned earlier, choosing to go to the granularity of a nanoservice comes with certain challenges. In a dynamic team with an ever-increasing number of nanoservices, thought has to be put into how to approach the following topics:

- Service sprawl, where we have lots of nanoservices performing the same or similar functions.
- Inter-service dependencies in terms of how we maintain which nanoservices have relationships with other services and data sources.
- Too big or too small, that is, when do we make the distinction about when the overhead becomes too burdensome?
- What is the usage pattern? Am I doing complex computational tasks, long-running tasks, or do I rely on a large amount of memory? Such patterns may be better suited for a microservice hosted in a container.

Some say that functions in the serverless world are the smallest level of granularity that we should abstract to. Next, we'll put our thinking hats on and see what we think may be coming up in our next architecture evolution.

Predicting what comes next

So, what is the next evolution after nanoservices? We've already seen applications being broken into smaller and smaller parts with the edition of repositories so that developers can share useful functions with others in the community.

I think we're going to see more sharing of things we can build into our applications, especially things we may not be specialists in building. I postulate that an Algorithms as a Service concept will emerge and become increasingly popular very soon. Developers who have knowledge in a particular problem domain or technology vertical will be able to share their models or the use of those models with others to achieve the same inferences.

A simple example could be a recommendation engine that predicts the likelihood of a customer purchasing a product, given their previous buying or browsing behaviors. Models could also be shared for good—think about a model that could detect a particular type of rare cancer in a photo of a number of cells. This model could be used by medical physicians to give an accurate positive or negative diagnosis, with the results of that feeding back into the training model.

This year (2019), we're seeing an explosion of new types of algorithms and new use cases. The intersection of machine learning and other technology areas has been made possible by the native integrations provided by AWS, connecting machine learning and artificial intelligence with areas such as IoT, big data, and mobile. There's no doubt that this will help drive the adoption of a new software architecture building block.

AWS has already launched its marketplace for models. AWS Marketplace for machine learning and artificial intelligence is a place where you can go to discover and buy algorithms for use in your own products or applications.

Summary

This chapter has been a reminder of the reasons behind hardware, compute, and software architectures evolving to where they are today. As we discovered, the progression of how we want to be less and less responsible for the hardware and compute we consume has been a large driver to abstracting management and responsibility away.

In the next chapter, we're going to explore some of the factors contributing to how designing and building applications has changed with the adoption of serverless architectures.

Questions

1. Which compute option gives you the best workload density?

   A) Virtual machines
   B) Containers
   C) Functions
   D) Bare metal

2. Which of the following is a benefit of an n-tier architecture?

   A) Defined and separated areas of responsibility
   B) Each tier can be scaled individually
   C) Controlled network isolation between tiers
   D) All of the above

3. What is the typical lifetime of a container?

   A) Minutes or hours
   B) Milliseconds or seconds
   C) Days or weeks
   D) Months or years

4. When creating virtual machines on a physical server, what must you take into account?

   A) Air temperature and humidity
   B) The type of workloads running on the physical host
   C) The amount of available CPU and memory

Further reading

- Introduction to serverless architectures: `https://martinfowler.com/articles/serverless.html`
- *Serverless Computing 101*: `https://hub.packtpub.com/serverless-computing-101/`
- Learn more about serverless in the following video, *Design Serverless Architecture with AWS and AWS Lambda*: `https://www.packtpub.com/virtualization-and-cloud/design-serverless-architecture-aws-and-aws-lambda-video`

Event-Driven Applications 2

To help you understand why the serverless mindset is so important, it's key to know about the underlying principles in play. In the previous chapter, we learned a lot about how applications had influenced the way that data centers and infrastructures were put together. Now, we will dig further into these application patterns, particularly those surrounding integration and transferring data. Serverless allows applications to be truly reactive so that they can respond to their surroundings, their bounded context, and things that are happening within their wider ecosystem.

In this chapter, you will learn about the basis of event-driven applications, the importance they have in the industry, and how serverless has influenced the way they are built. Regardless of the architectures of the environments you're working in, having clear and efficient patterns for transferring data will be invaluable.

In this chapter, we'll cover the following topics:

- Understanding modern applications
- Evolution of integration patterns
- Automation with serverless

Understanding modern applications

The logical move toward serverless technologies has also given rise to another paradigm in cloud computing. The following two factors form the basis of event-driven architectures—applications that can subscribe and react to changes within a wider ecosystem:

- **Event sourcing** is the model for storing the changes of state that a system goes through on an opinionated and real-time basis
- **Stream processing** is the consumption of these changes for further compute or storage

Many serverless services in AWS are inherently event-driven. Combine this with the fact that they are also highly scalable and resilient and we have the perfect recipe for building distributed systems in the cloud.

In the previous chapter, we learned about the challenges in scaling monolithic services and touched on the challenges in managing a distributed state. This section will cover the event-driven concept at a very high level and from an application context.

The first topic we will cover is distributed applications and the event-command pattern.

Event-command

Thinking past the days of large monoliths, now we talk about microservices. In the previous chapter we saw the benefits of distributing services so that components can be released independently, as well as the move away from the cyclomatic complexities that make releasing changes to a system hard.

But a distributed system isn't always the answer if you still have to centrally manage the orchestration, order of processing, and consistency of data. Microservices that are tightly coupled can introduce crazy amounts of dependencies, so you may find that you're actually no better off than when you had a monolithic architecture. What I'm alluding to here is the request-driven approach, which can be both synchronous or asynchronous. This is also known as event-command, where you're asking another system to do something based on something you have been asked to do:

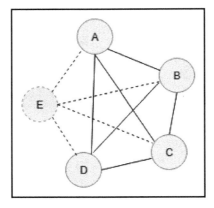

Tightly coupled microservices

To explain the underlying principles at play here, let's look at the example of RESTful APIs that front the functionality for a nano or microservice. Let's say we have a service that is responsible for creating new customer accounts for a storefront application. When a new request is received to create a new account, the service must call out to multiple other services that are responsible for doing their thing. Some of these could include the fraud service for checking the integrity of the request, the email service for setting up and validating their address, and the user profile service, which creates new entries in the ERP and CMS systems. This example includes loosely coupled services—they can all be deployed and maintained independently with their own data—but the caller service is still responsible for knowing how to communicate and request work from the downstream services. This creates a dependency on multiple levels as well.

These dependencies lead to questions that we may not have the answers to yet:

- Does the caller service wait for a successful response or have a timeout so that it can gracefully degrade a service in the event of a failure?
- How does the caller service maintain awareness of downstream REST interfaces if they are allowed to be changed independently?
- How can the caller roll-back any state that was changed if a transaction is interrupted?
- Can a service use a circuit breaker to disrupt the chain of events if a failure happens?

What we want to achieve is loosely coupled, modular services that have APIs and enable segregation of responsibilities and domains, but we also want to drive down these dependencies so that they become increasingly real-time. Instead of orchestrating and coordinating a dance of the services, what if the services only react to the things they are interested in?

This brings us to what we will cover in the next section: event-first. This is a different way of thinking about what an event communicates to the subscriber.

Event-driven or event-first

What we're talking about here is the shift to *event-first* thinking, which is more commonly known as *event-driven*. This hyphenated term will be written many times in this book. **Event-driven applications and architectures (EDAs)** are coupled with a programming model that has evolved over time.

The following evolution diagram shows integration architectures moving toward increasingly event-driven models.

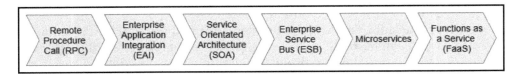

The spectrum of integration architectures

We'll get into this evolution and how it applies to the integration space soon, but the core premise here is the shift to an event-driven or event-first model. Applications today should be reactive and non-blocking to enable near-real-time services for customers. Event-driven services and components don't communicate directly with other services—in fact, they don't even necessarily know that other services exist. Instead of taking orders, they listen to events that they are interested in—events that mean something to them. When an event happens, the service springs to life to perform its job—*do one thing and do it well*—and in the process may maintain its own record of data or generate an event of its own. Other services may be interested in this event as well and update their data in order to be consistent with the new state.

What I'm explaining here is an eventually consistent gamut of services that all consume and publish events from a shard of an event stream.

In the following diagram, a producer puts an event on a stream that may be split across multiple shards or topics. One or more consumers may be subscribed to the shard and take an interest in a particular type of message being published:

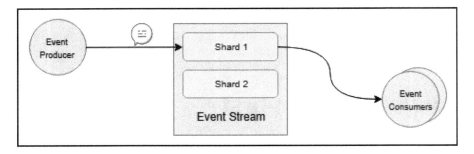

Producing and consuming messages on an event stream

Notice that there is no central orchestrating actor here. All the services can consume and react to an event at any point. This model only has the dependency on the event stream being available—services don't have to rely on other services being available in order to do their job.

 The evolutionary thinking here is that the subject of responsibility has been inverted.

It is now up to each microservice to figure out that some part of the ecosystem has changed and take action, rather than being explicitly told what to do via an instruction or command. Additionally, the producer or publisher of an event doesn't have to be concerned about the implementation of the consuming service.

An event can take the form of a state change or a notification and can be considered fact—the event has definitely already happened. Events should be well formatted to avoid ambiguity and to make sure a consumer can pick up a message with all the data that they expect. The **Cloud Native Computing Foundation** (**CNCF**), along with the community, have defined a standard format for events to ensure just that. CloudEvents (`https://cloudevents.io/`) was created to ensure the consistency of format, accessibility to consumers, and the portability of the platform. This is an emerging standard, so be sure to check out the link to the latest spec in the *Further reading* section.

Many services that are offered by AWS already follow an event-based triggering model to allow you to build massively parallel event-driven architectures. We'll learn about how we can use some of these services in Chapter 5, *Leveraging AWS Services*.

In this section, we've learned about the difference between event-command and event-first. This should help us understand specific implementations of event-driven models.

In the next section, we will focus on how the event-driven pattern has influenced integration patterns and how we move data between systems.

Evolution of integration patterns

Integration is the action or process of enabling communication of data between multiple systems. This can be achieved in many different ways and, over the years, these methods have evolved alongside the underlying technology. In this section, we will explore historic and current ways of implementing event-driven integrations.

Enterprise Application Integration

Enterprise Application Integration (**EAI**) is a concept that was spawned from the need to share data between multiple systems in the most efficient way. The premise behind EAI means creating an application (or suite of applications) to facilitate interactions between the many other applications that a business already has. Using the example of a retail store, they may have a **Customer Relationship Management** (**CRM**) system, supply chain system, and a payment system. All of these systems need to make decisions based on shared information. The contact information of a customer may be created or sourced in the CRM, and the invoicing system may also need this information to be able to create an invoice with the correct billing address:

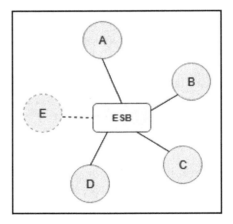

Adding an Enterprise Service Bus (ESB) to integrate systems

Historically, the best way to achieve information sharing was through EAI. This would involve creating an integration application that all the other applications can connect to in order to exchange data. Like System E in the preceding diagram, adding a new application to an existing set of applications is simple because the new system only needs to connect to a single integration application. As a concept, this is brilliant because it easily allows applications to exchange data, but before serverless technologies there were constraints on how EAI could be implemented.

In the early days, these integration applications would have been hosted on a single monolithic server. The applications being integrated only had to be concerned about connecting to a single specific server. The downside to this was that there was now a single point of failure when attempting to communicate between any system, assuming the integration application was being used to facilitate all interactions occurring with the applications. If the integration application had a problem or went offline, every system would be adversely affected.

One key element that EAI achieved was enabling system-to-system communication in an event-driven flow. The importance of this will be explained as we delve deeper into serverless and the effect it has had on integration methods and patterns.

In the next section, we will move on to a more specific version of EAI by introducing the **Enterprise Service Bus (ESB)**.

ESB

An ESB is a specific implementation of the EAI concept and is a modern method of achieving system-to-system communication. The key differences are that ESBs are broken down into smaller components that all work together to provide a single bus to facilitate interactions between different systems. ESBs forced communication from systems to align with **Service Oriented Architecture (SOA)** patterns to establish a common and standardized way of sharing data.

A key result of this is that event-driven integration patterns have become more favorable as the key concepts behind ESBs center around producing and consuming events.

The main advantage of using an ESB for integration is the idea that connecting new systems only requires configuration and minimal coding. For example, system **A** produces events on the **ESB** using a **Java client** and a SOAP-based transport but system **B** consumes the events with a **.NET client** using REST. If we add system **C** into the mix, and these systems also want to consume events using a .NET client and REST, we already have a component within the ESB that facilitates this; all we would need to do is implement some configuration to establish a working connection. Over time, we can build up our standard library of connectors, which gives us greater flexibility about the systems we integrate and also reduces the overhead incurred:

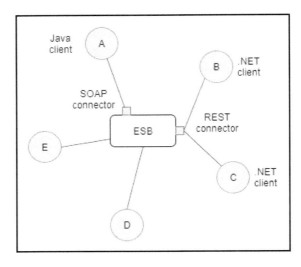

Reusing standard connectors in an ESB

On the other side of the coin, one disadvantage of this implementation is that ESBs are always on. When they're not busy, they are sitting idle, waiting for messages to be produced and published on the bus. ESBs are often built on large vertically-scaled infrastructure sizes to make sure that a bottleneck doesn't spike or a peak load doesn't occur. This is inefficient, especially if the quantity of messages being produced is minimal or sporadic. Digging into this further, using the previous example, let's say a new system is introduced (system **D**) that uses a **.NET client** and SOAP to produce messages. If system **D** produces significantly more data than the Java client using SOAP, then this component is spending most of its time waiting, whereas the .NET SOAP component receives most of the load. This highlights the inefficiencies of an application that is modular from a code component perspective, but not separately deployable by design.

That's where serverless enters the picture. In the next section, will explain how we can achieve the same result but with more efficient use of our infrastructure.

Serverless integration

Serverless integration is the next logical step in the enterprise application integration world. This concept builds on the foundations and learning of the previous EAI and ESB programming models and implements them through the use of architecture patterns with serverless technologies.

What we saw earlier was that not all integration components are used equally. Some connectors or transformations will always be used more than others, and their use will continue to change as consumers evolve their systems. So, what we need is something much like a microservice type model—something that is modular and can scale independently from other things.

Let's start with the previous example. In the serverless paradigm, we could have a lambda per client and completely decouple the internal workings of the ESB. In the past, you would have had different components spread across multiple distributed containers; today, though, we can build even smaller components that serve the specific function of interacting with consumers or producers:

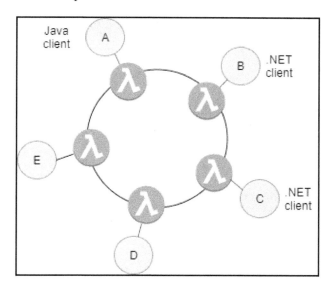

Connectors in an ESB replaced with serverless components

Now, not only can components be built smaller, they are also only triggered and executed as the result of an event. For example, in the previous example, we had System A using a Java SOAP-based client that created events infrequently. In a traditional ESB, this would have required an internal SOAP-based component to be sitting there, waiting for an event. Now, with the use of serverless technologies, the Functions as a Service or AWS Lambda service would only spin up when messages were being produced. This drives a more efficient event-driven integration application and saves costs because we only pay for the compute we use and not for when the system is idle.

Now, let's take this one step further. Previously, an ESB would have had many different components and used various different methods to transport messages or events internally within the ESB to other components; it would then have passed these on to the consumers. One way to do this is through the use of various messaging technologies, which will involve hosting a message brokering system alongside the ESB to help facilitate the internal workings of the ESB. This has now changed, with message brokering systems being turned into serverless services as well, which once again means you don't have the overhead of hosting an entire message brokering system yourself.

The following diagram applies this example to AWS services, with Kinesis hosting a data stream and the Lambda service acting as our event consumer:

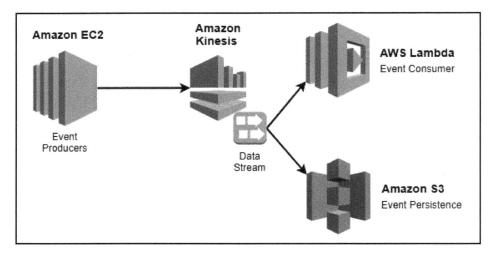

Producing messages on a serverless data stream with serverless consumers

What all of this means is that, through the use of serverless technologies, integration architectures are now significantly more efficient and require less overhead to manage and implement.

That concludes this section about integration patterns. We covered EAI at a high level and ESBs, and moved on to integration applications using serverless components. In the next section, we'll apply a serverless and event-driven mindset to automation.

Automation with serverless

We're shifting the focus here slightly from the previous sections. Another important area that has been impacted by serverless and event-first thinking is automation.

Groover, Mikell (2014), in *Fundamentals of Modern Manufacturing: Materials, Processes, and Systems*, described automation as follows:

> *"The technology by which a process or procedure is performed with minimum human assistance."*

In this section, we'll be covering the impact serverless technology has had on automation and how it has enabled a more reactive and event-driven automation approach.

Next, we'll go through the evolution from scripts on a server, to externalizing our configuration, right through to automating our infrastructure's creation.

Scripts on a server

Traditional software development for monolithic applications has always required additional operational tasks to be performed and is never as simple as build, ship, forget. Every organization (or even each individual application) will have unique tasks that are required to run the software, such as initialization and bootstrap logic, bespoke middleware configuration on a server, or even setting the correct default time zone on a server. In the past, these tasks were performed by one or many scripts that were either found on the servers themselves or hosted externally and placed on the server for execution. These scripts often perform critical tasks that are required by the application so that it can function correctly.

One of the major problems with this is that it makes these scripts intrinsically bound to both the application and the server on which the application is running. For example, say you have a Java-based application deployed on a Linux server and a .NET-based application deployed on a Windows server. Both of these applications would require some initialization once they'd been deployed to the server and, despite how similar their initialization is, the script would be completely different and would have to exist on both servers.

To achieve greater reusability of our automation scripts, we can externalize them into generic configuration directives that are run by a configuration management broker. We'll take a look at this in the next section.

Configuration management

Configuration is the next evolutionary step after hosting multiple scripts on a server and is especially important in the containerization world. The reason it's so important for containerization is the need for the containers themselves to be defined, as well as how the application will run on the container. A pertinent example of this is storing secure properties in a location external to the application and then accessing and pulling them down at runtime. This would typically be done by a script that is either sitting with the application itself in a container or on the server directly.

One consequence of having all these bespoke scripts or configuration files everywhere is that there is now a requirement for an entirely new concept of managing these automation scripts and configuration files. The scripts themselves are often running all the time on the server, performing a task when required, or they're on some kind of cron-type schedule to be executed at specific intervals. This is not the most optimized approach either; if you have a script performing a critical task required by an application and it is only running on a schedule, then the application either has to wait for the schedule to run or the schedule is running when it doesn't need to be, both of which are inefficient.

This inefficiency can then have a domino effect and require additional scripts or configuration to support the inefficiency of the initial script.

By introducing the serverless option, we can automate a lot of our traditional tasks using components we're already familiar with. We'll talk about this in the next section.

Automation as a Service

Nowadays, there are services, such as AWS CloudFormation or Terraform, which automate a significant amount of the configuration that's required for provisioning and running applications and infrastructure. Often, there is a requirement for some tasks to be performed that have the potential to be automated but are completely bespoke and not supported by the tools we mentioned earlier. This is where serverless really shines. Through the use of **functions as a service** (**FaaS**) tools such as AWS Lambda, you can convert your existing automation script into something generic and host it independently.

Let's take the original example of a Java application deployed on a Linux server and a .NET application on a Windows server. Here, you'd be able to write a generic script in any language (see the *Further reading* section for details about using your own runtime) and host it on a lambda function. Instead of using a specific DSL, we're now using the languages that we're already comfortable with. Then, the function can be triggered by any kind of event; for example, a successful deployment of an application triggers the initialization script, which reaches out to the hosted application.

Not only do these benefits apply to monolith-style applications, but also using serverless technologies and patterns for automation is almost a necessity when building, deploying, and managing serverless applications. Automating through the use of serverless technologies also enables a wider range of capability for more efficient automation. The efficiencies can be gained through making the automation event-driven. You no longer need a script on a weekly schedule to tidy up a server's logs; instead, you could fire an event when logs get to a certain size. By doing this, this event could trigger a Lambda with a script on it that truncates the logs.

The evolutionary part of automating or modernizing with serverless is that you can perform actions in the ecosystem that surround the server itself. You can automate every part of the server's life cycle and respond to changes in health or utilization. A great example of this is using EC2 Auto Scaling groups, where a pool of application servers can be horizontally scaled automatically, based on a metric threshold. The complete life cycle can be automated—terminating an unhealthy instance, deploying a new server, sourcing the application code, bootstrapping the runtime, setting up the load balancer, and monitoring.

That concludes this section. In `Chapter 7`, *Serverless Framework*, we will introduce a framework that you can use to maintain, develop, and deploy your automation projects.

Summary

In this chapter, we learned that we can translate our traditional and currently understood patterns into reusable event-driven applications to gain further insight into integration and automation. We also highlighted how the serverless mindset has been applied to evolving patterns to transform and move data between systems. The examples throughout this book will be heavily geared toward event-driven patterns, so it's great that we now have an understanding of the different types of event thinking.

In the next chapter, we will cover the very core of serverless compute—the function. We will learn how FaaS works in AWS and even have a go at creating a function of our own.

Questions

1. Adding new components to a large monolith can increase what?

   A) Code base
   B) Static coupling
   C) Cyclomatic complexity
   D) All of the above

2. What is the concept of providing application connectivity between two or more systems?

   A) Monolithic
   B) Extract, transform, load
   C) Enterprise Application Integration
   D) Enterprise Service Bus

3. What should an event producer and an event consumer use to exchange messages?

   A) Message broker
   B) Point-to-point integration
   C) Shared filesystem
   D) Email

4. A person walks into a room and switches on the light switch. The lights turn on. Is this an event-command or event-first pattern?

   A) Event-command
   B) Event-first
   C) Neither

Further reading

- Martin Fowler on microservices: `https://martinfowler.com/articles/microservices.html`
- Martin Fowler on events: `https://martinfowler.com/eaaDev/EventNarrative.html`
- The CloudEvents specification: `https://github.com/cloudevents/spec`
- Bring your own runtime to lambda: `https://aws.amazon.com/blogs/aws/new-for-aws-lambda-use-any-programming-language-and-share-common-components/`

Section 2: Getting Started with AWS Lambda Functions

2

The chapters in this section explain the details of AWS Lambda functions so that the reader will have all of the knowledge required to get started writing their first function.

This section comprises the following chapters:

- Chapter 3, *The Foundation of a Function in AWS*
- Chapter 4, *Adding Amazon API Gateway*
- Chapter 5, *Leveraging AWS Services*
- Chapter 6, *Going Deeper with Lambda*

The Foundations of a Function in AWS

3

This chapter is all about AWS Lambda. Lambda gives us a way to run code without having to manage servers. It's our most granular building block when it comes to building serverless applications and can be used in many different ways. It's important that you understand this chapter in particular because Lambda really shapes the way we do things in AWS—I guarantee that having this knowledge in your toolbelt will come in handy.

We're going to begin by learning about the characteristics of a function and some of the common areas we can use them in serverless applications. From there, we're going to dig into the security model and learn about the difference between invocation types and event sources. Then, we will learn more about the anatomy of a function and about the tools we need, all of which will lead to us deploying our first Lambda function.

We'll cover the following topics in this chapter:

- Learning about AWS Lambda
- Setting up security
- Invoking Lambda functions
- Anatomy of a Lambda function
- The programming model
- Writing your first Lambda function

Technical requirements

It would help if you have some experience using AWS and are familiar with its concepts. You will also need to understand at least one of the programming languages that we will use in this book. This includes Node.js, Python, Java, or C#. In order to write a function, you will need to have the following created or set up:

- An AWS account with an administrator IAM user
- The AWS CLI installed and configured

Learning about AWS Lambda

AWS Lambda is a fully managed service that fits into the serverless **Functions as a Service (FaaS)** category. As we mentioned earlier, this category is a subset of the event-driven compute architecture pattern and is the best way of achieving a serverless architecture. The FaaS model allows us to use, or more accurately rent, a compute share to run a discrete piece of code. This code includes one function that might make up one piece of a larger application.

In AWS, Lambda is the service that provides our FaaS. We can deploy our code and trigger it to run based on a predefined event. To learn about what is involved in this process, let's dig into some basic concepts underlying Lambda functions.

Fundamentals of a function

To set the scene for some more advanced details we'll find out about later on, we need to derive some understanding about the characteristics of an AWS Lambda function. For brevity, from here on, I'll refer to an AWS Lambda function as a function.

Simply put, a function is a piece of your own code that executes every time it is triggered by an event. A function can be written in many different programming languages, and you can also bundle any libraries or dependencies that the code needs. A function is executed within a runtime provided by AWS, on a platform provided by AWS, and hosted on an infrastructure provided by AWS.

You may include code in your function that performs any task you like, within the bounds of the execution model. For example, you may use it to regularly check on the status of a web page, run some processing on a file, or respond to an attribute that has changed in AWS and take action. You are responsible for writing, testing, and deploying the code running the logic.

 As an end user, there are no servers that you need to provision and manage yourself like there are with IaaS or Amazon EC2. This means you no longer have to worry about keeping your **Amazon Machine Images** (**AMIs**) up to date with the latest patch levels—this is done for you, and there are plenty of other benefits as well.

You do get the option to select how much memory is allocated to a function; this also governs the amount of CPU share that the function receives when it is executing. CPU share is allocated relative to the amount of memory selected. The minimum amount of memory you can allocate is 128 MB, but this goes all the way up to 3,008 MB (at the time of writing). This means you can be quite fine-grained about performance, with many options to tune and optimize. However, your choices do have cost implications, which we will explore shortly.

Invoking a function

We touched on the fact that a function is triggered by an event. Now, what does this mean? We'll talk about this in more depth later on in this section, but for now, you can think of an event as something that happens externally to the function. Because of a preconfigured mapping of that event to the function, every time the event occurs, a function will be triggered to invoke it. An example of this is something happening in S3, say PutObject, which would fire an event and trigger a Lambda function invocation. Events can also be created via the **software development kit** (**SDK**) or REST API.

You can trigger a function so that it executes once or a thousand times and the service will scale automatically to service the requests. This is also a great way to enable parallel execution. Say you had a batch job that required 5 minutes of processing per job. If you ran that job on a single-threaded server, you would need to wait until one job had finished to start the next. With a Lambda function, you can execute as many processing jobs as you required, and they will all be finished within 5 minutes. The scaling is transparent and there is no configuration that you need to do to enable it. As we mentioned previously, this is a characteristic (and one of the benefits) of a truly serverless service.

Pricing model

Let's segue straight into the next benefit: when the batch processing jobs from the preceding example have completed, there is no extra compute cost. With a server, you always pay for when it is running, but with AWS Lambda, you only pay for the amount of time the code is executing. The pricing model is actually a little more complex than that. Let's explore this further. With each Lambda function, you are charged per-request based on a combination of the following:

- How long the function executes (rounded up to the nearest 100 ms)
- The allocated memory that the function was configured with

AWS calls this combination gigabyte-seconds or GB-sec. You can find a pricing table showing the cost per 100 ms of execution here: `https://aws.amazon.com/lambda/pricing/`. Remember that there is still a storage charge to host the deployment artifacts in S3, as well as data charges for network ingress and egress.

An awesome thing about the **free tier** (`https://aws.amazon.com/free/`) is that you can do 1 million invocations per account per month (or the equivalent of 400,000 GB-secs) for free!

Ephemeral state

So, that's how a function can be invoked. What happens when the code finishes executing? When this happens, the function runtime is terminated. This includes access to the memory state and any temporary files that were created on the filesystem. In other words, everything is gone – state included. This means that if you need to maintain or keep track of a state, then this should be saved to a service that's external to the function, such as Amazon DynamoDB.

Consult the DynamoDB developer guide to learn more about how to persist state (see the link in the *Further reading* section), or check out `Chapter 5`, *Leveraging AWS Services*, where we will leverage other AWS services with Lambda.

Functions also have a finite execution time. There is a soft limit that you can configure yourself, and there is a hard limit of 900 seconds (15 minutes). If your function is still executing at this time, it will be terminated regardless. Some might say this is a limitation of the service, but actually this is a design decision that encourages you to build your applications within the bounds of a serverless architecture pattern.

High availability

AWS Lambda is also inherently fault-tolerant. A function can be configured to run inside one of your own VPCs or an AWS-managed VPC. If you choose to run in your own VPC, you can also choose which subnets a function can be executed in. If you have selected subnets across multiple **availability zones** (**AZs**), then the Lambda service will pick which subnet to execute the function in.

The Lambda service attaches an elastic network interface to the function during the initialization process before the code executes, and the function receives a private IP address. It's important to note though that a Lambda function can never be assigned a public IP address, so you can't make any inbound connections, nor can you make a function listen in on a port.

Service limits

Before we move on to use cases for AWS Lambda, let's quickly touch on some default resource limits. For each AWS account, there are specific limits for the service and runtime:

- For concurrency, there is a soft limit of 1,000 executions at a time. This can be raised by submitting a service limit increase request in the support center console.
- The size of environment variables can't be greater than 4 KB. You can have an unlimited number of envars, but the whole set cannot exceed 4 KB.
- The size of the invocation payload can be no greater than 6 MB for synchronous requests and 256 KB for asynchronous requests (invocations types will be explained later in this section). This means that, when you invoke a Lambda function, there is a limit to the amount of data you can include with the request.

Now that we've covered the fundamentals, let's apply this to some use cases to get an idea of how we can use Lambda.

Use cases

In serverless applications, I view Lambda functions as a way of providing the glue between services and integration components. It is one of the main building blocks in AWS and enables event-driven architectures to work on a massive scale.

Lambda is great for other uses, which are specified as follows:

- **Backend compute**: When applications and services need an engine to process business logic. A great example is using functions for the backend of an API. RESTful APIs are event-driven by nature and fit into the request and response model.
- **Web applications**: Everything from serverless static websites to more complex apps.
- **Data processing**: Lambda is perfect for real-time processing and serves to replace batch patterns by running massively parallel processing at the point of data creation. Check out `Chapter 10`, *AWS Automation*, where we will look at some of these architectures.
- **Chatbots**: Integrate a Lambda backend with your Amazon Lex to complement natural language processing with conversation logic and data wrangling systems.
- **Alexa Skills**: Use Lambda as the brain of your Amazon Alexa Skills.
- **Operations and automation**: Perform automatic remediation in response to events, run automated and scheduled tasks, and scan your infrastructure to maintain compliance levels.

The use cases are almost endless when you think about it, and I'm sure you might already have some ideas about where you want to use Lambda. Now that we've covered the basics, you should have a fairly good idea of what a function is and some of the things you can use Lambda for. Before you delve into development, let's learn about some important factors we need to take into account in order to keep our functions safe.

Setting up security

Let's talk about an important topic: how we secure access for entities that are invoking functions, as well as what functions can do while executing. These security features are used to secure the Lambda service itself and wouldn't necessarily be used to secure a web application.

Next up, we will cover the permissions model. You will learn about the difference between execution policies using IAM roles, as well as function/resource policies.

Execution policies

The first thing we should talk about is execution policies. These policies are attached to a service-linked role and define what AWS resources can be accessed by that role. The policy itself follows the same syntax as an IAM policy and works the same way. When creating a Lambda function, you're given a choice of attaching an existing IAM role or creating a new one. You can always modify the configuration to use a different role after creating the function, if you like.

When attaching a role to a Lambda function, we are defining exactly what AWS resources the function code has access to while it is running. To see an example of an execution policy, we need to create a role.

To create an execution role, perform the following steps:

1. Log in to your AWS account and head over to the IAM console.
2. Click on **Roles** | **Create role**.
3. Now, we need to choose which service will be using the role. Choose **Lambda** and click **Next**.

   In the background, this sets up a trust relationship that gives the Lambda service permission to use the role. This relationship is reflected in a trust policy document, represented in JSON, where a `Principal` is explicitly allowed to perform an action. The policy document for that relationship will look similar to the following code, and you will be able to find it in the role configuration after creating the role:

   ```
   {
     "Version": "2012-10-17",
     "Statement": [{
       "Effect": "Allow",
       "Principal": {
         "Service": "lambda.amazonaws.com"
       },
       "Action": "sts:AssumeRole"
     }]
   }
   ```

4. Next, we need to grant the role some permissions so that our Lambda function will be able to access AWS resources during execution. You can update these permissions any time without a new deployment of the function. Depending on the resources you want to grant your function access to, there might be a predefined managed policy that you can use. For example, if your function needs to call an endpoint in the API gateway, you might use the `AmazonAPIGatewayInvokeFullAccess` policy. On the other hand, since you might have very specific requirements for the policy, you can create your own and provide the JSON yourself. The following is an example of an execution policy document that would allow you to read records from a DynamoDB stream and also write log output to CloudWatch Logs. Choose a policy to use and click **Next**:

```
{
   "Version": "2012-10-17",
   "Statement": [{
     "Effect": "Allow",
     "Action": [
        "dynamodb:DescribeStream",
        "dynamodb:GetRecords",
        "dynamodb:GetShardIterator",
        "dynamodb:ListStreams",
        "logs:CreateLogGroup",
        "logs:CreateLogStream",
        "logs:PutLogEvents"
     ],
     "Resource": "*"
   }]
}
```

This is an IAM policy document that can be attached to a role. It states what API actions (for example, `GetRecords` in DynamoDB) the role is allowed or not allowed to perform, and which resources it is allowed to perform the actions against.

The preceding access control policy document states that the role attached to the function can list and read DynamoDB streams, as well as also set up a location in CloudWatch Logs to write log output into. This would be a suitable policy to attach if you were reading records from a DynamoDB stream event source mapping.

5. Optionally, you can tag your role with a key-value pair. Let's skip this and click **Next**.
6. Lastly, name your role and click **Create role**.

This will create a role that you can attach to a new or existing Lambda function. The next section will explain how we grant invocation permissions to other AWS resources so that they can trigger functions.

Function policies

Execution policies are not to be confused with function-or resource-based policies. These policies explicitly grant permission for another AWS service to invoke that particular function. You might notice that the previous policy did not mention the `lambda:InvokeFunction` action, and that's because an execution policy defines what the Lambda can do once it is executing.

You can also use a function policy to allow a service in another AWS account to invoke the function. Policies are added using the `AddPermission` action in the Lambda API, SDKs, and also by using the CLI.

Let's look at an example using the CLI:

```
aws lambda add-permission
  --function-name StoreMessageInS3
  --statement-id sns
  --action lambda:InvokeFunction
  --principal sns.amazonaws.com
```

This is a simple permission that allows the **Simple Notification Service** to invoke a Lambda function. This function is likely to be subscribed to an SNS topic, and the function will be invoked with the payload of a message that's been published to that topic.

We can also be more granular about our permissions. The following is an example of adding a permission to allow a specific ARN to invoke the lambda:

```
aws lambda add-permission
    --region ap-southeast-2
    --function-name GetRegionalForecast
    --statement-id forecast1
    --action lambda:InvokeFunction
    --principal apigateway.amazonaws.com
    --source-arn "arn:aws:execute-
api:southeast-2:"${ACCOUNT_ID}":"${API_ID}"/*/GET/weather/*/regional"
```

The source ARN is a particular Amazon API gateway method that is deployed in another account. This is an example of cross-account invocation.

It was important to learn how to secure our functions right from the beginning. Now, we understand the types of policy and permission we need to keep safe while developing and deploying code. In the next section, we will learn about the ways a function can be invoked.

Invoking Lambda functions

In this section, we're going to cover all the different ways we can invoke a Lambda function. We'll touch on which event sources can natively trigger a function and the types of execution that are supported. We will also go deeper into what resources are available to you during runtime.

Invocation types

So far, we've learned that Lambda functions are triggered by events. In the next section we'll show you exactly which events are supported as sources, while in this section, we're going to explore the different ways you can invoke a function.

At a high level, Lambda functions can be invoked using the following:

- A push
- An event
- A stream-based model

The push model is a synchronous type of invocation where you make a request for the function to be invoked and then wait for the function to come back with a response. You would typically use this when you need an answer right away, and you might expect some meaningful data in the response. An example of this would be when, paired with a GET method in API gateway, we need the Lambda to be the backend processor to fetch and return the data. The caller or requester of the HTTP GET method is expecting a 200 response with some data:

Invoking a function with an API gateway event

The asynchronous or event method for invoking functions is mainly used by other services in the AWS ecosystem to prompt a lambda function to fire as a result of an action on that service.

For example, when a new file is uploaded into an S3 bucket, you might want to invoke a function to perform some processing or metadata collection on the file. Within S3, you would create an event trigger on the S3 PutObject API action. The key thing here is that it is actually the S3 service itself that invokes the Lambda instead of your own code. This is why the resource policies that we learned about in the previous section exist – so that permissions can be granted to that service:

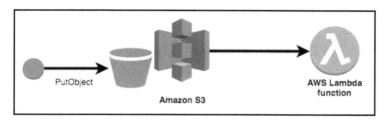

Invoking a function with a PutObject event from S3

The stream-based invocation model resembles a mapping between Lambda and an event stream, such as Kinesis or DynamoDB streams. In a way, this is a type of pull model as well, but it's not only polling that's involved here. To explain this model, we will use the Kinesis Data Streams service.

As events are produced or published on a shard in a Kinesis stream, the Lambda service is polling the stream. Once a preconfigured number of messages has been reached, the Lambda service invokes your function and passes the batch of messages, along with the event object, so that the function can consume and process them:

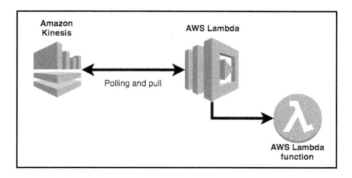

AWS Lambda polling for new messages on a stream

You can specify the invocation type as a parameter when calling the Lambda through the API or SDKs. The options you can use are as follows:

- **RequestResponse**: Use this to invoke the function synchronously and when you expect a response. The connection is kept open until the function returns a payload or terminates unexpectedly.
- **Event**: Use this to invoke the function asynchronously. The invoke API call will respond with 202 Accepted, meaning that everything's going well.
- **DryRun**: Use this type to check that all of your input parameters are valid and that your IAM user or role has the correct permissions to invoke the function. This will return an HTTP 204 No Content response if validated; otherwise, you will receive a 4xx or 5xx code that describes the problem.

The following is a simple Lambda function that invokes another Lambda function using the `RequestResponse` invocation type, and then logs the response. Don't worry too much about the syntax for now; we'll explain that very soon!

```
const aws = require('aws-sdk');
const lambda = new aws.Lambda();

exports.handler = (event, context, callback) => {
    let params = {
        FunctionName: mySecondFunction,
        InvocationType: 'RequestResponse',
        Payload: JSON.stringify(event)
    };

    lambda.invoke(params, (e, data) => {
        if(e) callback(e);
        else {
            console.log(data.Payload);
            callback(null, JSON.parse(data.Payload));
        }
    });
}
```

This Node.js function imports the AWS SDK and uses the `Lambda.invoke` API action to invoke a function. The function that it invokes is specified in the `params.FunctionName` parameter. We are also passing some arbitrary data to the function being invoked with the `params.Payload` parameter.

This is an example of invoking a function using the AWS SDK. Next, we will learn about what other methods there are.

Event sources

The following are the ways in which you can invoke a Lambda function:

- Via the AWS Lambda invoke API
- By using an SDK
- Event sources

We've already touched on the fact that various services in the AWS ecosystem can natively trigger a Lambda function to be invoked. A full list of services that support this can be found in the public developer guide for AWS Lambda, which can be found in the *Further reading* section. Event sources can also make use of the various invocation types; for example, Amazon SNS will invoke a function asynchronously, as well as Amazon Lex synchronously. Amazon SQS is message-based, so Lambda can read events from the queue.

A useful example to mention is the ability to trigger a Lambda function from a CloudWatch Event. One feature of CloudWatch Events is that you can create a rule to self-trigger on an automated schedule using cron expressions. This means we can run Lambda functions on a regularly scheduled basis – useful! Here's what it looks like:

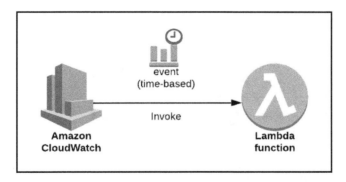

Time-based CloudWatch Event triggering a Lambda function

And here's the format for cron expressions:

cron(*Minutes Hours Day-of-month Month Day-of-week Year*)

We can translate this into a CLI command to create a CloudWatch Event rule. By doing this, we get the following response:

```
aws events put-rule --schedule-expression "cron(0 12 * * ? *)" --name
MyLambdaSchedule
```

Each service has a particular message event structure, and I recommend that you keep the documentation at hand when developing with an event source.

In the next section, we will describe the components that make up the execution of a function.

Execution environment

Let's explore some of the things that are available to us during execution. AWS publishes the current versions and kernel level of the underlying operating system in the documentation, and you can find these during execution if you really want to. Something else that's available at runtime is the SDKs for JavaScript and Python, so you don't need to bundle these with your deployment package unless you need a specific version. It's worth noting that these SDK versions can change at any time without notice, so you should continually test against the currently included version.

Depending on which runtime you choose to create your function with, there are three main execution components. You don't really need to be concerned too much about how these work, but they're good to know about when you dive deeper into creating your own runtimes. Let's go over these now:

- **Bootstrap file**: This is an executable wrapper file that helps with setting up the invocation environment. This includes finding the handler's name and dealing with the event object when triggering the function.
- **Runtime binary**: Once the bootstrap completes the initialization tasks, the runtime binary executes the actual function code.
- **Additional libraries**: These can vary between runtimes as needed. Typical libraries manage I/O, logging, and shared data.

It's also useful that the environment variables get initialized for you. You can find a full list and supported OSes and libraries here: `https://docs.aws.amazon.com/lambda/latest/dg/current-supported-versions.html`.

Speaking of environment variables, let's have a look at how to create our own.

Environment variables

A very useful feature of the AWS Lambda service is that you can specify your own environment variables to be set at the OS-level during each invocation. You can access these through your code.

This is a great way to parameterize certain variables that are likely to change throughout your code's life cycle, for example, the endpoint of a database.

This is also the perfect place for securing credentials so that they stay out of the code. Environment variables are encrypted automatically using the AWS **Key Management Service** (**KMS**). Using environment variables for credentials is one way to make sure they are secure, but maintaining these can get out of control quickly when you start deploying tens or hundreds of Lambda functions.

For larger deployments, it might make sense to manage credentials centrally. For this, a better strategy would be to use the Parameter Store in AWS Systems Manager or AWS Secrets Manager.

Let's dig into an example of setting up and accessing an environment variable. In the configuration screen for an existing function, there is a section called **Environment variables**:

Lambda function configuration options for adding environment variables

I've added some examples and clicked **Save**. Let's learn how to access and print these in code:

- Using Node.js, we can use methods from the console object:

```
console.log(process.env.DATABASE_ENDPOINT);
console.log(process.env.DATABASE_PORT);
```

- In Python, we need to import the os module and use the print statement:

```
import os
def lambda_handler(event, context):
    DB_ENDPOINT = os.environ['DATABASE_ENDPOINT']
    DB_PORT = os.environ['DATABASE_PORT']
    print('Database endpoint: ', DB_ENDPOINT)
    print('Database port: ', DB_PORT)
```

The preceding example has introduced a handler function – `lambda_handler()`. This important requirement ensures that a Lambda function works since it's the entry point for events. Let's dive in and learn how to write our own handlers.

Anatomy of a Lambda function

Okay, so we've talked about a lot of the characteristics of a Lambda function, but what about the code? What does a function actually consist of?

Handler function

First, we'll look at the handler function, the entry point for all Lambda functions. You choose your handler when creating the function. When the function executes, the service calls the handler function and passes in some event data and useful objects.

Let's have a look at the syntax for some handlers in different languages:

- Node.js:

```
exports.handler = function(event, context, callback) {
    callback(null, "executed successfully");
}
```

   The following is the fat-arrow syntax:

```
exports.handler = (event, context, callback) => {
    callback(null, "executed successfully");
}
```

- Python:

```
def handler(event, context):
    return "executed successfully"
```

C# and Java are a little different compared to Node.js and Python.

First, you specify a return type. If you're invoking the Lambda synchronously (`RequestResponse`), then this will be the data type of the object or thing you are turning. If you're invoking the Lambda asynchronously (using the event type), then you don't expect any data to be returned, so you can use a void return type.

You also need to specify the type of the incoming event data, and it's usually a string.

- The syntax for C# is as follows:

```
returnType handler-name(inputType input, ILambdaContext
context){
    return;
}
```

Because this is slightly more complex, let's look at an example that takes a string as input and returns the same string in upper case. This is an example of a `RequestResponse` invocation type:

```
public string Handler(string input, ILambdaContext context){
    return input?.ToUpper();
}
```

- The Java syntax is quite similar:

```
outputType handler-name(inputType input, Context context){
    return;
}
```

Let's put this into an example for an Event type of invocation:

```
public void handler(InputStream inputStream, OutputStream
outputStream, Context context)
        throws IOException {
}
```

Now, we'll look at context objects.

Event, content, and context objects

In this section, we'll look at objects that get passed to the handler on initialization. First off is the event object. This is a really useful piece of data and is necessary if you want to access the external inputs that the function was called with. This data is input to the `handler` function on initialization and provides information about the originating request. Additionally, the context object provides extra information about this, as well as methods that are supplied by AWS, that can help introspect the environment and other things.

If you're invoking a function through the API or SDKs, you can include some arbitrary JSON data along with it. This data is accessible during runtime through the event object. As an example, to invoke a Lambda function and include some data using the CLI, you could run something like this:

```
aws lambda invoke
    --invocation-type RequestResponse
    --function-name HelloWorldFunction
    --payload '{"hello":"world", "alice":"bob"}'
```

If another service invokes the lambda, that service will often include useful information in the event. For example, if you have an API Gateway backed by a Lambda function, when a request to an API Gateway method triggers the function, it will include a message event. In that event, you will find things such as the path of the method request, any special headers proxied to the Lambda, the HTTP method used, and the parameters from the path or query string. These pieces of data are useful when determining how to handle the request.

Each service will send an event object with a different format, so it's worth checking the Lambda documentation to see what you can expect: `https://docs.aws.amazon.com/lambda/latest/dg/lambda-services.html`.

The next thing to mention is the context object. This object provides some properties and methods that you can use to introspect the running environment. The object itself will be in a different format, depending on the runtime you choose, so it pays to check the documentation to see what's available. There are a couple of things to talk about here.

The first is the `getRemainingTimeInMillis()` method, which returns the number of milliseconds that remain for execution before hitting the preconfigured maximum timeout value. The reason that this is useful is that you can use this information to make a decision about whether you have time to do more work, or if you should recurse and spawn another function. It's also useful for when the client or consumer of the function is running something time-sensitive, such as an HTTP GET response or updating a view on a frontend web application.

You may wish to terminate a function early with an error if you know that processing will take a long time.

The next useful thing in the context object applies only to Node.js. JavaScript uses a combination of a **last-in-first-out** (**LIFO**) call stack, a **first-in-first-out** (**FIFO**) task queue, and an event loop to implement its concurrency model. It is possible to get into a situation where a Lambda function can terminate before all the background processes or callbacks are complete. If you think that could be a possibility, you could make some adjustments to your code (such as adding an await to function calls). It is also possible that a task in the queue or the stack could be holding up the hander's callback from being run.

In this case, the function is likely to reach its timeout period and terminate with an error. To avoid that, you can instruct Lambda to terminate the function after the callback is called with a nifty property called `callbackWaitsForEmptyEventLoop`. Set this to false if you wish, but note that any tasks remaining in the event loop will be processed on the subsequent invocation of the same Lambda instance. The details of this get complex quite quickly, so we will revisit Lambda instance reuse in Chapter 6, *Going Deeper with Lambda*.

The programming model

So, we've just learned what a Lambda function looks like and some of the utilities that you get at runtime. Now, let's look at options for writing, deploying, and testing.

Runtimes

As we mentioned previously, Lambda supports multiple runtimes and allows you to build functions using Node.js, Python, Java, Go, Ruby, and .NET (C# and PowerShell). AWS often adds support for more runtimes (check the latest here: `https://docs.aws.amazon.com/lambda/latest/dg/lambda-runtimes.html`), and recently released a feature that allows you to create your own custom runtime. This will allow you to bring your own language to Lambda using the Runtime API. We'll find out how this works in Chapter 6, *Going Deeper with Lambda*, so before we get ahead of ourselves, let's move on.

When creating a new Lambda function, you choose which runtime to use. You can't change the runtime once it is created – which isn't an issue – there are pretty much no use cases where you would need to change the runtime of a function after it's been created.

For runtimes that Lambda supports, there's a particular subset of versions that are supported. It's important that developers are using modern versions of runtimes that are current with the latest security and vulnerability updates. AWS has the same opinion and would rather not support an out-of-date runtime version along with its operating system and library dependencies. To make sure we are always developing against best practices, AWS deprecate versions of runtimes when they reach a certain stage in their life cycle.

Before starting deprecation, AWS will announce an **end of life** for a runtime. This is to notify you (via email) that it is about to be deprecated over two phases. The **first phase** is to remove the ability to create new functions using the deprecated runtime. You can still update deployed functions that use that runtime, but you can't create new ones.

The **second phase** removes the ability to update as well. There is a loosely defined **third phase** that Lambda may choose to use, and that is removing the ability to invoke the function altogether. There will be efforts to contact anyone in that situation prior to retiring the runtime.

Writing, building, and packaging

For the polyglots among us with options when it comes to what to write in, once we've chosen which language to write our function in, we have more choices about how to author a function. Let's talk about what's available.

The most simple method is to use the inline editor in the Lambda console. You can access this after creating your function and make direct changes to the code. Here's what the editor looks like:

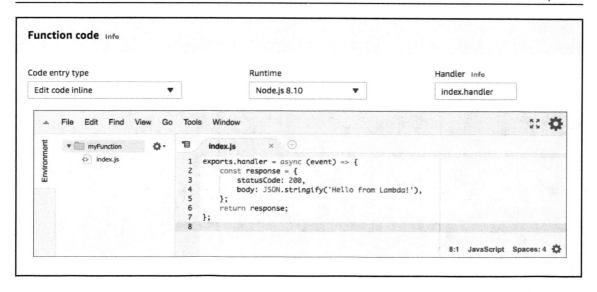

Screenshot of the code editor in the Lambda console

The editor is actually quite configurable since it has many user options. This is because it is actually a managed Cloud9 environment underneath (https://aws.amazon.com/cloud9/). One limitation of using the editor is that you can't include your dependencies or libraries, so it is mainly useful for ad hoc changes. Beware, though – it's very easy to make a change in the console and not update your copy in source control!

I mentioned AWS Cloud9 in the preceding section. Cloud9 is a recent addition to the AWS offerings and is a cloud-based **Integrated Development Environment** (**IDE**). You can write code in your browser and deploy it straight to Lambda. Cloud9 also supports collaborative coding for pair programming. Think of it as the Google Docs of word processors! Cloud9 is really useful because you can take all of your user settings and preferences with you when moving onto another device.

Most people have their favorite IDE, and one of my favorites is **Visual Studio Code** (**VS Code**), with the Material Theme Ocean High Contrast color theme and icon set. VS Code comes with a tabbed editor window and an integrated Terminal. How good does it look!

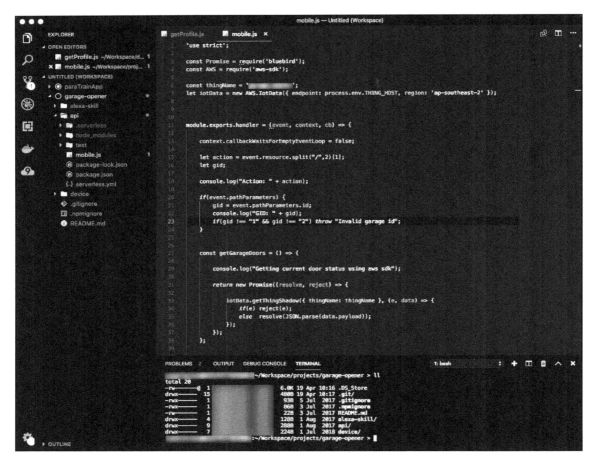

Microsoft Visual Studio Code editor

I've added some extensions to help with my development workflow. Some of these include linters for JavaScript and Dockerfiles, which assist me by highlighting syntax errors so that I can pick up on issues before deployment time. Another awesome extension that I use is called Live Sync for AWS Cloud 9. This was written by Ian Mckay in Australia and allows you to bring Cloud9 features into your VS Code experience. This is really cool if you want to make use of the collaboration and chat functionality, but don't want to change to an IDE that you're not used to. Check it out on GitHub: `https://github.com/iann0036/cloud9-sync`.

If you're developing in .NET, you might want to look at the AWS Toolkit for Microsoft Visual Studio: `https://aws.amazon.com/visualstudio/`. This extension has extra tools for building and deploying to Lambda.

So, now that we have our developer experience set up how we want it, we can move on to options for defining the project's structure. What I'm alluding to here are frameworks for writing and templating serverless applications. Now, these tools aren't a requirement for making a function work, but as you start to grow your serverless application with multiple Lambda functions, messaging systems, and data stores, you will quickly find that you need help.

An application framework brings a few benefits to your Lambda and serverless development:

- Centralizes the code for components of a serverless application
- Enables more control across a distributed development team
- Allows for local testing and debugging
- Encourages templating and reuse of code and libraries
- Give you extra tools to help with deploying, rollback, and management

There's a whole heap of frameworks that you can get started with, such as the Serverless Framework, AWS Chalice, Apex, and AWS **Serverless Application Model** (**SAM**), to name a few. We're going to cover my favorite framework in Chapter 7, *Serverless Framework*, but it's good to know that there are options available in this space.

In the meantime, let's look at what it means to run a build to make a deployment package without the help of a framework. For Python, Node.js, and Ruby, there are no compile steps that need to happen, so technically there is no build step here. Instead, we need to package our function and all the dependencies into a ZIP archive, ready to be uploaded to an S3 bucket. Note that the required dependencies should already be installed in the local directory before zipping. The command to ZIP may look something like the following for a Node.js function:

```
zip -r new-function.zip handler.js node_modules
```

For compiled languages, it's a little more complex. To build a Java function using Maven, we need to create a `pom.xml` file that has the appropriate project build configurations. Then, we can use the command line to build the project and create our Java archive file (`.jar`). The following is the file that will be uploaded to S3 for deployment:

mvn package

> More information on creating Java deployment packages, including an example using Gradle, can be found at `https://docs.aws.amazon.com/lambda/latest/dg/lambda-java-how-to-create-deployment-package.html`.
>
> For functions in C#, it's recommended to use the .NET Core CLI to create and deploy the project: `https://docs.aws.amazon.com/lambda/latest/dg/lambda-dotnet-coreclr-deployment-package.html`.

That covers the basics of writing and building functions. In the next section, we will learn how to deploy artifacts so that we can invoke our functions in Lambda.

Deployment

Now that we've got our deployment package sorted, we need to deploy it. Like everything else you do in AWS, there are options for deployment as well. Let's start with the most basic: using the Lambda console in the AWS Management Console. Perform the following steps to deploy:

1. First, we're going to update an existing Lambda function called `myFunction` using a ZIP file as a deployment package.
2. If we click on the drop-down list for the code entry type (shown by the blue arrow in the following screenshot), we can see the upload options that are available:

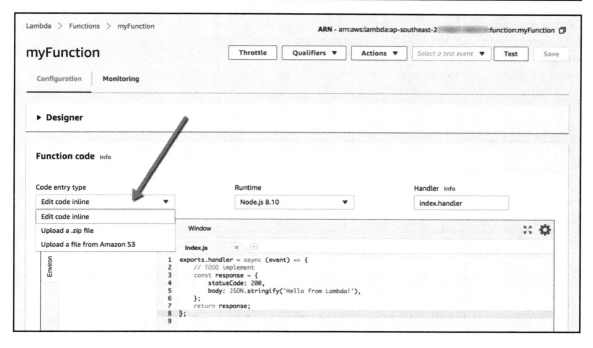

Lambda console showing the upload options for packaged functions

3. Let's choose **Upload a .zip file** and pick a `.zip` file to deploy.
4. When we click **Save** on the top right, the file will be uploaded and deployed.

So, what's happening in the background? When you hit the **Save** button, the file is uploaded through the browser to an Amazon S3 bucket that the Lambda service creates for you. Then, the Lambda service uses that newly uploaded object as a target for deployment and updates the code. The last option in the list – **Upload a file from Amazon S3** – simply lets you choose an object that has already been uploaded to S3.

Is the preceding code being overwritten? I hear you asking. Not quite – well, kind of, maybe. Versioning happens. When you create the first Lambda function, it is given the $LATEST version. What you need to do next is click on **Actions** and then **Publish new version**. The following screenshot shows where you can find this action:

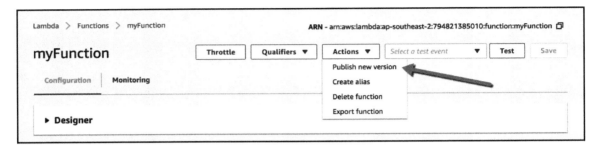

Lambda console highlighting where to publish a new function version

This will take whatever is in the $LATEST version and save it as a new version with a numerical value, starting with 1. Think of this as releasing a new major version, with $LATEST being the release candidate. Every new release gets its own **Amazon Resource Number (ARN)** so that you can manage or invoke it individually. You don't have to make use of this versioning functionality – you can use the $LATEST version forever and keep deploying over the top of it, but here's where it gets cool.

Aliases. You can arbitrarily add a name or a pointer to a version. These get ARNs as well, so you can invoke a specific version of the function by an alias. Okay; so how would this be useful? Let's look at a real-life use case, that is, the development life cycle of the function itself:

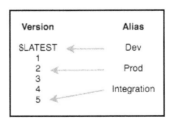

Version alias mapping to versions

Here, we can see we have created aliases for the various lifecycle stages that the function goes through. The **Dev** alias is pointing to **$LATEST** because that holds the most up-to-date code. The **Prod** alias is pointing to a previous version where the code has been tested and released for production use:

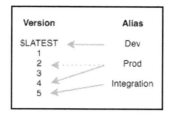

Releasing updated code to production by updating the version alias

This way, a production release is as simple as updating which version the alias points to. This is useful when all the environments are hosted in the same AWS account. For larger deployments, we may deploy ZIP artifacts across multiple accounts instead. We'll see what that looks like later on.

> It is recommended that a developer publishes a new version before updating $LATEST to avoid a potential race condition.

Here's where it gets even cooler. Let's say that, for the preceding production release, we wanted to mitigate some of the risks of deploying new code in a big-bang approach. Using aliases, we can choose to balance the traffic across two different versions in a weighted manner:

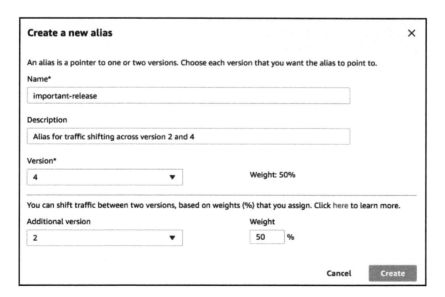

Creating a new version alias with traffic shifting enabled

When promoting *important-release* to Lambda function version 4, we can give it a weighting so that half the traffic goes to the new version and half goes to the other. This way, we can monitor any impact that the new version might have and take action where necessary.

Look for the START log entry in the function's CloudWatch Logs stream to find which version has been invoked.

We'll be exploring advanced deployment patterns in more detail and using the Serverless Framework in Chapter 8, *CI/CD with the Serverless Framework*. For now, we will move on and look at testing, monitoring, and debugging.

Testing, monitoring, and debugging

Now, you have a Lambda function deployed and ready to go. Let's test it to see if it works as expected! We're going to touch on the basic concepts of testing and debugging Lambdas and then delve more deeply into this in Chapter 6, *Going Deeper with Lambda*.

To test a function, we need to come up with an event object to invoke it with. If your function doesn't use anything from the event object, then this can simply be some arbitrary JSON data. If your function is being called by another service, then it's likely to be invoked with an event object of a known structure.

For example, here's a simplified event object from an SQS queue event source:

```
{
    "Records": [
        {
            "messageId": "19dd0b57-b21e-4ac1-bd88-01bbb068cb78",
            "receiptHandle": "MessageReceiptHandle",
            "body": "Hello from SQS!",
            "attributes": { ... },
            "messageAttributes": { ... },
            "md5OfBody": "7b270e59b47ff90a553787216d55d91d",
            "eventSource": "aws:sqs",
            "eventSourceARN": "arn:aws:sqs:ap-
southeast-2:123456789012:MyQueue",
            "awsRegion": "ap-southeast-2"
        }
    ]
}
```

The Lambda function is invoked with the details of one message from the queue. Presumably, the function would be performing some processing on `Records[0].body`. We can test our SQS message processing function by passing in our own data in this format.

To do so through the console, go to the Lambda console, find your function, and configure a new test event:

Lambda console showing where to create test event objects

Paste your event object in and give it a name. Once you've created the test event, you can use the **Test** button to invoke the function.

Before we check the output of our invocation, let's learn how we achieve the same thing using the AWS CLI:

```
aws lambda invoke
    --invocation-type RequestResponse
    --function-name myFunction
    --payload file://test-sqs-message-event.json
```

We can either pass the JSON inline with the command or specify a file that contains the data.

That's cool – we can invoke a function using our own inputs. What does the output look like? By default, each Lambda function comes with its own CloudWatch Logs log group. To write things to the logs, you can use the methods that are available on the `console` object or write out to `stdout` or `stderr`. The logs turn up fairly promptly in a log stream inside the log group associated with the function. A log stream is created for every new instance of the function. Predicting when a new instance of the function will happen can be fairly indeterministic, but we know that a new instance will be created if you update a function. We also know that the Lambda service can create new instances when scaling function for multiple concurrent invocations.

To look at some example output, let's head over to the CloudWatch console and look at the latest invocation of `myFunction`:

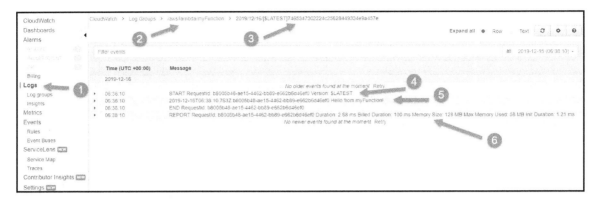

The CloudWatch console showing recent log output

I've scribbled over this screenshot, but for good reason:

1. Once you find the console for CloudWatch, head to the **Logs** page (1).
2. Find the log group corresponding to your function (2) – Lambda will create this group for you on the first invocation.
3. Click on the log stream with the most recent activity (3). Now, the console will show us all of the log output from the recent invocations.
4. In the preceding screenshot, we can see a single invocation, denoted by the `START`, `END`, and `REPORT` syntax.
5. We can tell which version of the function has been invoked as well (4).
6. Before invoking the Node.js function, I added a line to test the log output:

```
console.log("Hello from myFunction!");
```

7. This results in outputting a timestamp and our text (5).
8. Finally, when the function finishes execution and terminates, we get a report of some of the metrics for that invocation (6).

Before we move on to explaining those metrics, let's see whether we can achieve the same thing using the CLI:

```
aws lambda invoke
  --invocation-type RequestResponse
  --function-name myFunction
  --log-type Tail
```

```
--query 'LogResult'
--output text
outfile
| base64 -d
```

Here, we've added some options to the basic invoke command so that we can see the output of the logs. The log type of `Tail` allows us to get an object with log data, which we can extract with the query and output format. The `LogResult` data is `base64`-encoded, so we pipe the output through the `base64` program with a switch to decode (`-d` for Linux and Windows, `-D` for macOS).

The output is readable text in your command-line console that looks the same as what you would see in the CloudWatch log stream. Here's what the output looks like for me; it will be in a similar format for you but with different values and a different `RequestID`:

```
START RequestId: 87349dc3-49a2-4e5d-b02d-2fa4c317610e Version: $LATEST
END RequestId: 87349dc3-49a2-4e5d-b02d-2fa4c317610e
REPORT RequestId: 87349dc3-49a2-4e5d-b02d-2fa4c317610e Duration: 1.47 ms
Billed Duration: 100 ms Memory Size: 128 MB Max Memory Used: 55 MB Init
Duration: 106.83 ms
```

So, that was the basics of testing. These methods are useful for ad hoc or one-off tests, but ideally, we want to automate our testing in a pipeline.

Next, as promised, let's analyze some metrics that Lambda reports through CloudWatch. There are seven different metrics that are available out of the box for Lambda, as follows:

- **Invocation count**: The number of times a function is invoked.
- **Invocation duration**: The amount of time that a function took to execute in milliseconds.
- **Invocation errors**: The number of times that a function failed to execute, whether this is through handled exits from the code or unhandled errors such as reaching the configured timeout.
- **Throttled invocation count**: The number of times that a request to invoke a function was throttled due to hitting concurrency limits.
- **Concurrency**: This is a count of the number of functions that are concurrently executing in an AWS account.
- **Iterator age**: This applies to stream-based invocations where iterators are used to move through batches of messages.
- **Dead letter error count**: When there is an error writing to the Dead Letter Queue after failed invocations.

You can see these rolled up into a graph by using the CloudWatch metrics console. You can also create your own custom metrics using the AWS SDK. Maybe you want to track the number of new customer sign-ups or count the number of invalid data errors when processing a batch of messages. Let's have a look at these two examples using Node.js and Java SDKs.

For a Node.js Lambda, follow these steps:

1. First, you need to define the imports that the function will need to run:

```
const AWS = require('aws-sdk');
const cloudwatch = new AWS.CloudWatch();
```

2. Then, create the data object that you want to publish as a metric:

```
const metric = {
    MetricData: [{
        MetricName: 'NewCustomerCount',
        Dimensions: [{
            Name: 'NewCustomers',
            Value: successfulSignup
        }],
        Timestamp: new Date(),
        Unit: 'Count',
        Value: 1
    }],
    Namespace: 'Customers'
};
```

3. Finally, use the `PutMetricData` action from the CloudWatch API to send the metric data to CloudWatch:

```
cloudwatch.putMetricData(metric, (e, data) => {
    if (e) console.log(e, e.stack);
    else console.log(data);
});
```

For Java, there are a bunch of imports to make:

```java
import com.amazonaws.services.cloudwatch.AmazonCloudWatch;
import com.amazonaws.services.cloudwatch.AmazonCloudWatchClientBuilder;
import com.amazonaws.services.cloudwatch.model.Dimension;
import com.amazonaws.services.cloudwatch.model.MetricDatum;
import com.amazonaws.services.cloudwatch.model.PutMetricDataRequest;
import com.amazonaws.services.cloudwatch.model.PutMetricDataResult;
import com.amazonaws.services.cloudwatch.model.StandardUnit;
```

The code looks as follows:

```java
final AmazonCloudWatch cloudwatch =
AmazonCloudWatchClientBuilder.defaultClient();
Double validation_errors = Double.parseDouble(args[0]);

Dimension dimension = new Dimension()
    .withName("DataValidationErrors")
    .withValue("Errors").build();
MetricDatum datum = new MetricDatum()
    .withMetricName("DataValidationErrorCount")
    .withUnit(StandardUnit.Count)
    .withValue(validation_errors)
    .withDimensions(dimension).build();
PutMetricDataRequest request = new PutMetricDataRequest()
    .withNamespace("Customers/DataErrors")
    .withMetricData(datum);
PutMetricDataResult response = cloudwatch.putMetricData(request);
```

Often, an easier way to achieve metric collection is to simply log the value or occurrence out to `stdout` or `stderr`. Then, you can set up a metric filter in CloudWatch Logs to search for a preconfigured pattern. The filter will search incoming logs in your log group and increment a metric when a match is found. This is also a more efficient way of collecting data because you aren't using compute time within the function to make the API request.

What happens when a Lambda function fails to complete execution for some reason? In `Chapter 6`, *Going Deeper with Lambda*, we'll talk about what it means when function execution results in an error, and how we can rectify this. In the next section, we'll learn how to write our first Lambda function.

Writing your first Lambda function

Finally, we're here. We've reached the section where you get to put together everything you've learned to see what a Lambda function looks like, and also deploy one yourself. Well done for getting this far! After completing this chapter, you'll have all the knowledge you'll need to go and create functions for your own projects and blow your colleagues away with your new cutting-edge technology insights and wisdom.

Hello, world! in the console

In this section, we're going to create a Lambda function in Python using the AWS Management Console. Since Python code doesn't need to be built, we'll create a function that needs no dependencies so that we can use the inline editor.

Fire up your AWS account and head over to the Lambda console. If you haven't created any functions, you'll be greeted by the home screen. Have a read if you like, and when you're ready, click the **Create function** button.

We're going to create our function from scratch, but it's worth noting the other options there. Chances are that there will be a blueprint for what you're trying to do, so it pays to remember to check the list of samples before creating functions:

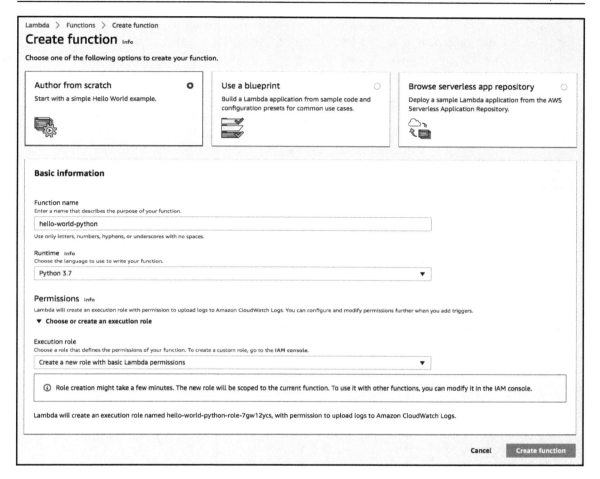

Creating a new Lambda function using the console

Perform the following steps to create your Lambda function:

1. Enter an appropriate name for your function and select a Python runtime.
2. For the permissions section, we don't need our Lambda to be able to do very much, so we'll let the service create an IAM role for us with a basic policy document.

Note the execution role name in case you have to update the policy later. Hit **Create function** when you're done.

3. Next, you should be presented with the Lambda function console, including all the options for connecting event sources, the incline editor, environment variables, and then a few options for how the function executes. Use the editor to add the code, as follows:

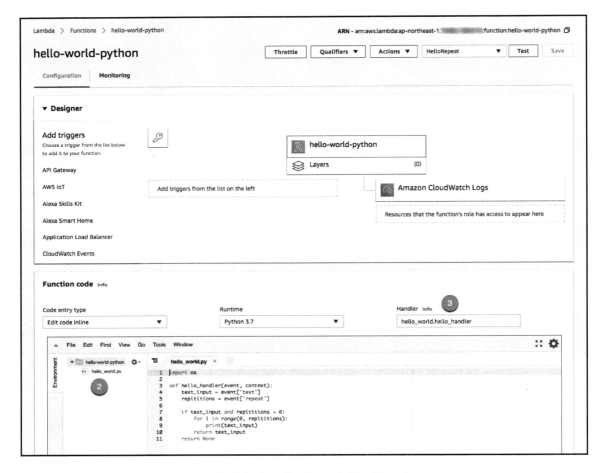

Overview of a function configuration screen in the Lambda console

4. Let's boost the function to 512 MB of memory with a 10-second timeout (1).
5. We should rename the default file (2) and update the pointer to the handler (3).

6. We don't need to configure the event source since we'll be invoking the function ourselves, with our own event:

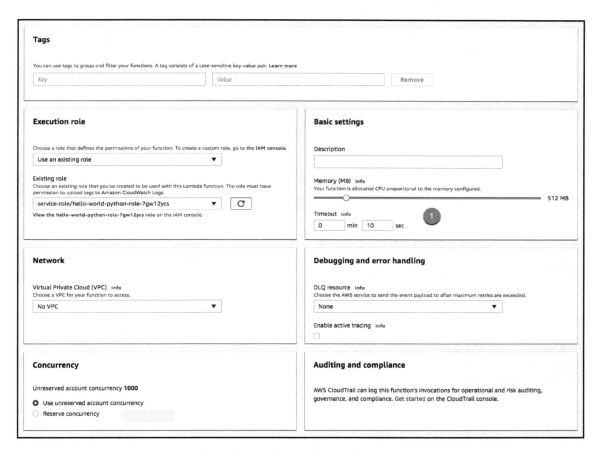

More configuration options on the *Function Configuration* page

7. Next, we'll set up our test event so that we can pass in the values that the function is expecting. We're passing in a JSON event object with a text string to print and an integer with the number of times we want it to be printed:

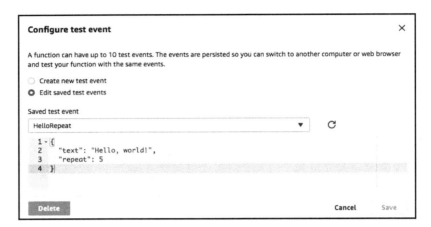

Creating a new test event object

8. Finally, let's invoke our function. Hit the **Test** button and have a look at the output:

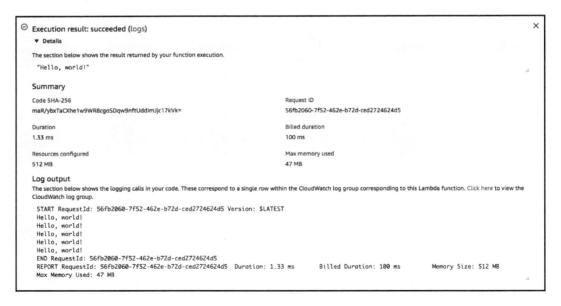

A snippet of the Lambda console showing the results of an executed Lambda function

At the top of the preceding screenshot, we can see the response data that we were expecting. We also get some information about how long the function took to execute, as well as the resources it consumed. This information can help you fine-tune your function configuration. At the bottom, we can see our log output, which is an extract from the log data stored in CloudWatch Logs.

That's it! You've successfully created a Lambda function from scratch and invoked it with a test event!

Hello, world! using the command line

That was fun – let's do another one! However, in this section, we're not going to touch a browser at all. Instead, we'll be running commands in a bash Terminal using the AWS CLI. This is a less wizard-like method and I think you'll find it much easier. In this example, we're going to use Node.js. Let's get started:

1. First, let's write some function code in our favorite IDE:

Creating a Lambda function in Visual Studio Code

This is as simple as it gets – the function will return a message and the event that was originally passed in when invoked.

2. Zip up the function, ready for deployment:

```
zip helloworld.zip index.js
```

3. We will need to select an execution role for the function when we issue the create command, so let's grab the ARN of the default Lambda role. Remember this value for the next function:

```
aws iam get-role
    --role-name lambda_basic_execution
    --query 'Role.Arn'
    --output text
```

4. Now, we have everything we need to create a new function:

```
aws lambda create-function
    --function-name hello-world-nodejs
    --runtime nodejs8.10
    --role
arn:aws:iam::${AccountNumber}:role/lambda_basic_execution
    --handler index.handler
    --zip-file fileb://helloworld.zip
```

5. And boom! Our function has been created:

```
{
    ...
    "FunctionName": "hello-world-nodejs",
    "CodeSize": 286,
    "MemorySize": 128,
    "FunctionArn": "arn:aws:lambda:ap-
southeast-2:${AccountNumber}:function:hello-world-nodejs",
    "Version": "$LATEST",
    "Role":
"arn:aws:iam::${AccountNumber}:role/lambda_basic_execution",
    "Timeout": 3,
    "Handler": "index.handler",
    "Runtime": "nodejs8.10",
    ...
}
```

Let's invoke it. The last argument in the following command is a file to which the output of the execution will be written. We are also passing in an arbitrary piece of JSON data for the event object:

```
aws lambda invoke
    --function-name hello-world-nodejs
    --payload '{ "text": "Hello!" }'
    output.file
```

We can get the output in a nice format with the help of the JSON encoder/decoder extension for Python:

```
cat output.file | python -m json.tool

{
    "message": "Hello, world!",
    "event": {
        "text": "Hello!"
    }
}
```

This is the JSON data the function responded with. It's in the exact same format and structure we programmed it with.

And that's it. Once you become familiar with this method, it will be a quicker and easier way to manage Lambda functions with fewer clicks.

Summary

Well, there you have it. In this chapter, you learned about the fundamentals of how a Lambda function works in AWS. We covered quite a lot of thing: the permissions model, the three types of invocation, event source options, the code structure of a function, and what is available during execution. We also learned how to write, build, and deploy a function and, hopefully, you were successful in invoking your first Lambda function.

If you're developing and deploying solutions to AWS, it's really important that you learn how Lambda functions work and how to write your own. They will undoubtedly be a useful component in building future solutions.

In later chapters, we're going to explore a development life cycle for Lambda functions and explore some more advanced concepts. In the next chapter, we'll add another component that complements our Lambda compute capability.

Questions

1. Event-driven compute and architectural patterns have evolved to abstract away the runtime from the developer so that they can focus on writing business value into their code. Such a pattern is called what?

   A) Platform as a Service (Paas)
   B) Infrastructure as a Service (IaaS)
   C) Functions as a Service (FaaS)
   D) Mobile Backend as a Service (MBaaS)

2. When creating a Lambda function, there are a number of configurable options. Which of the following is NOT a directly configurable option?

   A) CPU cores
   B) Memory allocation
   C) Runtime
   D) Execution timeout

3. Lambda functions can be written in what programming language?

   A) Node.js
   B) Python
   C) Java
   D) Go
   E) C#
   F) Ruby
   G) All of the above

4. What would be a good method for enabling multiple environments for a Lambda function?

   A) Deploy multiple copies of the function
   B) Use environment aliases to point to a particular version
   C) Always use the $LATEST version

5. What might be the issue if you are getting permission errors when trying to access an S3 bucket from a running Lambda function?

   A) The bucket doesn't exist
   B) The bucket was created in another region
   C) The resource policy doesn't allow S3 to invoke the function
   D) The execution role doesn't allow access to the bucket

6. Why do I keep receiving HTTP 429 status code responses when using the Lambda Invoke API?

    A) The request concurrency limit has been exceeded
    B) The Lambda function doesn't exist
    C) The request is in the wrong format
    D) The Lambda function terminated unexpectedly

Further reading

- In-depth article on serverless architectures: `https://martinfowler.com/articles/serverless.html`
- AWS Lambda development guide: `https://docs.aws.amazon.com/lambda/latest/dg/welcome.html`
- AWS Software Development Kits: `https://aws.amazon.com/tools/#sdk`
- Python SDK documentation: `https://boto3.readthedocs.io/`
- DynamoDB developer guide: `https://docs.aws.amazon.com/amazondynamodb/latest/developerguide/Introduction.html`
- Hands-on Serverless Architecture with AWS Lambda: `https://www.packtpub.com/virtualization-and-cloud/hands-serverless-architecture-aws-lambda-video`

Adding Amazon API Gateway 4

In this chapter, we're going to add Amazon API Gateway to the mix and talk about why this service is such a good fit for Lambda. By adding an API gateway to our Lambda solutions, we are also introducing some features and benefits that will help to make our architectures production-ready. These features are centered around API management, which can help with things such as throttling and quota management, monetization of your APIs, and added security functionality. One of the additional benefits of using Amazon API Gateway over other options is its native integration with Lambda along with many other integrations in the AWS ecosystem.

We'll go over some of these features and then build on the knowledge learned from the previous chapter to explain how to create an API backed by a Lambda function.

We'll cover the following topics:

- Serverless APIs—build, deployment, and use cases
- WebSocket APIs
- How to secure your API with IAM, Cognito, and custom authorizers
- Overview of API management including deployment options
- Building your own API with Lambda using the console and the AWS CLI

Technical requirements

To get the most out of this chapter, it would help if you understood at least the basics of RESTful API web services and architectural styles. There's a link in the *Further reading* section for a quick-start tutorial if you need to brush up. For the authentication and authorization topics, you will need an understanding of OAuth standards such as OpenID Connect and how they work.

Introducing Amazon API Gateway

Amazon API Gateway is another component in the serverless arsenal from AWS. It is used to create and manage RESTful and WebSocket APIs in front of your backend functionality.

In this section, we'll dig into the features and benefits, see what our deployment options are, and review some common use cases.

Serverless APIs

There are several reasons for using an API Gateway, and the first is to abstract the implementation of your application or service away from the client. This is to allow you to have greater flexibility in how the business logic and processing are built, and so that the client doesn't have to understand the underlying data structures or storage layer.

In `Chapter 1`, *The Evolution of Compute*, we covered the basics of a microservice, and an API gateway is an integral part of enabling microservices to function. This is because an API layer serves as a common, structured, and predictable way of communicating with a service. The API specification or interface can be published so other microservices and consumers know how to request information and know what format the response will come back in. This is a key premise for a RESTful service.

Another reason for a gateway component is to offload the responsibilities for authentication, authorization, and certificate management. This can lighten the load on a microservice and allow the implementation to be reused for other microservices. This also helps the developer to focus on building the business logic needed for the service.

An API gateway, and especially Amazon API Gateway, can protect your service against attacks because of the way it was designed. Amazon CloudFront sits in front of API Gateway to filter requests and distribute traffic across edge locations. One of the benefits of leveraging CloudFront is that it also has AWS Shield built-in as standard. Shield protects against layer 3 and 4 **Distributed Denial-of-Service** (**DDoS**) attacks.

 The layers referred to are the seven layers of the **Open Systems Interconnection** (**OSI**) model. Check the *Further reading* section for a link to more information.

As in the following diagram, we see that Amazon API Gateway has network and transport layer DDoS protection out of the box. It also has some controls for layer 7 attacks, including the ability to set usage plans so requests can be throttled after a configurable request rate. Also available is Amazon **Web Application Firewall** (**WAF**), which can mitigate common web-based attacks at the application layer (layer 7):

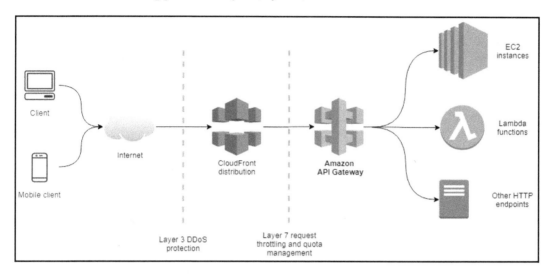

Enforcing the layers of protection

So, it's clear that a combination of Amazon API Gateway and other AWS components is a formidable security mechanism for publishing APIs. The reason I usually talk about security when I first introduce a technology is that it should be one of the first aspects of a service that a technology option is evaluated on. If an option can't adequately secure your workload, that's the end of the story.

There are several other benefits as well. Continuing the theme of this book, API Gateway is serverless. You will be familiar with this already—API Gateway is a managed service with no infrastructure you have to manage yourself. Scaling is also taken care of, with the ability to transparently scale from 1 request per second to 10,000 (a default limit that can be increased). APIs can be deployed and published very quickly, and high availability is inherent.

Let's check out what a typical deployment could look like at a high level:

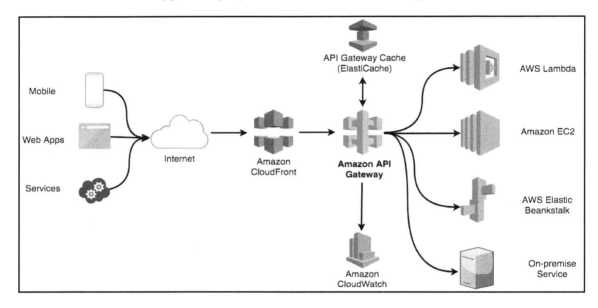

A high-level overview of a typical API Gateway deployment with an edge-optimized endpoint

The preceding diagram shows several clients traversing the internet to reach CloudFront, which provides the edge connection. The integration with API Gateway here is internal; you can't actually view the distribution that API Gateway created in the console. A cache is available should you want to reduce the requests to your backend. The implementation under the hood is Amazon ElastiCache but again, we don't get to view the details of what API Gateway creates in the ElastiCache console. API Gateway is natively integrated into CloudWatch, sending metrics and logs to a central location for a consistent experience across the services. Lastly, on the right-hand side, we can see several options for backend integrations. API Gateway can natively invoke Lambda functions—we'll explore this in-depth in this chapter.

Also, an interesting point to note is that you can create an integration with any HTTP endpoint. This includes services running on your data center provided there is network connectivity. In an upcoming section called *Securing an API*, we will also show you how to integrate API Gateway with Amazon Cognito for authentication and authorization.

Amazon API Gateway can act as a service proxy, which is an interesting concept. This functionality allows you to create an HTTP endpoint to expose an AWS service as a backend. What this enables you to do is apply your own RESTful API definitions with all of the additional benefits of web-type security controls and traffic management. And you can skip your compute layer altogether. An example use case could be when you need your frontend web application to store some data, such as comments on a thread or messages in a chat. Using DynamoDB as a service proxy integration point would allow you to implement a CRUD-like API that the frontend can directly interface with. There are plenty of other useful examples as well, and we'll have a look at some of those in the *Use cases* section.

So, what happens when we connect up a Lambda as a backend integration? At a high-level view, here is the sequence of events performed by API Gateway:

1. Receives the request
2. Authenticates and authorizes the request
3. Applies the mapping template
4. Invokes the Lambda function
5. Applies output mappings to translate the Lambda response if required
6. Responds to the client

Let's take a quick look at what options are available for authentication and authorization. We'll go into detail later in the *Securing an API* section:

- First, there are API keys. These are long-lived keys that you can issue and attach to a set of permissions. To use a key to access an API, you need to add it to a header called `x-api-key`. It is not advisable to use API keys as a primary means of securing an API because of the risk of the key being leaked. Instead, they are more suited for use in development and testing environments where you are not using production data.
- Another option is to use a scoped IAM credential and sign the HTTP request using **Signature Version 4 (SigV4)**.
- The next option, and probably the recommended option in most cases, is to use Amazon Cognito (`https://aws.amazon.com/cognito/`).
- Finally, you can also create your own authentication and authorization implementation with the use of Lambda authorizers.

You can also pair API key protection with the other methods if you need to, and it is definitely recommended that you pair the use of API keys with a stronger authentication method.

As far as pricing goes, you're in luck—it's pretty cheap. Following the serverless model, you only pay for what you use. The free tier includes one million API requests per month for free for a year. If you pair that with the free tier Lambda invocations, then it's likely you won't be paying anything at all to run a simple RESTful API.

When you go over that amount or your account is older than a year, then the API Gateway cost is $3.50 per million requests. It is tiered pricing, so the more you use, the cheaper it will be but note that the next tier is at 1 billion requests per month! Also note that the pricing and tiers vary between regions, so check on the pricing page to find your region. Caching, data transfer, and CloudWatch all have additional costs as well.

Something to be aware of before going into production with an API is the account-level service limits. By default, API Gateway has a maximum throughput that is throttled to 10,000 requests per second with a burst capacity of 5,000 requests. Clients will receive an HTTP 429 response if this happens. The limit can be increased with a support request. Another limit to be aware of is the payload size. The maximum amount of data you can send with a request is 10 MB, and this cannot be increased. There's a trap for young players here as well. The maximum payload size of a Lambda request is 6 MB, so you will find that requests will fail if the payload is over 6 MB even though they are within the valid size for API Gateway.

Deployment options

Next, we're going to run through the options for the different endpoint types. The underlying implementation and network connectivity will depend on the option you pick, so it's important to know what you need before deploying.

The first option follows the example given in the previous section: edge-optimized endpoints. An edge-optimized endpoint is a deployment that leverages the CloudFront global distribution network and is useful if you have clients connecting from multiple locations around the world. API requests are sent to the nearest CloudFront point of presence, or edge, which can improve latencies for connections. At the time of writing, there were 189 edge locations across 37 countries.

The next is a regional endpoint deployment type, which is similar to the first option but doesn't come with a CloudFront distribution by default. You can still create and connect your own distribution to an endpoint; doing this would give you the flexibility of being able to manage your own.

Finally, a long-awaited feature is the private endpoint type. This enables you to create an API endpoint inside your own VPC. Previously an API endpoint was public by default, so the introduction of this feature allows you to deploy API Gateway so it can be used by private resources in your subnets. This endpoint type uses VPC endpoints, so you will need to create and apply a resource policy that allows API invocations from your own source VPC.

As shown in the following, the endpoint type can be selected when you're creating a new API:

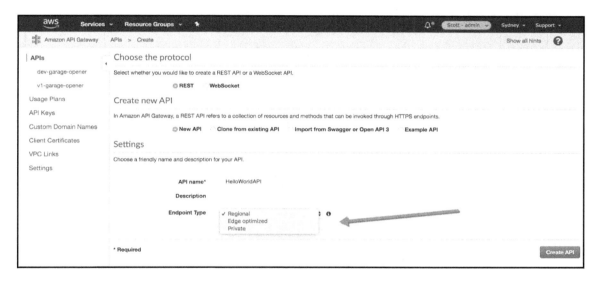

Screenshot of API Gateway console, creating a new API

Another relatively new feature is the ability to create WebSocket APIs—more details on that next.

WebSockets

A recent addition to the feature set of API Gateway brought the ability to create WebSocket APIs. In the last screenshot, you can see that there are now two options for the types of API you can create. Because it is such a new feature, I wanted to cover it in depth in its own section.

Let's start by reviewing what WebSockets are and why they're so useful for frontend clients. WebSocket is actually a transmission protocol built on TCP (`https://tools.ietf.org/html/rfc6455`) and allows a two-way, long-lived connection between client and host. The protocol is now supported by most modern browsers.

The words long-lived don't gel well with serverless compute—think about the timeout for a Lambda. Usually, a Lambda will be invoked by an event, do some compute, and respond before terminating and erasing state. The content views in the frontend of a website can't often handle the state being so ephemeral. The state needs to persist at least for the length of a web session, so the content view doesn't change unexpectedly and lose information. That's where the new API Gateway connection model can be useful.

For an overview of how a WebSocket API works with API Gateway, study the next diagram. It shows an example of a view that gets updated by a client:

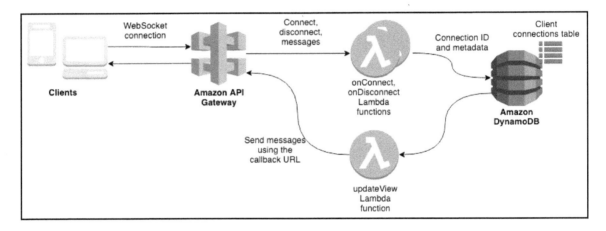

Overview of a WebSocket API using API Gateway

Amazon API Gateway maintains the WebSocket connection with the client and fires off events to Lambda when certain things happen during the life of the connection.

Two Lambda functions are triggered when the client connects and disconnects, and then one to update the view:

- `onConnect`
- `onDisconnect`
- `updateView`

When the view is updated, the `updateView` Lambda function is triggered to make the updates and to update all of the connected clients. The clients are updated using the Management API (see version 2 of the API reference), with details of the connected clients persisted in a DynamoDB table. There's a link to both versions of the Management API reference in the *Further reading* section.

So now we understand the basic characteristics of API Gateway, let's talk about some use cases before delving more deeply into the details.

Use cases

We've covered the preceding WebSocket use case for API Gateway, so let's explore a few more at a high level. Some of the examples are not strictly serverless but we're looking to get a broad understanding of where this technology is useful.

The first use case to cover is the Serverless API model, where all of the components that you use live within the serverless category in the AWS ecosystem. You can build a RESTful API backed by Lambda that stores documents or state in a DynamoDB database.

The following shows the request flow with API Gateway exposing a RESTful API and Lambda used as the compute backend, which performs actions on a DynamoDB table:

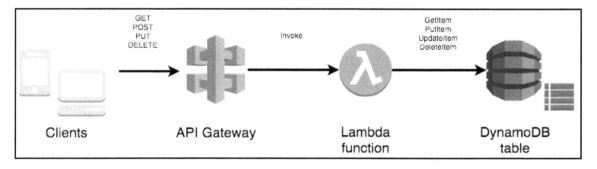

Flow of a REST request to an API

This is a really simple model and there is surely an unlimited number of examples you can apply this to. If the type of processing or compute that you need to do is multi-step or needs greater control or orchestration, you can use API Gateway in front of AWS Step Functions. Invoking a method on Gateway can kick off a workflow in Step Functions that can invoke Lambda functions.

In this example, we have added API Gateway in front of step functions to add our layer of API management and give us the flexibility to implement our own logic or transformations before the execution of a state machine. This example doesn't need to include a DynamoDB table because our state is stored in a Step Functions state machine. Lambda is used as our compute provider:

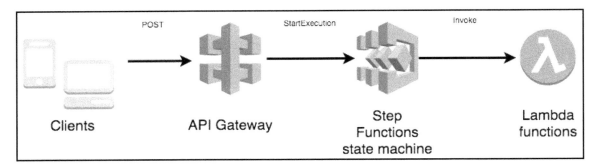

Flow of a REST request as a proxy to a Step Functions state machine

API Gateway also enables APIs for container-based microservices. You could roll your own container orchestration on EC2 with an API in front.

The following example shows **API Gateway** in front of a compute workload. The auto scaling group contains EC2 instances running containers, with the load and session durability being provided by an **Elastic Load Balancer**:

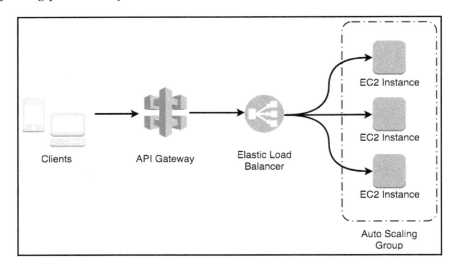

Using API Gateway in front of a server-based workload

Or you could pick from one of the many managed container platforms that AWS offers such as Amazon ECS, Amazon EKS, AWS Fargate, or Amazon Elastic Bealkstalk (for Docker). The diagram for these examples would look much the same as the preceding. Container platforms also use EC2 for their compute workloads but are managed by a separate control plane.

Before we finish, let's look at one additional use case that is slightly different: securing a backing AWS service by setting up a service proxy. Every service in AWS has a public API. Sometimes, you want to expose the functionality of that API to your clients. You might also want to augment or restrict parts of the API, and you will definitely want to add your own web security controls.

The following diagram shows an example of using API Gateway as a service proxy to Amazon Kinesis:

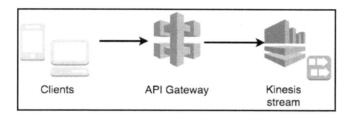

| Clients | API Gateway | Kinesis stream |

Using API Gateway as a service proxy to Kinesis

This is a way to enable clients to publish events directly into Kinesis using the `PutRecord` method. You might want to use this design to ingest clickstream events or for IoT devices. As discussed earlier, using API Gateway in front of any service can abstract the implementation of the underlying compute or data store. This makes the implementation modular and flexible, allowing you to migrate the backend to something else without significantly impacting the consumer. For the preceding Kinesis example, you might want to migrate to another event-sourcing solution such as Kafka in the future. Keep this in mind when building your own APIs because, as your technology options evolve, you want to maintain flexibility and agility so you can change your systems to make use of the benefits of newer technology.

That was an introduction to Amazon API Gateway, deployment options, and some common deployment patterns. Next is an important topic—how to secure our APIs.

Securing an API

Security of the resources you are trying to protect is an important topic, and that's why we are covering it before getting into explaining how to build and deploy APIs. API Gateway is often used as a security appliance as a front door for client connections. This is a good idea, so it pays to familiarize ourselves with our options.

In this section, we will cover IAM permissions, authentication with Amazon Cognito, Lambda authorizers, and certificate management.

IAM permissions and policies

The first option to cover is the IAM authentication method for securing APIs. To clarify, there are two main ways to use IAM:

- The first is to provide administrative access to create, update, maintain, and delete APIs.
- The second is to control which entities can invoke or execute an existing API—this is the component that this section is focused on.

The benefit of using IAM for access control is that it centralizes our authentication and authorization concerns to a single service. Those of us who have been using AWS for a while will also be very familiar with the IAM service as it is integrated with almost everything. Changes we make to roles or policies can also be made without redeploying any API code, and the changes are instant without causing outages. This also gives us the ability to quickly disable any roles or issued credentials during a security incident. The downside of using IAM is that each of your clients will need an IAM user or role. This isn't so bad for internal clients or services, but it isn't suitable for securing web-based APIs.

To enable a client to make a successful request to an API, there must be an IAM policy attached to an entity that permits such an action. The action to allow is called `execute-api:Invoke`. The API also needs to be created or deployed using the method property authorization type set to `AWS_IAM`.

The following JSON shows the format of a policy document with some allowed permissions included:

```
{
    "Version": "2012-10-17",
    "Statement": [
        {
            "Effect": "Allow",
            "Action": [
                "execute-api:Invoke"
            ],
            "Resource": [
                "arn:aws:execute-api:${region}:${account-id}:${api-
id}/${stage}/${METHOD_HTTP_VERB}/${pesource-path}"
            ]
        }
    ]
}
```

In the preceding policy document, you can clearly see we can be very specific about the API Gateway methods that the user is allowed to invoke, right down to path level. You can also specify the HTTP method, which gives you the flexibility to give access to the POST method and deny access to the DELETE method for a particular path, for example.

When an IAM user is created you can also generate security keys—namely, an access key, and a secret access key. Now, to invoke an API gateway method using your newly minted IAM credentials, you will need to sign the request using SigV. The process for signing the request is quite complex so I recommend that you use the AWS SDKs or another library in your chosen language to do the job for you instead of rolling your own.

We've just learned about the way we can secure an API using the IAM method. The implementation of authentication is made more simple with the help of Amazon Cognito, which we will cover next.

Authentication with Cognito

Amazon Cognito is a managed service that provides a mechanism for authenticating and authorizing users for the web. We'll be covering the two main components for user management—user pools and identity pools. Each component is different and you can pick the one that suits your needs best or even use both. When I first used Cognito, I thought it was performing magic, and it totally is, so I'm excited to be able to share this service with you!

Cognito was designed to provide authentication, authorization, and user management capabilities. For the authentication part, users of a protected service can be local or federated to identity providers such as Facebook or Google for social identities, or your own enterprise identity provider. Authentication is implemented with a token-based standard with OAuth 2.0 support. For authorization, Cognito can be used to enable fine-grained access control. User management includes a full range of user lifecycle controls including a user directory; it can store user data against a profile, and it exposes metrics for analytics and security.

As mentioned early, there are two ways to federate users for authentication. Cognito User Pools can federate with social media accounts—Amazon, Facebook, and Google are supported. It can also create and manage users within the User Pool itself, like a local user profile. Once the user has signed into the identity provider, a set of **OpenID Connect (OIDC)** tokens are returned to the client, including an ID token, access token, and a refresh token:

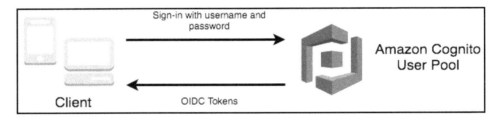

High-level authentication flow with Cognito with OAuth

How this works with API Gateway is shown as follows:

1. When you've created an API, you head over to the **Authorizers** section and create a new authorizer.
2. User Pools itself don't deal with authorization—this is implemented in your own code using scopes. You will need to have a user pool already created and ready to select. The **Token Source** field tells API Gateway which request header it should look for a token in:

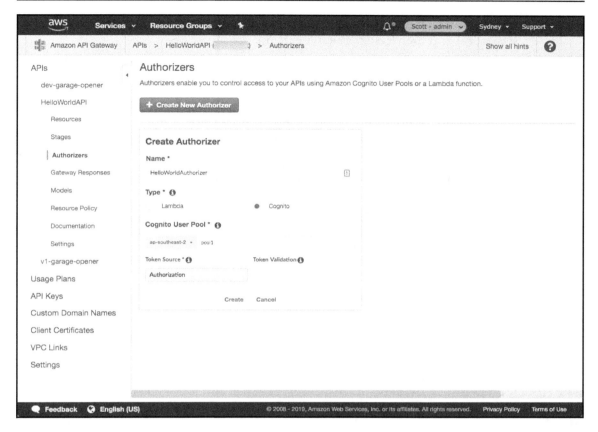

API Gateway console showing where to create a new Authorizer

3. You can then configure a new or existing method to use the new authorizer to protect the resource.

You will need to refresh the API Gateway console after creating the new authorizer for it to show up as an option.

4. Once the change has been deployed, sending requests to that method now means you need to include your token (which is actually a **JSON Web Token (JWT)**) in the authorization header.

5. API Gateway will decode the JWT to check its validity (pool ID, issuer, and signature) and then invoke the integration:

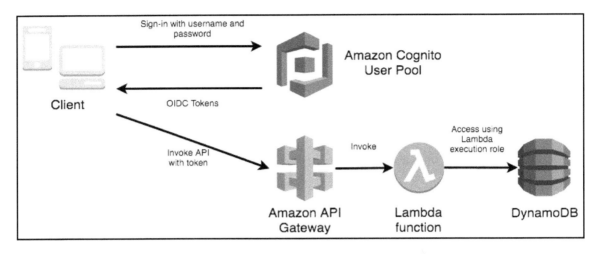

Using a Cognito type Authorizer with API Gateway

Alternatively, Cognito Identity Pools can provide temporary scoped AWS credentials for accessing resources using IAM. These credentials are assigned to a role, so they can have an associated policy document predefined. Using this method allows the client to directly access other AWS resources using those IAM credentials, and this is the main difference between User Pools and Identity Pools. When we add API Gateway to the mix using Identity Pools, we should be protecting methods with the AWS_IAM authorizer type. It is also important to note that when using a Lambda backend, we can now use the client's IAM credentials to call AWS resources on their behalf instead of using the Lambda execution role. This allows for a more fine-grained approach.

Let's run through the scenario of a client that has already been through authentication with a user pool. This is an example of using both User Pools and Identity Pools together. The client has received the OAuth tokens back, but wants to directly access DynamoDB. DynamoDB supports IAM for access control, so we need to go to Identity Pools to swap our tokens for some IAM credentials.

The following diagram shows the flow for signing in, receiving a token, and then exchanging the token for AWS credentials:

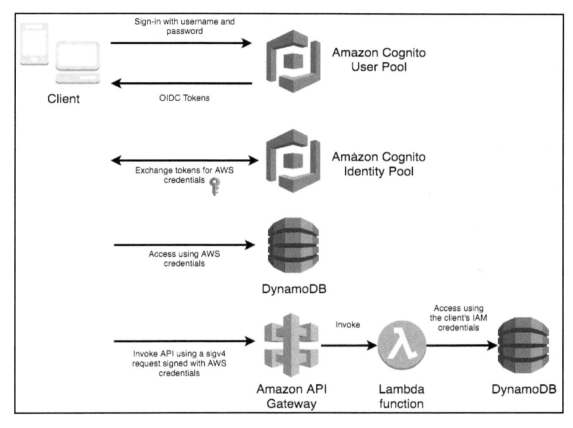

Exchanging OIDC tokens for temporary scoped AWS credentials

We can see in this example that, once we have the AWS credentials, then we can either access the AWS resources directly (if the IAM policy allows) or make a request to an IAM-protected API Gateway method.

So, that's pretty cool and rather useful. Say we had some additional requirements and needed to implement our own authorization logic instead of using IAM. Maybe we have to check with another authorization provider before being able to decide whether or not to grant access to the requestor. The next section explains Lambda authorizers, which we can use to add more logic to our authentication and authorization flows.

Lambda authorizers

Using a Lambda authorizer is another option to secure access to your APIs. You can use this mechanism if you want to implement something custom that is not covered by API Gateway or Cognito features. You might have extra fact checking and injection to perform or you might need to further validate the origin of a request. By using a Lambda authorizer, you can also separate your authorization logic from the business logic inside a Lambda function, and then go on to reuse that authorization logic for other APIs. This keeps your code base nice and clean and allows you to separate responsibilities if the authorization logic were to be maintained by another team, for example, a SecOps team.

Lambda authorizers are invoked before the integrated backend Lambda function to facilitate checking before your code runs. They are natively invoked by API Gateway and return a policy document describing the permissions that the client has or doesn't have. Basically, you need to assemble and return this yourself. It's the same policy document as IAM uses with allow and deny statements. Additionally, you can include some extra context to pass to your backend integration. Note here that the format of the values is all strings and not JSON objects.

Let's take a look:

```
{
    "principalId": "${user-identity}",
    "policyDocument": {
        "Version": "2012-10-17",
        "Statement": [
            {
                "Effect": "Allow",
                "Action": "execute-api:Invoke",
                "Resource": "arn:aws:execute-api:${region}:${account-
id}:${api-id}/${stage}/${METHOD_HTTP_VERB}/${resource-path}"
            }
        ]
    },
    "context": {
        "string": "value",
        "number": "1",
        "boolean": "true"
    }
}
```

When API Gateway receives the policy document, it is cached for up to an hour. This is so API Gateway doesn't have to check every time a new request is received from the same client, which improves the latency of the request. Let's have a look at that authorization flow:

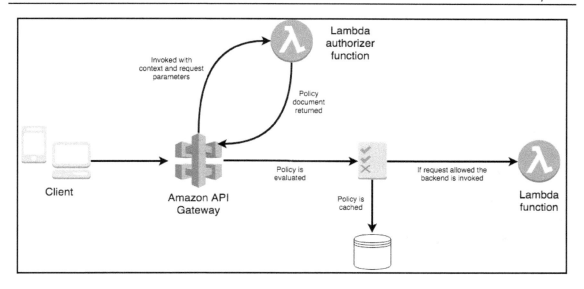

The authorization flow for a custom Lambda authorizer

Great, so we learned some extra functionality for when we need a more flexible authorization implementation. Now, let's have a look at how we secure the endpoint itself at the transport layer. For that, we need to use certificates to secure the endpoint, and there's more about that in the next section.

Certificates

A security section wouldn't be complete without mentioning certificates and domains. Specifically, what options do we have for bringing our own SSL/TLS certificates and creating custom domain names?

When you create a new API, the endpoint starts with a domain provided by AWS:

```
https://api-id.execute-api.region.amazonaws.com
```

This endpoint is also protected by a certificate issued by Amazon. When we deploy our own APIs, we want the endpoints to match our own domains—at least in production, for example, `https://api.mycompany.com`.

Thankfully, **AWS Certificate Manager** (**ACM**, `https://aws.amazon.com/certificate-manager/`) is integrated into API Gateway, so we can use our own SSL/TLS certificate. To do so, we need to create or import a certificate (PEM-encoded) into ACM.

If you're planning to create an edge-optimized API, then the certificate needs to exist in the us-east-1 region.

Once you have a certificate registered and available, we can head over to the API Gateway console to create our own custom domain name. Creating a new custom domain name makes changes to CloudFront distributions, so make sure you have the appropriate permissions to do so.

The following screenshot shows where to add your custom domain name and where to select the certificate hosted in ACM:

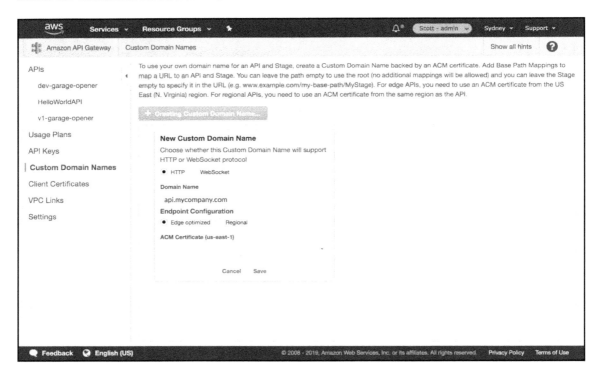

The API Gateway console showing where to create a custom domain name

Here, you get to choose between a domain name for REST or WebSocket API.

Note that you can't associate a custom domain name with both API types or use custom domain names for private endpoint types.

The drop-down field for ACM Certificate will populate with the existing certificates available for you to choose from. A key thing to note that, after creating the domain name, you will need to update your DNS to point to the API's CloudFront distribution for edge-optimized APIs or the API endpoint for regional APIs.

API Gateway also can generate and use client-side SSL certificates for mutual authentication. This is a more advanced topic that you can read about in the AWS documentation; see the link in the *Further reading* section.

That concludes our topic about securing APIs, where we went through the standard options supported by API Gateway. We should now better understand how easy it is to make an API more secure and get started building these into our solutions. Moving on to the next section, we will learn how to build and deploy APIs.

Building, deploying, and managing APIs

Now that we know how to properly secure our APIs, the next thing to do is learn how to build and deploy APIs. Additionally, there are a bunch of controls that will make managing APIs possible.

We're going to explore some of the options and concepts, then in the next section, we'll pull it all together to deploy our very own API.

Building APIs

After covering an introduction to API Gateway, there are a few more concepts and details to learn before we create our own API. We'll start by reviewing the concepts then explain some of the ways to create and build APIs.

An API built and deployed to Amazon API Gateway is made up of resources, methods, and integrations. To show examples of what these look like in the console, we're going to use a real API that has been built to control the garage doors at home.

Don't worry, this API has the proper security controls in place:

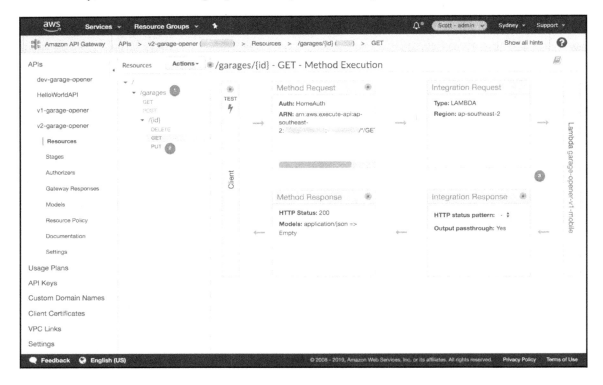

The API Gateway console showing the method execution page for a GET method

First up are resources, which are the logical entities that make up the path of an API. You can see at point number (**1**) on the preceding screenshot that I have created /garages, which is the superset for all of my garage IDs in /{id}. The curly brackets are to denote a variable. Under each resource, there are several methods (**2**). This is a combination of the resource path and an HTTP verb and can be considered in REST as an action or operation on that particular entity. For example, I can send a GET request to /garages/2 and expect to see all of the details that are relevant to the garage with ID = 2. We have clicked into the **Resource** page and clicked on a particular method, so we are presented with the method execution overview. This shows a nice representation of the request/response flow when an API is invoked. Around point (**3**), we can see the details of the integration; in this case, it is with a Lambda function.

Let's click into the **Integration Request** and see what's available. This page shows us a drill-down of all of the options available; see the following screenshot:

← Method Execution   /garages/{id} - GET - Integration Request

Provide information about the target backend that this method will call and whether the incoming request data should be modified.

Integration type ○ Lambda Function ❶

○ HTTP ❶

○ Mock ❶

○ AWS Service ❶

○ VPC Link ❶

Use Lambda Proxy integration ○ ❶

Lambda Region ap-southeast-2 ✎

Lambda Function garage-opener-v1-mobile ✎

Execution role ✎

Invoke with caller credentials ❶

Credentials cache Do not add caller credentials to cache key ✎

Use Default Timeout ☑ ❶

▶ URL Path Parameters

▶ URL Query String Parameters

▶ HTTP Headers

▶ Mapping Templates

The integration request options for a GET method

Here, we can see the options for changing the type of integration; note that we have a Mock type available. This is a common feature of API Gateways and integration solutions and allows a developer to create an API without the implementation of business logic so that other teams can develop against the expected API response in parallel.

The next feature is Lambda proxy integration, which allows a builder to pass everything from the request straight to the Lambda without manipulation or transformation. To use this, you can set a path variable of `{proxy+}` with a method of `ANY` (which means all methods). This functionality will detach the API specification from the implementation and allow for greater flexibility in Lambda development since it will accept any path and method. The downside is that the client now has to know a lot more details about what is built in the backend because they can't check an API specification for the supported requests.

Further down the page, we see some hidden sections to create data mappings. These are input mappings and you can also create output mappings during the Integration Response flow. Using mappings is a way to transform requests into support for your integrations and can be used in reverse to support a client. An example of this is transforming a response from JSON into XML. There's a specific syntax for creating models to map templates; we're not going to get into that in this book.

Moving on, the following are the ways in which we can build APIs using API Gateway in AWS:

- The API Gateway console is a good way to prototype ideas, run ad hoc tests, and visually check on the current state. If you were building and deploying regularly to production, then you would hopefully be using a continuous integration pipeline to facilitate that. In that situation, you need something more powerful than the console.
- The API Gateway CLI is useful for making changes quickly or programmatically. Like the console, commands can be issued on the fly without a whole lot of change governance.
- Infrastructure as Code is possible using AWS CloudFormation. This is when you declare the details of an API in a template written in JSON or YAML. The template file is then deployed to the CloudFormation service, which takes care of creating or updating the AWS resources. Infrastructure as Code is great because you can store the templates in source control, which enables versioning by design and allows multiple parties to work on the build. Approving a new release to be deployed becomes a matter of reviewing the difference created in the pull request.

- Some builders prefer to define their APIs in an industry-standard specification format. API Gateway supports importing APIs written within Swagger, or the OpenAPI specification as it's now called. There are also extensions for the OpenAPI specification to support authorizer types and the data mapping functionality.

- Finally, in my opinion, the best workflow for developing APIs with Lambda and other resources is to use an application framework. Examples include AWS Serverless Application Model, Serverless Framework, AWS Cloud Development Kit, and the AWS Chalice microframework. These are really good because it allows you to pair your API definitions with your implementation code. Serverless Framework is particularly awesome because it can take your Lambda code and event mappings, create a CloudFormation template, bundle everything up, and deploy them. It also comes with a CLI for deployment and management. This really is the best of all of the options for building production APIs.

Now we understand the concepts involved when we talk about building APIs using API Gateway. After we build something, we need to be able to deploy it so that users can interact with the service. We'll cover deploying APIs in the next section.

Deploying APIs

Once we've written an API implementation and declared the infrastructure that should be created, how do we deploy it? When deploying things, we need options to support a software development lifecycle, so that we can safely promote artifacts through the various environments using an appropriate release method. We'll be covering Continuous Integration/Continuous Delivery pipelines in a later chapter. For this section, however, we need to understand the native capabilities and features of Amazon API Gateway when it comes to deployment.

The way that API Gateway separates deployments of an API is by using stages. To be clear, we're talking about separating a deployment of a single API here and not creating an entirely new instance. Stages can be used for an API's lifecycle, to move changes through or to enable different settings (caching and throttling) for different deployments. You can use as many or as few stages as you would like (10 is the default soft limit) and use them for whatever you need. For example, you could use them to enable versioning for your API. The syntax looks like this:

```
https://<domain-name>/<stage-name>/<resource-path>
```

So, the example of how versioning could be implemented would be `https://api.mycompany.com/v1/widgets` and `https://api.mycompany.com/v2/widgets`.

Another feature that comes with using stages is stage variables. These work sort of like environment variables for your APIs. You can store things for configuration or extra context, and then reference them using the curly bracket syntax, for example, `${stageVar}`. You might use a stage variable to abstract an element that changes across lifecycle environments. This would allow you to reuse code and inject specific values at deploy time.

Notice here that I haven't mentioned an example of how you could use stages as lifecycle environments—that is, `dev`, `uat`, or `prod`. You might be tempted to do this, but a better idea is to have separate instances of the API for each environment. Often, in larger deployments, these instances might even be in different accounts. Separating environments into their own instances allows you to apply different security guard rails, administrator access controls, and configuration elements such as log levels.

Okay, we've already run through what the console looks like for building APIs, so let's fire up our command line and run through a deployment using the CLI. This command assumes the resources, methods, integrations, and stage have been created:

```
aws apigateway create-deployment
    --rest-api-id ${api-id}
    --stage-name ${stage-name}
    --description 'My first deployment'
```

As far as deployment commands go, this is fairly straightforward. This will deploy any changes you have made to the specified stage.

Releasing code to production can often be a risky endeavor. If it goes wrong, then real users can be negatively affected, which could impact customer churn rate and revenue. Thankfully, with the create-deployment command, the deployment is pushed without downtime and existing requests won't be disconnected. But there's always a possibility that your backend code implementation has a problem or hits an edge case that wasn't expected or tested. Surely, there's a less risky method to releasing code? Well, there is. It's called a canary release—a method of rolling out the deployment slowly so it's available to a handful of users first. Vital service metrics can then be monitored using your tooling, and then you can make a decision to roll back the deployment if error rates rapidly increase or you become confident enough to decide to roll out the change to the rest of the user base.

So, how does this work with API Gateway? When you have deployed an initial release to a production stage and you want to make a change with a canary release, you need to create the canary release in the stage configuration. This will give you options for the percentage of traffic that is split across the base release and the new release:

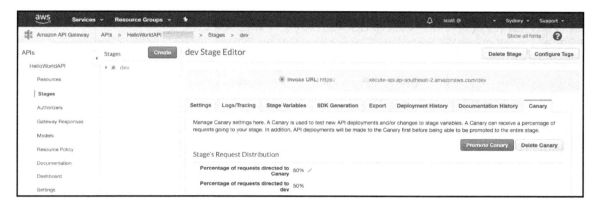

The API Gateway console showing the options for creating a canary release for the dev stage of an API

API traffic is split at random to maintain the configured ratio. Once it's deployed, you can make changes to it in the same place in the console or use the CLI. Let's see an example of updating the traffic percentage to 25% using the CLI:

```
aws apigateway update-stage
    --rest-api-id ${api-id}
    --stage-name ${stage-name}
    --patch-operations
op=replace,path=/canarySettings/percentTraffic,value=25.0
```

There is also another step to finally promote the canary release into the new production base release. Check out the AWS documentation for examples of how to do that. Once a deployment has been completed, there is a cool feature that helps you to kickstart the consumption of your API. You might want to publish this along with your API specification on your developer portal. I'm talking about generating the SDK for your API, and that is done through the console or CLI. API Gateway will generate SDKs in a supported language: Java, JavaScript, Java for Android, Objective C or Swift for iOS, and Ruby.

We've covered some of the details for deploying APIs to API Gateway. Later on, we're going to cover an application framework that combines building, testing, and deployment to create a really useful toolset. We'll also cover in-depth how this framework would be integrated into a CI/CD pipeline in Chapter 8, *CI/CD with Serverless Framework*. Stay tuned for that!

Once we have deployed our API, we then have to switch our focus to managing the API while it is in use. The next section will teach us about the benefits of throttling and managing the number of requests to our service.

Throttling and quota management

Part of the management functionality that API Gateway provides is the ability to control traffic. This can be achieved through throttling the rate of requests and the total number of requests. One reason you might want to throttle requests through your API Gateway is to protect your backend integrations from sudden spikes in load. Maybe the backend architecture has performance bottlenecks, like a monolithic database with limited max connections, or maybe there is a lead time in scaling EC2 instances to handle the new load.

Throttling and quotas in API Gateway can be configured when using API keys by creating a usage plan. This allows the key to be metered and then your traffic rules are applied once the configured threshold has been reached.

The following screenshot shows an example of an API usage plan, which describes the thresholds at which the traffic rules kick in:

API usage plan settings in API Gateway

Requests exceeding the limits are responded to with an `HTTP 429 Too Many Requests` status code. You can also set the throttling limits at the method level by configuring the stage settings, shown as follows:

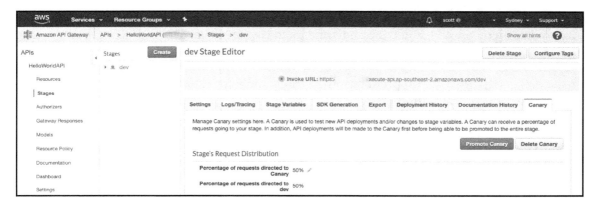

The options for setting throttling limits in an API stage

And finally, each AWS account has a default limit applied that can be increased by submitting a service request. The soft limit is set to 10,000 requests per second with a burst capacity of 5,000 requests. So, what does this burst capacity mean, and how is it measured and applied?

> Request usage limits are applied in the order of the most specific (API keys) to the least specific (account level).

API Gateway uses a token bucket algorithm to implement the throttling logic. There are two components to the algorithm:

- **Burst capacity**: This is the maximum size of the token bucket.
- **Rate**: This is the number of tokens (or requests) that get added to the bucket.

The details of the token bucket algorithm get too complex for this section, but there are some great resources online if you want to know more. The next thing we need to think about after deploying our API is monitoring usage metrics, logging activity, and exceptions—see in the next section.

Monitoring and logging

Next up, let's investigate what services and features are available to help us operate our APIs once deployed. We're talking logs and monitoring. Straight out of the box, there is a set of CloudWatch Metrics that are collected as soon as a deployed API starts executing. After you deploy an API, a new option appears in the pages list for your API called Dashboard. Here, you will find a basic dashboard showing some metrics. You can find and manipulate the metrics views a little better in the CloudWatch console. Here, you can also create alarms that can fire on predetermined thresholds, for example, if the 5XXError metric rises above a bad number.

When developing any kind of software, it's always a good idea to have event logs and exception logging. This is so you can trace the transactions or things happening in your system, which is also extremely useful for troubleshooting. Without API Gateway logs, we would be missing a piece of the puzzle that might be crucial to resolving the root cause of an incident. API Gateway can log its access logs to CloudWatch Logs. To set up logging, you first need to give the API Gateway service an ARN of an IAM role to use.

The next steps shows where to input this information:

1. Click **Settings**.
2. Then, input the ARN into the **CloudWatch log role ARN** field:

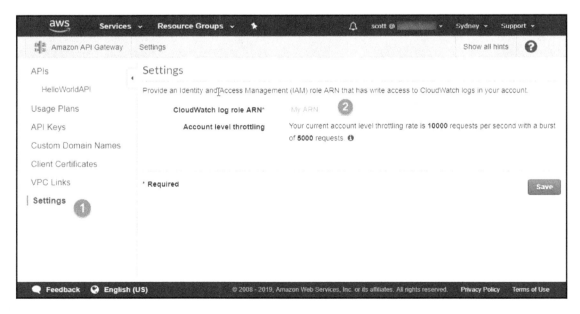

The API Gateway console showing where to input the configuration for API logging

This is enabled in an odd location, so it might trip up some users. You only need to configure this role once, per account. Then, you can set up logging in the stage settings.

The following shows the stage settings, where we find the **Logs/Tracing** tab:

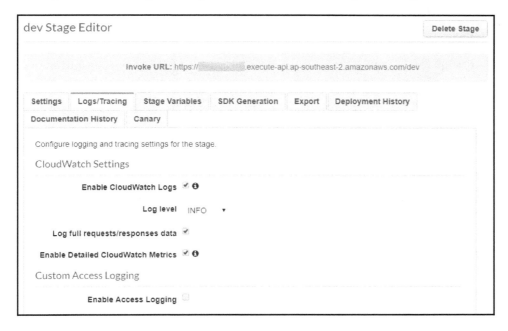

API stage settings showing where to enable logging for the stage

Once the logs are streaming into CloudWatch Logs, a lot of people choose to ship these to another service such as Elasticsearch for further analysis. Third-party log analytics tools such as Splunk or Sumologic have integrations as well.

Now we understand how to enable logging for our APIs, we'll move on to writing and deploying our very own.

Building a Lambda-backed API

Alright, we're getting to the fun stuff! We're about to piece together what we've learned in this chapter to create an API of our own. We'll use the Lambda function from the previous chapter as an integration point for a new RESTful API.

Then, we'll fire some test messages and see what we get!

Hello world using the console

For this section, we'll create a new API and smoke-test it using GUI-based tools. This is the best way to introduce the required steps, and it's good to be able to see the feedback straightaway on the console.

Let's create a new RESTful API:

1. Create a new API with a regional endpoint type and give it a useful name. The API will be created but with no resources or methods—let's change that.

2. Make a new resource by clicking **Actions** | **Create Resource**. Don't worry too much about the resource name or path, we're not trying to create the most RESTful API in the world here.

   The following screenshot shows where to find the **Create Resource** action:

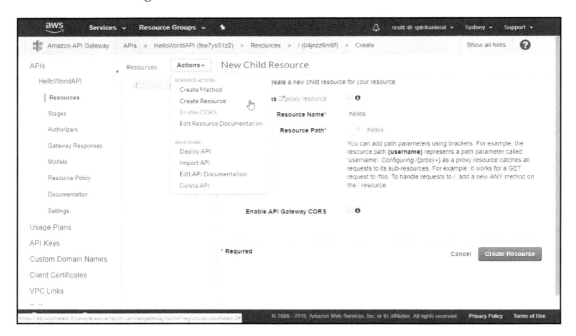

Creating a new child resource for an API

3. Next, we need a new method, so we can perform actions against the resource we just created. Let's go with a simple GET method. There's a little tick icon that appears when creating a method—it's hard to see and you need to click it to confirm the method type.

The following shows the settings I've used for the GET method. We want to connect this new API to use our Lambda function as a backend integration, so specify the function you created earlier and click **Save**:

How to connect our GET method to our Lambda function

API Gateway will automatically add the IAM permissions that are needed for API Gateway to be allowed to invoke your Lambda function.

It's good practice to make ourselves an API key to use when doing our development. We might only be using test or public data during this process but it's important to still control the traffic to the endpoint.

To be able to enable some basic API management, we first need a usage plan, so let's create one:

1. Log in to the management console and head over to the API Gateway console.
2. Click on **Usage Plans** and create a new plan using values that you think would be sensible.

I'm going to pick a request rate of 100 requests per second with a burst capacity of 500 requests. Because we only have one developer working on this API, I'm also going to limit the total quota down to accepting only 1,000 requests per day.

The following shows an example of my usage plan. You can copy my settings or use your own sensible values:

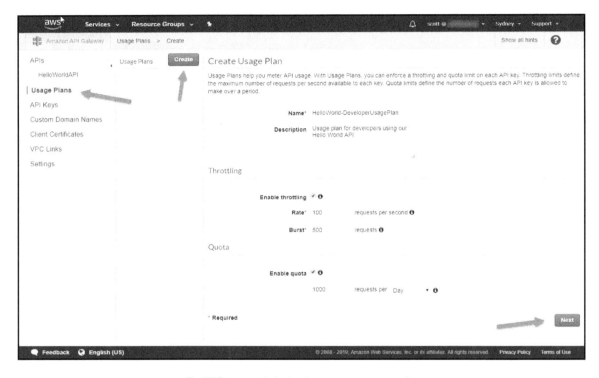

The API Gateway console showing where to create your own usage plan

We can skip adding an API stage for now but we'll need to come back to this later to associate the usage plan with a stage.

3. On the next screen, let's create a new API key and include it in this new usage plan. You can also create keys any time using the **Usage Plan API Keys** screen:

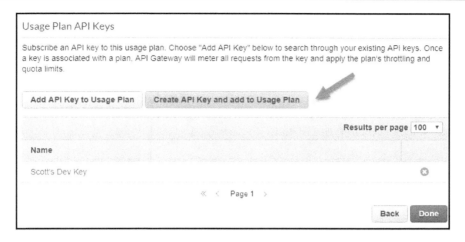

Adding your API key to a usage plan

Cool, now we've got a credential to call our API with. You can find the value of the key under the **API Keys** screen:

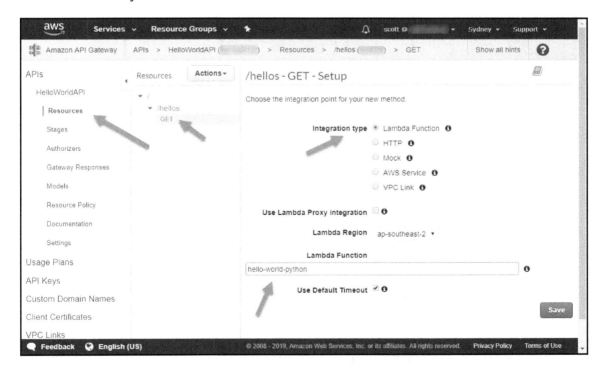

Where to find your newly created API key

Great, so we've created our new resource, method, usage plan, and API key. Feel free to click around and explore the options for the method execution as well. Before we deploy or publish our API, let's make sure that the resource is properly secured with the API key we created:

1. In the **Method Execution** screen, click into **Method Request**. Change **API Key Required** to **true**. The following screenshot indicates which settings to update. Remember to click the little tick when done:

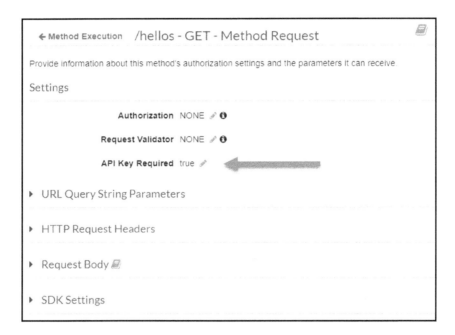

Screenshot showing where to secure an API resource using an API key

2. Now, we will create a new stage and deploy it to our endpoint. Click **Actions | Deploy API** and create a new stage called dev. Done! That's how simple it is to author a new RESTful API and deploy it to an endpoint.
3. The last thing we need to do is hook our usage plan up to the new stage so we can access it with an API key. Head back over to the **Usage Plan** page, select the plan we created, and follow the steps to add an API stage to the plan.

Okay, it's time to test it. I'm going to use a tool called Postman to send a GET request to our resource. Notice here that I've included the API key as the value of the x-api-key header. You'll need to do the same with your key.

The following shows Postman with an example request to my API. The bottom section shows the response data:

An example request to our API using Postman

Oh no! It's responded with an error. Looking at the logs of the function execution in CloudWatch Logs, we can see the error trace.

I've included a screenshot of my log output in CloudWatch logs. It looks like there is an issue at line 4:

Subset of CloudWatch log entries from our function execution

Our function code is expecting two input fields, text and repeat. The code doesn't know how to handle it when those fields aren't present and therefore terminates the execution. Let's add a line to our function so that it returns something when there is no input. Given that we are now using this function as a backend to a RESTful API, we should also make sure we are returning a JSON response.

Let's extend the hello-world-python function code a little bit and save it:

```python
import os, json

def hello_handler(event, context):
    if not event:
        return {
            "body": "Hello, world!"
        }
    text_input = event["text"]
    repetitions = event["repeat"]
    if text_input and repetitions > 0:
        response = {}
        for i in range(0, repetitions):
            print(text_input)
            response[i] = text_input
        return {
            "body": response
        }
    return None
```

Now when we perform the same request in Postman, we get a nice HTTP 200 response and our message. What we have managed to do here is make changes and redeploy our backend implementation logic independently of our API Gateway deployment. That's pretty cool. We also saw what happens when we make a mistake and where to troubleshoot errors. Don't be afraid to deploy often and make lots of mistakes—it's all part of the fail-fast mentality.

After we have developed and deployed via the management console a few times, we start to wonder whether there is a more efficient workflow for development. There absolutely is. In the next section, we will see how we can build on our example but this time using the AWS command-line interface.

Hello world via the CLI

Next, we're going to extend the API we built in the previous section. We're going to use the command line entirely to create a new method, deploy it to a `dev` stage, and fire off some test requests. If you haven't created your API key and usage plan yet, go back to the last section and do that before progressing.

Using your AWS CLI, let's create a new `POST` method under the resource we've already created. Substitute your IDs into the following command:

```
aws apigateway put-method
    --rest-api-id ${api-id}
    --resource-id ${resource-id}
    --http-method POST
    --authorization-type NONE
    --api-key-required
```

This new method should also be connected to the same Lambda function that we're using for our backend. Notice here that we have to issue another command to add the integration. The console steps do this as part of the method setup:

```
aws apigateway put-integration
    --rest-api-id ${api-id}
    --resource-id ${resource-id}
    --http-method POST
    --type AWS
    --integration-http-method POST
    --uri
arn:aws:apigateway:${region}:lambda:path/2015-03-31/functions/arn:aws:lambd
a:${region}:${account-number}:function:hello-world-python/invocations
```

The URI option is the location of the endpoint for event source integration. This is a unique value and is used to relate the API Gateway event source to your Lambda function. The date in the path refers to the Lambda service API version.

Now, we need to add our method response as follows, replacing the `${}` placeholder with your values:

```
aws apigateway put-method-response
    --rest-api-id ${api-id}
    --resource-id ${resource-id}
    --http-method POST
    --status-code 200
    --response-models application/json=Empty
```

And then we have the integration response:

```
aws apigateway put-integration-response
    --rest-api-id ${api-id}
    --resource-id ${resource-id}
    --http-method POST
    --status-code 200
    --response-templates application/json=""
```

Deploy the API again to our dev stage:

```
aws apigateway create-deployment
    --rest-api-id ${api-id}
    --stage-name dev
```

We also have to add a permission statement to Lambda to allow API Gateway to invoke our function. This was done for us when using the console, which is why we didn't have to do this step in the previous section:

```
aws lambda add-permission
    --function-name hello-world-python
    --statement-id hello-world-api-allow
    --principal apigateway.amazonaws.com
    --action lambda:InvokeFunction
    --source-arn "arn:aws:execute-api:${region}:${account-id}:${api-id}/*/POST/hellos"
```

This time, to test our new method, we're going to use a command-line utility called httpie and pass in a JSON request body. You can also use any other HTTP client—cURL is another popular one:

```
supremay@dellnax-ub:~$ http -v POST https://            .execute-api.ap-southeast-2.amazonaws.com/dev/hellos
x-api-key:                                     <<< '{"text": "Hello, world!", "repeat": 5}'
POST /dev/hellos HTTP/1.1
Accept: application/json, */*
Accept-Encoding: gzip, deflate
Connection: keep-alive
Content-Length: 39
Content-Type: application/json
Host:            .execute-api.ap-southeast-2.amazonaws.com                    <------- Request
User-Agent: HTTPie/0.9.8
x-api-key:

{
    "repeat": 5,
    "text": "Hello, world!"
}

HTTP/1.1 200 OK
Connection: keep-alive
Content-Length: 120
Content-Type: application/json
Date: Sun, 12 May 2019 02:32:52 GMT
X-Amzn-Trace-Id: Root=1-5cd785d4-ba448b70222a4b84316b11c6;Sampled=0
x-amz-apigw-id: ZjHZNGw9ywMFwYg=
x-amzn-RequestId: 3de5f84d-745e-11e9-92a2-837a373f1b35

{
    "body": {
        "0": "Hello, world!",
        "1": "Hello, world!",
        "2": "Hello, world!",         <------- Response
        "3": "Hello, world!",
        "4": "Hello, world!"
    }
}
```

Example request to our API using httpie and bash —the request and response are shown

And that's it! Congratulations on creating your first completely serverless API using API Gateway and Lambda.

You can see from the CLI steps that the console is actually doing a lot of the setup for us and this makes for a more seamless experience. In a later chapter, we'll introduce Serverless Framework to make it even easier to develop our API Gateway setup alongside our function code.

In this section, we have progressed our understanding by creating our own APIs using the console and the CLI. When you've comfortable with what we have built, move on to the *Summary* and *Questions* sections.

Summary

There we have it. We've added Amazon API Gateway to AWS Lambda and other services to implement real-world serverless API architectures. Covering security at the start was important because, without properly securing our services, we can't safely offer functionality to our customers and consumers. We also learned about some of the API management functionality that Amazon API Gateway can bring to our solutions; these are key when we're planning a production implementation and when we want to expose our compute service via a RESTful API. Finally, we created an API of our own using the console and the CLI. Later on, we will show you an application framework that will make creating and maintaining APIs much easier.

In the next chapter, we going to be delving more deeply into more components of serverless architectures. We'll explore some examples of other AWS services such as Amazon S3 and Amazon DynamoDB to see how we can leverage these to our advantage.

Questions

1. Which type of API endpoint is NOT a valid endpoint type?

   A) Regional
   B) Edge-optimized
   C) Public
   D) Private

2. Amazon API Gateway can connect to on-premise integrations.

   A) True
   B) False

3. Which is the best method for authenticating federated users of your API?

   A) API Keys
   B) Custom authorizer
   C) Amazon Cognito
   D) AWS Lambda
   E) Active Directory

4. If a backend is experiencing a performance bottleneck, what are some options to mitigate the issue? (Choose two)

A) Caching
B) IP blacklisting
C) Load balancing
D) Throttling requests
E) Deploying another API

5. What are some metrics that are available in CloudWatch?

A) Latency
B) 5xx errors
C) Cache hit count
D) Count
E) All of the above

Further reading

- RESTful API tutorial: https://www.restapitutorial.com/
- HTTP status codes: https://tools.ietf.org/html/rfc7231, https://www.restapitutorial.com/httpstatuscodes.html
- OSI model explanation: https://www.youtube.com/watch?v=vv4y_uOneC0
- API Gateway pricing: https://aws.amazon.com/api-gateway/pricing/
- API Gateway service limits: https://docs.aws.amazon.com/apigateway/latest/developerguide/limits.html
- API Gateway Management API reference for version 1 and 2: https://docs.aws.amazon.com/apigateway/latest/developerguide/api-ref.html
- How to SigV4 sign a request: https://docs.aws.amazon.com/general/latest/gr/sigv4_signing.html
- Setting up client SSL certificates: https://docs.aws.amazon.com/apigateway/latest/developerguide/getting-started-client-side-ssl-authentication.html#generate-client-certificate

5
Leveraging AWS Services

As our journey in creating our own serverless application continues, we need to look at some of the other components that are available. Along with requiring the compute power from Lambda, we also need to be able to persist data or state for longer periods of time. Additionally, when our applications become more complex, we need a way to orchestrate the distributed transactions and decision making.

In this chapter, we'll introduce a component that we can use to store data objects, a NoSQL database, and a workflow tool. We'll look at each object from two perspectives:

- Using them as an event source
- Leveraging their use from an SDK

All of the components are serverless and will help you build out more functionality in your serverless applications.

In this chapter, we will cover the following topics:

- Using Amazon S3 with Lambda
- Using Amazon DynamoDB with Lambda
- Using AWS Step Functions as an orchestrator

Technical requirements

This chapter isn't going to go into the advanced details about how to use each service; instead, we will focus on how to use the services with Lambda. It would help if you had some prior knowledge of the following:

- Amazon DynamoDB
- Amazon S3
- AWS Step Functions

There are resources in the *Further reading* section if you need to get up to speed.

Using Amazon S3 with Lambda

S3 (short for **Simple Storage Service**) is a fully managed object storage service that you can use to store objects. It is inherently fault-tolerant, durable, and is said to have unlimited storage capacity.

In this section, we'll discover how to create an event source trigger from S3 and how to upload and download objects using the AWS SDK.

Revision

Let's have a bit of a recap to see why S3 would be such a good fit for storing objects in a serverless application. First, why am I talking about objects in a storage system instead of files? S3 is an object storage system as opposed to block storage with a file system layered on top. Each piece of data is considered an object, and these are stored with their metadata in a flat pool of storage. This is distinct from a filesystem since filesystems are hierarchical in the way in which files and folders are designated. Because of this flat design, an object storage system has an advantage when it comes to scaling capability and data retrieval performance.

This flat design is fine in theory, but, in practice, we do need to group objects into areas for easier management and organization of data. For this, we can use S3 object prefixes, which look much like a folder! An example object prefix include `raw-data/` or `processed/`, which comes before the key name. Objects with the same prefix will be grouped into the same area. From an application development point of view, we don't need to know about the nuances of supporting and interfacing with the filesystem. S3 has a public API that we can use to perform management tasks, as well as object storage.

S3 comes with all the benefits of a serverless service. There is no need to run your own storage clusters or worry about how much redundancy you're building in. Its capacity is limitless. Here's a random fact for you: Amazon actually orders their storage in kilograms, not data volume. Bandwidth is high and there is no aggregated throughput limit, so there is no need to worry about S3 being a performance bottleneck in your account.

As an added benefit, you can also enable versioning on your objects in order to protect them from accidental overwrites and other cases. S3 integrates with AWS Key Management Service so that you can protect the objects in your bucket with strong encryption.

Finally, to give you flexibility in the solutions you build, S3 has several storage classes that have different characteristics:

- **Standard**: Objects are replicated across a minimum of three availability zones within a region.
- **Standard with infrequent access**: Lower price point than standard for a lower availability SLA.
- **One zone with infrequent access**: Data stored in a single availability zone for lower availability and durability, at a lower cost.
- **Glacier**: Designed for long-term storage for data archiving and backups.
- **Glacier deep archive**: Even lower-cost storage designed to archive data for years.
- **Intelligent tiering**: Automatically moves your data between the storage classes to achieve a price that is optimized for your data access patterns.

Now that we are up to speed with the S3 service, let's move on and learn how we can use it as an event source for Lambda.

S3 as an event source

In a previous chapter, we talked about the types of invocation for Lambda functions and how other services in the AWS ecosystem can trigger a function to be executed. Now, it's time to learn a little more about how this applies to S3 and see how we can create one ourselves.

The example in this section and the next is a trivial exercise to show that we can enable some processing to happen when an object is uploaded to a bucket in S3. Setting the scene, let's say we have users who are uploading photos into an S3 bucket. We want to classify these photos and move them into another location within the bucket. We also want to extract and store the metadata of the photo, such as the EXIF and a timestamp. Storing this data in a database is a good idea because we are planning to be able to run searches against the metadata later down the line.

Connecting an action on an S3 bucket to a Lambda function is the first task for enabling the event-driven approach that's used by serverless applications. Let's take a look:

1. To do this, in the S3 console, we need to navigate to the **Properties** tab of a bucket.
2. Under the **Advanced settings**, you will find where to create an event and set up a notification to occur when the event happens.

Let's see what this looks like for our example. In the following screenshot, we have set up a new event that triggers when new objects are created under the specified prefix and suffix:

Adding an event to an S3 bucket

Under the **Send to** dropdown, we actually have three options to choose from:

- SNS topic
- SQS queue
- Lambda function

These options give us the flexibility to change our architecture, depending on what we need. For example, we may use an SNS topic so that multiple message consumers can subscribe to the new object event.

If you create the event in the console, a new permission will be added for you to allow S3 to invoke Lambda. You'll also be able to see the new connection in the Lambda console. This is easy to try yourself, so create a new bucket and set up a new Lambda function to try it out. There's a good Lambda blueprint to get started with called `s3-get-object`. The code in this function will actually download or get the object from the location it was uploaded to. This is useful when we want to perform further processing on that object.

When everything has been created, we get the following sequence of events. An object is created in the bucket using the `putObject` API action, which causes an event that triggers our Lambda function:

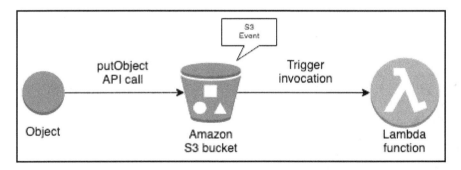

Event trigging sequence

That's the basics of how to integrate S3 with Lambda and enabling our function to respond to events that happen in S3. When the function is executing, we may need to interact with an S3 bucket even further. We might have to download the new object, run some processing, and then upload the resulting object to the same bucket. In the next section, we will learn how to use the AWS SDK to interface with S3 from code.

Interacting using the SDK

We just put together an example of how a Lambda can be triggered and automatically get the new object. We want to do more processing on the file and then upload it to a different location in the same bucket—one that doesn't trigger an event. The following diagram shows this new functionality, where the Lambda function is performing the `putObject` API action using the SDK:

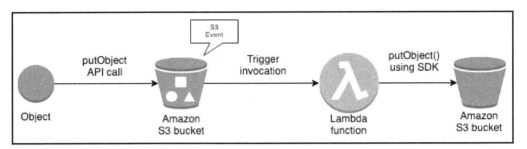

Adding more actions to our event triggering sequence

For the upload, we're going to leverage the API operations in our SDK to put or upload the object into a folder called `photos-processed`.

Let's walk through some examples in different languages to get an idea about what is involved.

For Node.js, you can use either the `upload()` or `putObject()` method. The upload method has some extra parts in it that can automatically switch over to perform a multi-part upload when the file is over a specific size. This parallelizes the upload to increase performance. It can also handle retries when there are errors. The details are created in a params JSON object that is passed into the upload function. Pass the upload function an object with the required parameters: bucket name, key (directory and filename), and the actual object being uploaded. The upload function is part of the AWS SDK and handles the actual upload to the S3 bucket, as shown in the following code. We handle the success and error conditions in the same function:

```
const params = {
    Bucket: 'my-photo-bucket',
    Key: 'photos-processed/' + filename,
    Body: photo-file
};

s3.upload(params, (err, data) => {
    if(err) console.log(err);
```

```
        else console.log(data);
});
```

In Python, the SDK is called Boto3 and for uploading, we can use the `upload_file()` method:

```
import boto3
s3 = boto3.client('s3')
s3.upload_file(photo-file, 'my-photo-bucket', 'photos-processed/' +
filename)
```

Java is a little more complex. Once the `s3Client` object is set up, we can use the `putObject()` method. The following example would upload a JPG file called `my-photo` to the `photos-processed` directory in the bucket called `my-photos-bucket`:

```
AmazonS3 s3Client = AmazonS3ClientBuilder.standard()
    .withRegion(yourRegion)
    .withCredentials(new ProfileCredentialsProvider())
    .build();

PutObjectRequest request = new PutObjectRequest("my-photos-bucket",
"photos-processed/" + fileName, new File(fileName));
ObjectMetadata metadata = new ObjectMetadata();
metadata.setContentType("image/jpeg");
metadata.addUserMetadata("x-amz-meta-title", "my-photo");
request.setMetadata(metadata);
s3Client.putObject(request);
```

The C#/.NET example is quite lengthy. I recommend that you consult the documentation for the scaffolding code in this language.

Here's a pro tip for high-use buckets: If you regularly exceed 3,500 TPS on a bucket, you should start to distribute your key names across multiple prefixes. Avoid starting key names with the same prefix or adding a suffix that increments. Add some randomness at the beginning of the key name, such as a hash of the date/time.

In this section, we learned how to upload files into S3 using the AWS SDK for various languages. Another useful service we could use with our example is DynamoDB. We'll introduce this in the next section.

Using Amazon DynamoDB with Lambda

So far, we covered object storage, but how about that metadata storage we were interested in? We could use the Lambda function to extract the metadata from the photo file and then upload that as a separate file to the same bucket, but that would make searching across the objects a challenge. Instead, what would be more useful is a database to persist the information. Because we're not dealing with relational data, a NoSQL document and key-value store is a perfect fit. Our natural choice from here is to use the serverless NoSQL database, Amazon DynamoDB.

In this section, we will learn about the concepts of DynamoDB, find out how to trigger a Lambda function with DynamoDB, and dive into how to use the SDK to make queries.

The basics

Amazon DynamoDB is a fully managed serverless database service that you can use to provision tables, create indexes, and store data. It has extremely scalable performance and supports event-driven programming models. DynamoDB is often referred to as the petabyte storage database because its performance scales consistently and predictably, no matter how much data you load in. Like S3, writes to the database are replicated to three availability zones within a region, and you can specify in your queries whether you want a strongly or eventually consistent read operation.

One of the core premises of using DynamoDB is that you can focus on running your business instead of being distracted by having to feed and water your database.

DynamoDB tables are structured into the following concepts

- **Items (1)**
- **Attributes (2)**
- **Values (3)**
- **Keys (4)**

The following is an example of our photo-metadata table. I've highlighted the concepts from the preceding list:

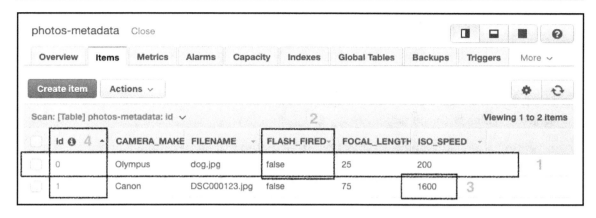

DynamoDB console showing items in a table

An item can be considered as an entry or row, such as an RDMS database. An attribute is one particular field. The benefit of a NoSQL database is that the data can be unstructured and not follow a defined schema. This means that each item within a table can have a different set of attributes.

An important thing to get right is the partition key and sort key. Let's take a look at these in more detail:

- The **partition key** is a mandatory piece of information that uniquely identifies an item. It is also used to help distribute the data using an internal hashing function under the hood. The details get complex quite quickly, so I recommend that, if you have tables that will grow to over 10 GB, you should consider doing further investigation into choosing the right partition key.
- The **sort key** is an optional key that you can set that allows you to run smarter queries. Both the partition key and sort key make up a composite primary key that is sorted by the sort key.

You can also have an alternative partition and sort key by using a **Global Secondary Index (GSI)**. This is an index that is updated asynchronously when changes happen to the table. The GSI is inherently eventually consistent because of the asynchronous nature of the update. This means that when a table is updated, there will be a lag time before the GSI receives the propagated update. Your application should be designed to handle situations where it might not receive the most up to date data from a query to the GSI.

The use cases we will look at in the next section follow the fundamental ideas of the event-driven pattern, where an update to a database table will trigger some compute to happen. After that, we will learn how to save data to a table using the SDK.

Triggering a Lambda function

In order to react to the changes that happen in a table, we need to know what the changes are. That's where DynamoDB Streams come into play. A stream is like a message queue or notification topic that you can subscribe to in order to learn about the changes that are made to a table. Messages on a stream are asynchronous, arrive exactly once, and the stream itself scales with the table.

After creating a new stream on a table, DynamoDB will publish a number of change records on the stream in response to items in the table being inserted, deleted, or updated. A change record will include the old item, the new item, the primary key, and the type of change that was made to the item.

Here's an example message with one change record. We can see that the difference in the two images is that the value for the FLASH_FIRED key changed to true. The following change record has been simplified for brevity:

```
{
    "eventID": "1",
    "dynamodb": {
    "OldImage": {
        "id": { "N": "2" },
        ...
        "FLASH_FIRED": { "BOOL": false }
    },
    "Keys": { "id": { "N": "2" } },
    "NewImage": {
        "id": { "N": "2" },
        ...
        "FLASH_FIRED": { "BOOL": true }
    },
    "eventName": "MODIFY"
    "StreamViewType": "NEW_AND_OLD_IMAGES"
}
```

The data on a stream lasts for 24 hours, and a Lambda consuming from the stream can have an unlimited number of retries.

Let's have a look at how to create a stream on an existing table. If you don't already have one, create a new photos-metadata table:

1. Navigate to the DynamoDB console and click **Create table**. You can use the following configurations to create your table:

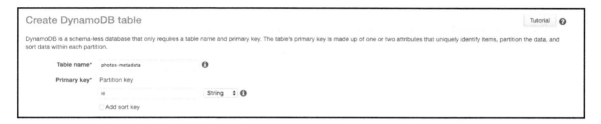

Creating a new table in DynamoDB

For this example, we will create a new stream on the photos-metadata table.

2. On the table overview page, click the **Manage Stream** button and enable a stream with a view type of **New and old images**. Your view should look similar to the following:

Table configuration page in the DynamoDB console, indicating where to create a stream

This creates a new stream with its own ARN to refer to. Choosing the **New and old images** view type means that, when a new event is triggered by a table update, the event object that goes into the stream will contain both the original item and the updated item with the associated values. You can also choose to have just the old items, just the new items, or just the attributes. The following diagram shows a high-level view of what happens when an item is added to a table that has a stream enabled:

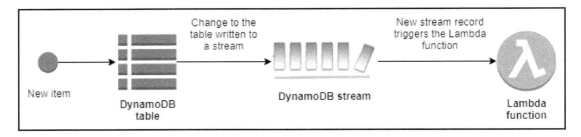

The event-driven sequence when connecting a Lambda function to a stream

Now, let's create a new Lambda function so that we can hook it up to our new stream:

1. First, we'll need to make sure that the execution role that we assign to our Lambda has the appropriate permissions. It's likely that you'll need to add a statement to the policy document to allow the function to access the stream:

```
{
    "Effect": "Allow",
    "Action": [
        "dynamodb:DescribeStream",
        "dynamodb:GetRecords",
        "dynamodb:GetShardIterator",
        "dynamodb:ListStreams"
    ],
    "Resource": "arn:aws:dynamodb:${region}:${account-id}:table/photos-metadata/stream/*"
}
```

2. Create a new lambda function. I've called mine processMetadata and used a blueprint called dynamodb-process-stream. This will save me some time in writing the implementation.

3. Next up is selecting the trigger:

Function configuration showing the DynamoDB trigger

When you click on point number (**2**), a configuration box will appear where you can select which table to listen to, the batch size, and the starting position. These are some new configuration elements that need some explanation. Batch size is the number of records that are passed to the Lambda function every time there is a change triggered. This number can be up to 1,000 MB or up to 6 MB in total size. There are two options for the starting position:

- Latest, where all the new records are included from the tail of the stream
- Trim horizon, where the Lambda receives all the records in the stream shard

4. When you've added the new trigger, remember to hit **Save.**
5. Test the new integration by adding an item to your table!

Just like how we learned about S3, we are going to move on from event sourcing to interacting with the service via the SDK. In the next section, we will learn how to add data to a table in DynamoDB.

Interacting using the SDK

Switching tack a bit, let's talk about how we can programmatically add data into our new table from a Lambda function (or any other compute provider using an SDK). We'll step through the methods that are required to insert and query the data in a table. To get a good range of implementations, we'll give examples for Python, Node.js, Java, and C#. Like any other function, while using the SDK, we need to make sure we have it imported. For these examples, I'm going to assume we have imported it already and set our region correctly.

The first language to cover is Node.js. Here's how to insert a single item and then retrieve that same item. Notice that the number values are strings, but the Boolean value is not. The code following has a params object to set up the payload, and then uses the `putItem` API action from the AWS SDK for DynamoDB:

```
let ddb = new AWS.DynamoDB({apiVersion: '2012-08-10'});

let params = {
    TableName: 'photos-metadata',
    Item: {
        'PHOTO_ID': { N: '1' }
        'FILENAME': { S: 'myphoto.jpg' }
        'FOCAL_LENGTH' : { N: '25' },
        'ISO_SPEED' : { N: '200' }
        'CAMERA_MAKE': { S: 'Olympus' }
        'FLASH_FIRED': { BOOL: false }
    }
};

ddb.putItem(params, (err, data) => {
 if (err) {
 console.log("Error", err);
 } else {
 console.log("Success", data);
 }
});
```

Assuming all is going well, we will have that item inserted into our photos-metadata table. To get this item, we can use the `getItem` method and identify the item using our primary key. Alternatively, we can query for the data if we think there might be more than one item being returned.

Here's a simple call to get our existing item:

```
let ddb = new AWS.DynamoDB({apiVersion: '2012-08-10'});

let params = {
```

```
        TableName: 'photos-metadata',
        Key: {
            'PHOTO_ID': { N: '1' }
        }
    };

    ddb.getItem(params, (err, data) => {
        if (err) console.log("Error", err);
        else console.log("Success", data.Item);
    });
```

This will retrieve all the values for the item. To filter this down, we could use the `ProjectionExpression` parameter to get only the value we need. This will help you optimize your usage of DynamoDB.

The same scenario in Python is much the same:

```
    dynamodb = boto3.client('dynamodb')

    dynamodb.put_item(
        TableName='photos-metadata',
        Item={
            'PHOTO_ID': { 'N':'1' },
            'FILENAME': { 'S':'myphoto.jpg' },
            'FOCAL_LENGTH' : { 'N': '25' },
            'ISO_SPEED' : { 'N': '200' },
            'CAMERA_MAKE': { 'S': 'Olympus' },
            'FLASH_FIRED': { 'BOOL': false }
        }
    )
```

You can also pull the table name out and set that as an object:

```
    dynamodb = boto3.client('dynamodb')
    table = dynamodb.Table('photos-metadata')

    response = table.get_item(
     Item = {
     'PHOTO_ID': '1'
     }
    )

    return response['Item']
```

The Java example has lots of imports that I've left out for brevity:

```
final AmazonDynamoDB ddb = AmazonDynamoDBClientBuilder.defaultClient();
PutItemRequest request = new PutItemRequest();
request.setTableName("photos-metadata");

Map<String, AttributeValue> map = new HashMap<>();
map.put("PHOTO_ID", new AttributeValue().withN("1"));
...
map.put("FLASH_FIRED", new AttributeValue().withBOOL(false));

request.setItem(map);
try {
    PutItemResult result = ddb.putItem(request);
} catch (AmazonServiceException e) {
    System.out.println(e.getErrorMessage());
}
```

To get an item using Java, we need to use the following code:

```
private static void retrieveItem() {
    Table table = dynamoDB.getTable(tableName);
    try {
        Item item = table.getItem("ID", 303, "ID, Nomenclature,
Manufacturers", null);
        System.out.println("Displaying retrieved items...");
        System.out.println(item.toJSONPretty());
    } catch (Exception e) {
        System.err.println("Cannot retrieve items.");
        System.err.println(e.getMessage());
    }
}
```

Finally, let's look at the .NET examples. The following code uses the `Amazon.DynamoDBv2` namespace:

```
var client = new AmazonDynamoDBClient();

var request1 = new PutItemRequest
{
    TableName = "photos-metadata",
    Item = new Dictionary<string, AttributeValue>
    {
        { "PHOTO_ID", new AttributeValue { N = "1" }},
        { "FILENAME", new AttributeValue { S = "myphoto.jpg" }},
        ...
        { "CAMERA_MAKE", new AttributeValue { S = "Olympus" }},
        { "FLASH_FIRED", new AttributeValue { BOOL = new
```

```
DynamoDBBool(false) }}
    }
};

client.PutItem(request1);
```

Getting two attributes of the item, while specifying that we want read consistency, can be done with the following code:

```
private static AmazonDynamoDBClient client = new AmazonDynamoDBClient();
Table photosMetadata = Table.LoadTable(client, "photos-metadata");

private static void RetrieveItem(Table photosMetadata)
{
    {
        AttributesToGet = new List<string> { "PHOTO_ID", "FILENAME" },
        ConsistentRead = true
    };
    Document document = productCatalog.GetItem("1");
    PrintDocument(document);
}
```

The preceding code snippets are examples of how we can put and get items in a DynamoDB table. There are plenty of other operations we can do via the SDK as well. For now, you have learned enough of the basics to get started. Consult the documentation to find out more about the available options.

The next section introduces another service that can help take your serverless application development to the next level.

Using AWS Step Functions as an Orchestrator

Now, we will move on and take a look at another service that has recently entered the AWS ecosystem. In AWS Step Functions, you can build state machines that provide the next layer of integration on top of Lambda. State machines are an excellent way to orchestrate the flow of entire serverless applications. The state can be externalized from our compute layer and tracked throughout its life cycle. When your workflow requirements are more complex than what a single Lambda function can provide by itself, look to Step Functions.

In this section, we will learn more about Step Functions at a high level and gain insights into where it might be useful.

State machines with Lambda

Ok, so, Lambda is good. It's great, in fact. It is amazing at doing one thing well, and that is running the compute for a nano or microservice. But as we already know, serverless applications are more than just one disparate microservice: they can be made up of tens or hundreds even—and that's not forgetting the messaging and event sourcing systems that help with the flow of communication between other interfaces and compute. How do we make sure a transaction can traverse through this fruit salad of services, end to end, to ensure that the output is successful and errors are handled? This is where state machines are super helpful.

AWS Step Functions provides state machines that can orchestrate serverless applications and enable the workflow logic that a transaction would need in a modern microservice application. In this section, we'll cover some core concepts and explain how you can get started with building your own state machines using Lambda. We'll be keeping it fairly high level because this can be quite a deep topic.

Here's an example of how a state machine can be visualized through the console. Yes, it's the example that we worked with in the previous sections, but with more functionality.

The following diagram is representative of the state machine or workflow:

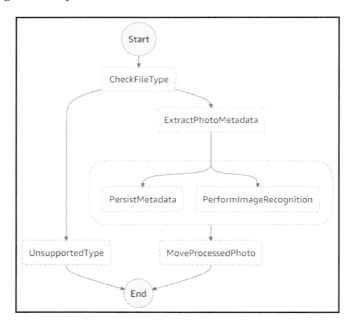

Graphic representation of our state machine, found in the Step Functions console

In order to understand what is going on here, let's kick off with a few key concepts. The entire workflow shown in the preceding diagram can be defined in JSON, which allows you to store infrastructure as code in source control. CloudFormation is also supported for defining and declaring Step Functions resources. Every run through of a workflow is called an execution, and we can kick those off using the CLI, SDKs, or Step Functions API. You can execute one or ten thousand state machine executions and they will all run in parallel, and all of them can be monitored from the console.

There are seven different state types that an execution can be in. Each type has its own configurable parameters that you can choose in the console or include in your JSON definition. Here are the seven different states:

- A **task** is one unit of work. The resource we've chosen to do this work is a Lambda function:

```
"ExtractPhotoMetadata":{
    "Type": "Task",
    "Resource": "arn:aws:lambda:us-
east-1:123456789012:function:photosMetadata",
    "Next": "ProcessPhoto"
}
```

- A **choice** is where you can add logic to branch out the tasks in an execution. You might decide to do one thing instead of another, depending on the output of a Lambda function.

- **Parallel execution** is when you can fork and run two or more tasks in parallel, and then join their output for the next change in state. In the following example, we are adding our metadata to DynamoDB at the same time as another function is running to perform image recognition to classify what is in the photo:

```
"ProcessPhoto": {
    "Type": "Parallel",
    "Next": "MoveProcessedPhoto",
    "Branches": [{
        "StartAt": "PersistMetadata",
        "States": {
            "PersistMetadata": {
                "Type": "Task",
                "Resource": "arn:aws:lambda:us-
east-1:123456789012:function:savePhotoMetadata",
                "End": true
    }}}, {
        "StartAt": "PerformImageRecognition",
        "States": {
            "PerformImageRecognition": {
```

```
                    "Type": "Task",
                    "Resource": "arn:aws:lambda:us-
          east-1:123456789012:function:classifyImage",
                    "End": true
          }}}]}
```

- A **wait** state is an artificial delay of a trivial length. You might use this when we're waiting for another service to start up before polling. We don't have a reason for this state in our example, so let's move on.

- A **failure** state stops the execution and flags it as a failure. This is like a script exiting with a non-zero condition. In our example, we want to exit if our function checking the file types returns an error for an unsupported type:

```
"CheckFileType": {
    "Type": "Task",
    "Resource": "arn:aws:lambda:us-
east-1:123456789012:function:checkPhotoFileType",
    "Next": "ExtractPhotoMetadata",
    "Catch": [ {
        "ErrorEquals": ["UnsupportedType"],
        "Next": "UnsupportedType"
    }]
},
"UnsupportedType": {
    "Type": "Fail",
    "Cause": "UnsupportedPhotoType",
    "Error": "File type not a supported photo"
}
```

- Conversely, a **succeed** state is when an execution stops with a successful outcome. You can specify this in any state by using the end field:

```
"End": true
```

- Finally, a **pass** state is when the input is simply passed to its output without doing any work on the data. We don't have any of these in our example.

Where does the state exist during transitions? Well, it lives in the machine, that is, in JSON objects that are passed from state to state.

In `Chapter 7`, *Serverless Framework*, we'll introduce an application framework that can simplify the job of creating and maintaining state machines in code. Step Functions also integrates with other services. We'll find out more about this in the next section.

Integrating with other services

So far, with Step Functions, we've covered integrations with Lambda. This service can orchestrate the inputs and outputs of data from other services as well. More services are being added to the supported list over time. Some of the latest services to be added as integrations to Step Functions are as follows:

- Amazon ECS and AWS Fargate
- Amazon DynamoDB
- Amazon SNS and SQS
- AWS Batch and Glue
- Amazon SageMaker

These give you much greater flexibility in how you create serverless applications because you can take both the interface and the decision logic out of your Lambda functions and externalize that into the workflow. What that means is that, now, your function won't have to take care of sending a message to an SQS queue, or getting an item from a DynamoDB table, including dealing with all of the error handling and logic associated with it. Step Functions can do this for you and then inject the data as input into the next function execution or step in the workflow.

Another benefit is that you have more options to use for compute, including Elastic Container Service. You could use Step Functions to provide the service layer between microservice containers running in an ECS task.

So, you can clearly see that this could be a crucial service that can combine many building blocks into an application. The next section will give you a head-start for developing your own state machines on your local computer.

Step Functions Local

Before we wrap up, it's worth mentioning an alternative method for developing Step Functions workflows that isn't directly in AWS. It's possible to download a local version of Step Functions so that you can write code on your own machine. This artifact comes as a .jar file or a Docker image. All you have to do to start a container is pull the image from Docker Hub. Let's get started:

1. Use the following command to download the image from Docker Hub. It is assumed you have Docker installed:

```
docker pull amazon/aws-stepfunctions-local
```

2. Run it, publish the port mapping, and you'll be away:

```
docker run -p 8083:8083 amazon/aws-stepfunctions-local
```

There are actually a few environment variables you have to set inside the running container. Check out the links in the *Further reading* section, where you will get an idea as to where you can find the details on this.

To interact with the locally running service, you will also need to have the AWS SAM CLI Local installed and running. This is because the SAM CLI provides a local version of the Lambda service so that you can test your code while writing.

Once all the services are running, use the `--endpoint` option in the AWS CLI to reference your deployment endpoint, like so:

```
aws stepfunctions --endpoint http://localhost:8083 create-state-machine
```

That's it! Work on your state machine definitions locally and then deploy these to AWS. This is a good development method if you have an intermittent communication with AWS for some reason, and it shouldn't replace a non-production type of environment.

In this section, we learned that it is possible to run some AWS services locally for development purposes. This is an easy way to get started writing your own state machines.

Summary

In this chapter, we've explored three services that you can use to trigger Lambda function executions. We also had a look from another perspective, that is, how we can leverage those services from within a function execution. These are just three examples from a whole range of services that can be used. I hope this paints a picture of just how useful Lambda can be, and I hope you will agree that Lambda is truly the glue that connects services together.

In the next chapter, we will dive deeper into the more advanced characteristics of Lambda so that you can learn how to use it more effectively in your solutions.

Questions

1. Which S3 storage class will choose the optimum storage class for your usage patterns?

   A) Standard
   B) One zone with infrequent access
   C) Glacier
   D) Intelligent tiering

2. Which is a valid service for receiving S3 events?

   A) Lambda
   B) Simple queue service
   C) Simple notification service
   D) All of the above

3. What is the maximum batch size for DynamoDB streams?

   A) Unlimited
   B) 1,000 records
   C) 50 records
   D) 1 record

4. Step Functions Local can be used offline.

   A) True
   B) False

5. The best way to stitch together services to create application workflows is to use what?

   A) Simple queue service
   B) Lambda
   C) Step Functions
   D) Simple workflow service

Further reading

- Learning DynamoDB: `https://aws.amazon.com/dynamodb/getting-started/`
- DynamoDB design: `https://aws.amazon.com/blogs/database/choosing-the-right-dynamodb-partition-key/`
- Step Functions tutorial: `https://docs.aws.amazon.com/step-functions/latest/dg/getting-started.html`
- Step Functions Local, configuration options: `https://docs.aws.amazon.com/step-functions/latest/dg/sfn-local-config-options.html`

6
Going Deeper with Lambda

Now that we've learned how to do the basics of invoking a Lambda function and using AWS services from within an execution, it's time to take things to the next level of understanding. In this chapter, we're going deeper into some of the more advanced aspects of Lambda development to help you build better solutions. We're going to touch on some points that will help you use Lambda to your full advantage.

In this chapter, we'll cover the following topics:

- Bringing your own runtime to Lambda
- Lambda layers
- Environment variables
- Secrets management
- Concurrency and reuse
- How to structure a function

Technical requirements

For the topics we will talk about in this chapter, you will need at least some development experience in your chosen language. It would help if you also had experience building and deploying Lambdas in a production environment and are looking to gain efficiencies in what you do. At a minimum, you need to have read and understood the foundations of this chapter.

Bringing your own runtime to Lambda

The first topic we'll cover is intended to give you the flexibility to write Lambda functions in a language that you are the most comfortable with. Adopting Lambda doesn't mean you have to learn to code in an entirely new language, but there are some steps we need to take to enable a runtime that doesn't come out of the box.

Throughout this section, we will learn what is involved in using the relatively new custom runtime feature and run through an example.

Runtime API and bootstrapping

The Lambda service now provides a new runtime interface that helps us get more information about invocation events, and also allows us to submit an execution response. This functionality was made available when AWS released the ability to create a function using a custom runtime. This is where you can essentially bring your own language interpreter (a binary file or script), packaged in your deployment package or separately deployed as a Lambda layer. What this allows you to do is write your handler and logic in your preferred language, and then have this bootstrapped by Lambda.

In your code, you must implement the runtime API. This will allow you to interface to the Lambda service to send responses, send errors, or check the invocation data to see if there is a new event to process.

The paths you will be most interested in during the initial stages are as follows:

- `/runtime/invocation/next`: Call this to get the next event and some metadata about the request.
- `/runtime/invocation/$REQUEST_ID/response`: Call this to post your response from the handler.

In order to initialize the runtime environment, we need to create a bootstrap file that we'll include in our deployment package, along with the function code. This is an executable file that the Lambda service will run in order to invoke your function handler. The file sits in a continuous loop that calls the Runtime API endpoint to get the invocation data. It then invokes the function handler to get the response data and sends that response data back to the Lambda service.

Here's an example of this in bash:

```
#!/bin/sh
set -euo pipefail

# Initialisation: load up the hander and set the root
source $LAMBDA_TASK_ROOT/"$(echo $_HANDLER | cut -d. -f1).sh"

while true
do
    HEADERS="$(mktemp)"
    # Invocation data: get the next invocation event
    EVENT_DATA=$(curl -sS -LD "$HEADERS" -X GET
"http://${AWS_LAMBDA_RUNTIME_API}/2018-06-01/runtime/invocation/next")
    REQUEST_ID=$(grep -Fi Lambda-Runtime-Aws-Request-Id "$HEADERS" | tr -d
'[:space:]' | cut -d: -f2)

    # Run your handler function, passing in the invocation data
    cd $LAMBDA_TASK_ROOT
    RESPONSE=$(echo $EVENT_DATA | ./bin/lci hai.lo)

    # Response: call the runtime API to return a response to the Lambda
service
    curl -X POST
"http://${AWS_LAMBDA_RUNTIME_API}/2018-06-01/runtime/invocation/$REQUEST_ID
/response" -d "$RESPONSE"
done
```

The example is included in bash for brevity, and you can create this file in whichever language you like as long it can be executed using your provided runtime. Along with managing the response and processing the event and headers, the bootstrap file also needs to manage error handling.

Remember to chmod 755 your bootstrap file!

In the execution environment, there are three environment variables that will be immediately useful when you're writing your own bootstrap file:

- AWS_LAMBDA_RUNTIME_API: The host and port number for the runtime API
- LAMBDA_TASK_ROOT: The location of the directory containing the function code
- _HANDLER: The function handler, as defined in the Lambda configuration

Implementing a bootstrap file is not a simple undertaking, and it's best to consult the documentation from here. A word of warning before you delve too deeply into providing your own runtime – you're messing with a layer of abstraction that Lambda provides. This abstraction is one of the core benefits of using serverless functions as a service, that is, not having to manage your own runtime. You will need to manage your own runtime life cycle and compatibility from that point on, so think carefully before committing to that.

Now that we've learned about the components and stages of bootstrapping a runtime, let's put it together and create our own example.

Putting it all together

Let's step through a real-life example of this. By the end, we should be able to have a Lambda function working using our own custom runtime. The example we will use is creating a function using lolcode, just because it's an easy example and it's hilarious. There is one limitation in that we will still need to write our bootstrap file in bash because lolcode doesn't support accessing environment variables, and, therefore, we wouldn't be able to process events. We will still need to bundle our lolcode interpreter because, understandably, this isn't included in the base Lambda execution environment. Hopefully, in keeping it simple, everyone can follow along to see what is happening.

First of all, we need to sort out our interpreter, making sure that we can create a binary so that we can package it in our Lambda deployable. Lambda uses Amazon Linux as the underlying environment, so I'm going to fire up a Docker container running this OS so that we can build our binary. We'll only need to do this once:

```
docker pull amazonlinux
docker run -it -v ~/Desktop/lolcode-lambda:/root amazonlinux /bin/bash
yum -y install git cmake make gcc gcc-c++
git clone https://github.com/justinmeza/lci
cd lci && cmake . && make
```

Awesome – our interpreter binary has been built and is ready at our bind mounted location. Find the file called "lci" and copy that into your workspace:

```
cp ~/Desktop/lolcode-lambda/lci/lci ~/Workspace/lolcode-lambda/bin/
```

Next, we need to create a bootstrap file. Use the file that we provided in the previous section and save it as bootstrap in your workspace. Remember to make it executable!

```
chmod 755 bootstrap
```

The last file we need now is our actual function code—here's a lolcode function I created earlier!

```
HAI 1.2
    HOW IZ I HANDLER
        I HAS A EVENT ITZ A YARN
        GIMMEH EVENT
        CAN HAS STDIO?
        VISIBLE SMOOSH "HEAZ UR EV KK:: " AN EVENT MKAY
    IF U SAY SO
    I IZ HANDLER MKAY
KTHXBYE
```

Lolcode is a fun and hilarious language to write things in. This function takes the event data that was piped in when the code was run, creates a variable, and then concatenates a string to print to stdout. Check out the lolcode specifications document here to decipher what's going on: https://github.com/justinmeza/lolcode-spec/blob/master/v1.2/lolcode-spec-v1.2.md.

Now, we should have three files that are arranged like this:

```
lolcode-lambda
├ bin
    └ lci
├ bootstrap.shj
└ hai.lo
```

It's time to package up the files and deploy them to a new Lambda function. The following commands will compress the files into a ZIP file and then create and deploy a new Lambda function:

```
zip -r function.zip bin bootstrap hai.lo

aws lambda create-function
    --function-name lolcode-runtime
    --zip-file fileb://function.zip
    --handler hai.lo
    --runtime provided
    --role arn:aws:iam::${account-id}:role/lambda_basic_execution
```

With the following command, we can invoke the function with some data. We can use some arbitrary input as the payload data:

```
aws lambda invoke --function-name lolcode-runtime --payload '{"text":"OH
HAI!!!!1!"}' response.txt
```

Okay, so the finer details of the lolcode function don't really handle JSON very well and using bash as a bootstrap file is kind of cheating, but this exercise was more about following the process so that you can create your own. With all the languages that are available to you, this process can get quite complex, and you can find some examples that have been made by other developers on GitHub.

Using your own runtime is quite an advanced feature. When your development progresses to advanced levels, you may also be interested in efficiency. In the next section, we will explain how to reuse code across multiple Lambda functions using layers.

Enabling code reuse through layers

When we are building a distributed serverless application, we often use many Lambda functions to make up all of the functionality that's needed to deliver a service to a user. Depending on our demarcation point for what constitutes a micro or nano service, we can be developing tens (but usually not hundreds) of Lambda functions. There might be multiple teams responsible for producing the microservice logic and function for their domain. Usually, there are common systems of record, monolith integration platforms, event topics, or third-party SaaS services that each microservice might need to reach out to. It's not efficient if every team has to write their own connector library to interface with a common system. Instead, we should aim to reuse as much common code as possible. Perhaps we could have a repository of organization-specific libraries to interface with internal systems and perform common tasks. For maximum code reuse, Lambda has a layering feature called Lambda layers where you can share code across multiple functions.

We'll dig into what Lambda layers are in the next section.

Understanding Lambda layers

Let's say we are developing multiple Python functions. Each function uses a number of Python modules that are packaged and deployed with the code each time you create or update a function. A lot of these modules are likely to be common across the Lambda functions, so we are duplicating the amount of storage space that's needed for each function. This has an impact on cost and function initialization performance since each time an execution is scheduled on a new host, it needs to pull the deployment package from S3. It also has an impact on the manageability of module versions if they are spread across multiple locations.

The following diagram shows two Lambda functions, both using the same libraries (**A** and **B**), but each have been deployed individually:

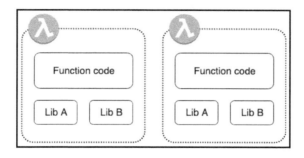

Lambda functions with individually deployed libraries

To address these inefficiencies, Amazon introduced Lambda layers. A Lambda layer is a ZIP file that contains the libraries, modules, binaries, and other data that you want to share between functions. An example might be **Lib A** and **Lib B** from the preceding diagram. The layer can be referenced from multiple lambda functions, much like we do for other modules and libraries.

Here is a diagram showing **Lib A** and **Lib B** now separated from both Lambda functions and into a layer. Each function references the layer and can access both libraries:

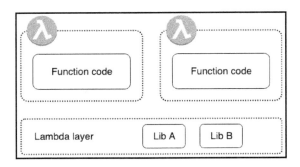

Lambda functions with the libraries deployed as a layer

Another benefit is that you can now separate the build, test, and deployment process of your business logic from your other libraries or dependencies. You might have another team developing and providing a library or SDK to access their service, and this could be worked on independently and then published as a layer for other development teams to consume. This allows the team writing the business logic to iterate and release faster. Lambda layers supports resource-based IAM policies, which means you can also publish layers to multiple accounts or organizations or even publicly.

Each layer gets its own identifier, an **Amazon Resource Number** (**ARN**), and can also be versioned much like a function. The layers themselves are immutable, which means that, if you're using a layer in your Lambda, you can't make changes to it, which may affect other functions using the same layer. When including a layer in your Lambda, the package is extracted into the /opt directory of the Lambda runtime. The directory structure under that will be particular to the runtime you are developing against. You can reference up to five layers per function, and the overall size of the function, including the layers, can be up to 250 MB when unzipped. One of those layers can be a custom runtime. Typically, the interpreter binary of a custom-built runtime can be in the megabytes size range. Lambda layers are a really good way of sharing around these binaries to keep your deployment size down. If you reference multiple layers, you can also specify the order in which the layer is installed.

Because all of the layers are unzipped in the /opt directory, there is potential for a layer to override the files of another layer, so choose your order carefully.

An example of how you might use multiple layers could consist of three types:

- **Dependencies**: One or more layers with shared libraries, middleware, or common code
- **Management**: Another layer that adds security or monitoring functionality
- **Custom runtime**: Sharing your runtime binary and bootstrap file

Now that we understand what a Lambda layer is, we can create our own.

Using a Lambda layer

Let's have a go at creating our own Lambda layer using the console and then see if we can share it with another account. For this example, we're going to create a layer in Python that simply passes a message back to our handler. Let's get started:

1. We'll start by writing the code that will make up our layer. The following is a super simple function that returns a message:

```
def provide_message():
    return "Hello Lambda learners!"
```

2. Save that file as message_vendor.py, in a folder called python. This is important because our layer gets extracted into the /opt directory. The directory is automatically added to the path variable, making it easily accessible to our actual function. We must make sure we are following the directory structure that's required for our runtime.
3. ZIP up the directory and file ready for upload. The following command will help you here:

```
zip -r layer.zip python/
```

4. Jump into the Lambda console, navigate to the **Layers** page, and click **Create layer**.

5. Fill in the layer configuration and upload your ZIP file. The compatible runtimes option is to make things easier when you're choosing from the list of layers to add to your function from the console. It doesn't serve much purpose other than that. The following screenshot gives you an idea about what your layer configuration should look like:

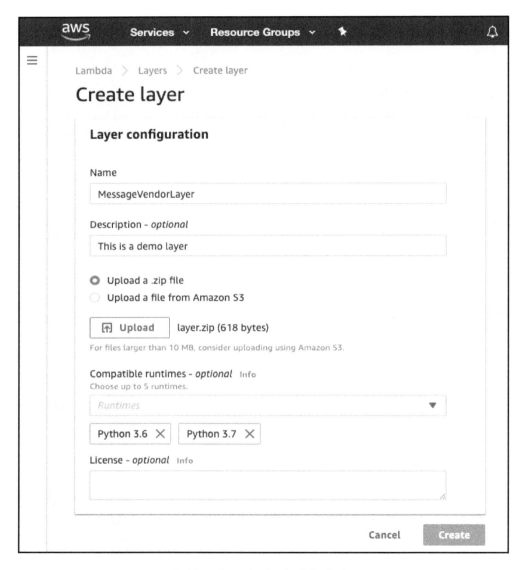

Lambda console – creating a layer for a Python function

6. After you've created the layer, we next thing we need to create is the function. Like you've done already, create a Python 3.7 function from scratch and jump into the configuration screen. We're going to attach our layer to our new function.

7. As you can see, we don't have any layers attached at the moment, so let's open the Layers configuration page and click **Add a layer**. The arrows in the following screenshot show where you can find the necessary buttons:

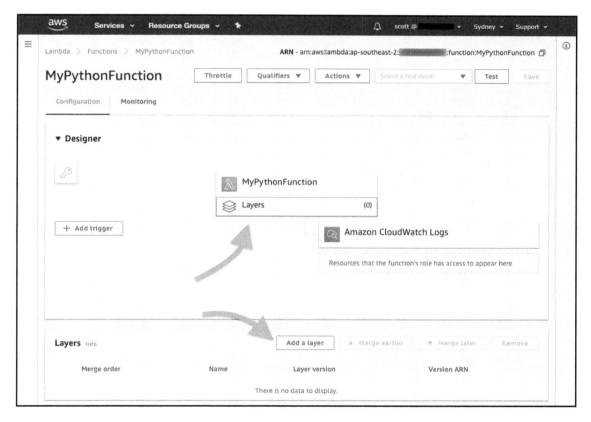

Lambda console showing where to find the layer configurations

8. In the Layer selection screen, we can see that there are two options. The first is that we can pick from a list of layers that are available to us in our account already, including the useful layer that AWS provides. The second option is that we can also enter an ARN of another layer that might exist in another account.

9. Attach our new layer and **Save** the function configuration.

10. Next, we'll replace the boilerplate function code with our own. Use the following function in place of the default Lambda function code:

```
import message_vendor as msg

def lambda_handler(event, context):
    message = msg.provide_message()
    return {
        'statusCode': 200,
        'body': message
    }
```

What we're doing here is importing the layer as a new variable and then calling the function inside the layer to retrieve a message. Go ahead and test it to see if it works!

Assuming the execution ran successfully, you should be treated to a green response in the console with our returned data, as shown in the following example:

```
  ⊘  Execution result: succeeded (logs)

     ▼ Details

        The section below shows the result returned by your function execution.

        {
          "statusCode": 200,
          "body": "Hello Lambda learners!"
        }
```

A snippet of a successful function execution using layers

As an extension exercise, to show that a layer can be used across multiple functions, you can use another Lambda function and test that they can both be invoked simultaneously.

You can add multiple lambda layers to a function and also specify the order they are processed in. Be careful, though – a layer that is applied later in the order can override files that have already been extracted to /opt.

If you're developing Lambda functions for a larger organization, you may be working in a multi-account environment. It would be helpful if we could centralize where the layers were deployed to or hosted. Then, we could share access to the accounts that needed it. With this approach, we can reduce the amount of code we need to deploy, thus avoiding duplication, sprawl, and versioning nightmares. In the next section, we'll explain how to add permissions so that other accounts can access a central Lambda layer.

Sharing a Lambda layer across multiple AWS accounts

To share a layer between accounts or even publish it publicly, you need to use the AWS CLI or the API, as this is not supported in the console yet. We add permission statements using the `AddLayerVersionPermission` API action, which is similar to the way we do it with Lambda functions.

The following command is what we use to share a Lambda layer with another account:

```
aws lambda add-layer-version-permission
    --layer-name MessageVendorLayer
    --version-number 1
    --statement-id sharingWithOneAccount
    --principal 123456789012
    --action lambda:GetLayerVersion
```

What the preceding command will achieve is sharing version 1 of our layer to the AWS account with ID `123456789012`. You could replace this principal with a * if you wanted to share it with *any* account. The consumers of your layer would enter the ARN as part of the attachment process we saw earlier. Only do this if you intend your layer to be available publicly, however.

 This is a great way to share work across accounts and make the most of the code we have written ourselves, or from other teams who have developed their own. In the next section, we'll home in on exactly where layers are useful.

Use cases for Lambda layers

As we can see, there are almost endless use cases that you can imagine. This really gives Lambda some extra flexibility and will help developers deliver code faster. At a high level, these use cases fall into three categories:

- Custom modules, libraries, or functions that can be used by multiple functions
- Third-party dependencies
- Static data that can be shared with multiple functions

A connection you have probably made already is how ideal Lambda layers are for distributing custom runtimes. If you are going to the effort of bringing your own runtime to Lambda, then you're likely going to run more than one function using that custom runtime. Lambda layers are the perfect way to share the custom runtimes across functions.

I encourage you to use layers in your own Lambda development for any of the use cases in this section. In the next section, we're going to explore the aspects and considerations we need to make when using Lambda in production.

Operationalizing

When we get to deploy our functions into a production environment, there are a few things to be aware of, such as the limits on concurrency and how failed invocations are handled. If we don't know about these things, they might trip us up when something goes wrong, requiring much more troubleshooting time than required.

In this section, we'll have a look at concurrency, observability, service limits, and also learn about some tools and tricks that will make our lives easier for reusing code across multiple environments.

Using environment variables

Environment variables in Lambda functions are exactly what they sound like: operating system-level key-value pairs that are dynamically passed to a function and set during instantiation for availability during runtime.

The idea behind environment variables is that you can modify the operational behaviors of the function's execution between your various environments. For example, you might have a different source database for development, test, and production environments that your function needs to communicate with. By abstracting the connection string into a variable, you are allowing the rest of the cost to be reused across each deployment.

Environment variables are encrypted at rest by default using an AWS KMS key, and the Lambda service decrypts this information when it is passed in during the instantiation phase. You can also specify your own KMS key if you wish. It might sound like this would be a good place to store secrets to pass into the function, but there's a better method to do that, which we'll get to in the next section – secrets management. Environment variables are best used to dynamically modify configuration.

Let's have a look at where to add an environment variable to our function using the management console:

1. Jump into the Lambda console and find a function to use for this example.
2. Scroll down your function page. You will find the following section:

Screenshot of the environment variable configuration in the Lambda console

You can also set environment variables using the CLI. We can use the following command to add environment variables to an existing function:

```
aws lambda update-function-configuration
    --function-name MyPythonFunction
    --environment Variables={dbPort=5432}
```

You can also specify environment variables when you're creating the function by using the same --environment option.

There's no limit to the number of environment variables you can set, but the total size of all key-pairs combined cannot exceed 4 KB.

Now, let's have a look at how we might access and set these variables for use during runtime. Each language is slightly different:

- Node.js:

```
const DB_HOST = process.env.dbHost;
const DB_PORT = process.env.dbPort;
```

- Python:

```
import os
DB_HOST = os.environ['dbHost']
DB_PORT = os.environ['dbPort']
```

- Java:

```
final String dbhost = System.getenv("dbHost");
final String dbport = System.getenv("dbPort");
```

- C#:

```
var dbHost = Environment.GetEnvironmentVariable("dbHost");
var dbPort = Environment.GetEnvironmentVariable("dbPort");
```

Using these simple steps is a great way to add extra environmental context to a function's execution. Now, you should have all you need to start using environment variables in your Lambda functions!

Next, we'll learn how to deal with a similar element of environmental context, that is, secrets management.

Secrets management

Just like environment variables are the configuration that's been abstracted away from the source code, we should do the same with secrets. Obviously, these must not be part of the source code and, instead, should be injected during runtime. It's also a good idea to externalize secrets from the function configuration so that they can be reused by other functions in the future. This is part of the reason why we don't use Lambda environment variables to hold secrets.

In AWS, we have two choices for achieving this:

- AWS Systems Manager Parameter Store
- AWS Secrets Manager

Let's start with the Parameter Store. This service is a component of the AWS Systems Manager suite of services that are designed to make life easier when it comes to operationalizing your solutions. Parameter Store can store both configuration items and secrets as key-value pairs, and the data can be encrypted or plain. Items are added to the Parameter Store in a hierarchical way, so, when you're creating the name for your item, you specify the name and the path; for example, all of your database connection parameters for the development environment might be under `/app1/dev/database/connection`. To get the actual parameter for the port, you could request `/app1/dev/database/connection/port`, or, more efficiently, you could use the `getParametersByPath()` API method and specify down to the connection to get all of the parameters under that. Check the SDK documentation for your language to see how each method works.

Moving over to AWS Secrets Manager, we find that this service is more focused on managing the secret itself. Secrets Manager can store a secret and then automatically rotate it periodically on a schedule that you specify. It also has integrations with some of the other AWS services and can trigger a password rotate, set it with a new randomly generated password, and then update the entry.

The similarities between these two services are as follows:

- Both can encrypt your secrets and store them safely
- Both are key-value stores

The only significant difference to call out is cost. Parameter Store is free to use and can store up to 10,000 parameters at a size of up to 4 KB each. Secrets Manager, on the other hand, is $0.40 per secret per month, plus $0.05 per 10,000 API calls. This might not sound like a lot, but it adds up when you have hundreds of secrets with millions of Lambda invocations. This is where you would want to make use of the inherent caching that comes from smart container reuse – which we'll get to later in this section.

Moving on from the environmental context, the following sections will address some of the things we need to be aware of when running at high volume or in production environments.

Concurrency and error handling

The next pieces of information you should be aware of before putting any Lambda-backed solutions into pasture include how to manage execution concurrency and when things go wrong.

 Quick definition check: concurrency is invoking the same Lambda function more than once at any given time.

Lambda comes with an out of the box limit of 1,000 concurrent executions per account. While this might seem low, when you have something that is potentially limitless in scale, all you're doing is shifting the performance bottleneck to the next component. There aren't many RDBMS systems that can handle millions of transactions per second, so let's step back and see how we're managing our data, queries, and throughput before raising that concurrency limit (which can be done by raising a support request). Our options are to either match our Lambda execution rate with the throughput of the downstream resources or enforce more appropriate batch sizes upstream. Both of these options are examples of rate-limiting and differ in the stack, where the limit is being applied.

On our Lambda function configuration page, which can be found in the console, we can actually reserve some of the concurrency for that function to use since the limit is account-wide and applies to all the functions running in that account. If you had a particularly busy function that's being used by another application or team, that could result in the throttling of your function if you reach the service limits, unless you had reserved some capacity. However, be aware here—if we set a reserved concurrency of 200 executions, the total number of concurrent executions for that function can't exceed this. So, treat this function configuration setting as a new limit (that you can change at any time through configuration):

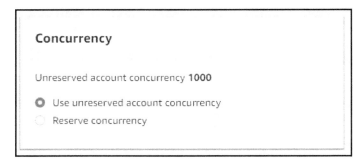

Setting the reserved concurrency for a Lambda function

Now that we understand our limits and how to tune them to our advantage, what we need is a way to monitor concurrency so that we can take action if it approaches the limit.

To do this, Lambda gives you two CloudWatch Metrics to keep an eye on:

- `ConcurrentExecutions`: This is available as a metric for each function, and can also be used as an aggregate of the execution counts for all the functions in the account. If you're running too close to the service limit, you can expect some functions to be throttled if you hit the limit.
- `UnreservedConcurrentExecutions`: Again, this is an aggregate of execution counts, but, this time, the functions with reserved concurrency are excluded.

Okay, let's take some more moments now to look at a situation where we are reaching our limits and invocations are being throttled. What do I mean by throttle? In Lambda, the term throttle refers to something that happens when a function is invoked but does not get executed, usually because a service limit has been exceeded. What actually happens when a function is throttled is different, depending on the source of the event.

Here are the three throttling behaviors for each invocation type:

- For functions that are invoked **synchronously** and subsequently throttled, the client will receive an `HTTP 429` error code with the `TooManyRequestsException` message. The client is then responsible for managing retries from there.
- If functions are invoked using the **asynchronous** invocation type and are throttled, Lambda will automatically retry the invocation twice more, with random delays between retries. On the third failure, the event can be redirected to a Dead Letter Queue.
- Things get more complex if you are throttled during **stream-based** invocations, so check the documentation for the latest handling logic.

There is another metric to watch as well, called *Throttles*, which is a count of invocation requests that didn't quite make it to execution, specifically because of a throttling event. If this metric goes above zero, your clients may be experiencing an impact on the service.

Regarding Dead Letter Queues, these are either an SQS queue or SNS topic that you create and configure yourself, and then assign to be the DLQ of a particular function in the function's configuration. For asynchronous invocations, if none of the retries succeed, then the event will be sent to the DLQ. This will give you a record of all the failed invocations and their error parameters. The idea behind having this is that your unprocessed events aren't lost; you have the record and you can choose what action to take from there.

While concurrency is a characteristic of Lambda that we should call out specifically, observability is a larger objective to meet. This is looking at the service or solution you are providing as a whole and pinpointing measurable characteristics. We'll learn more about observability in the next section.

Observability

Observability is something that we need in order to troubleshoot, debug, monitor, benchmark, and optimize our serverless applications. With the many distributed components that make up a serverless application, we need a way to track the performance of a single transaction throughout the system. This gets really hard when the compute we get from Lambda is so ephemeral, and when functions can be chained with asynchronous or parallel invocations. Observability can encompass event logging, metrics, and tracing. We've already covered a lot of logging and metrics so far, so let's dig into options for traceability.

Most third-party **Application Performance Management** (APM) tools rely on an agent or daemon being present on the host that is running the application. With Lambda, you can't easily install such a thing and there's also no compute that can happen in the background.

Each execution of a Lambda function sends logs to CloudWatch Logs, which is good, because we can find a request ID and some execution timings. We can also code into our function to log a correlation or transaction ID so that we can line up the logs from all the other components to get a picture of a single transaction. Hopefully, our APM can get all the necessary source data from these logs.

To get even more information about our function executions, we could use AWS X-Ray. X-Ray is a service that is really good for digging deeper into the execution of a function to help diagnose where valuable execution time is being spent. It works by listening to trace statements that you send to the X-Ray API from within your function. From there, the service puts a nice service graph visualization together so that you can see all the services and downstream resources that your function is calling, as well as their timings.

The following is a screenshot of the X-Ray console and shows a trace of a transaction moving through a distributed serverless solution:

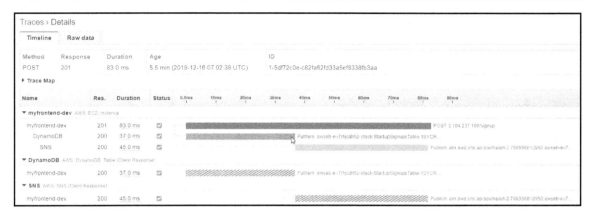

Screenshot of an application trace in the X-Ray console

You can enable X-Ray tracing in your Lambda function by simply ticking a box. You'll find this in the function configuration section. This will only create traces for the function's execution and won't follow any external calls that are made by the function code during execution:

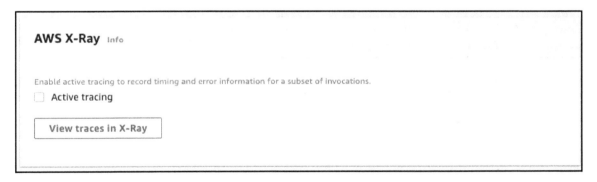

Screenshot of where to enable X-Ray in the Lambda console

It's likely that you'll also need to add permissions for accessing X-Ray to the execution role attached to your Lambda. The actions that you will need to allow are as follows:

```
"xray:PutTraceSegments",
"xray:PutTelemetryRecords"
```

It's also possible to enable X-Ray tracing if you are deploying functions via CloudFormation. Here is a snippet for a Lambda function that has X-Ray tracing enabled. Add this to the properties block of your function declaration:

```
Properties:
  TracingConfig:
    Mode: Active
```

Finally, if you are using the Serverless Framework, you can enable X-Ray tracing in `serverless.yml`. Here's an example function configuration:

```
functions:
  helloWorld:
    handler: handler.helloWorld
    tracing: Active
```

I mentioned earlier that these methods would enable tracing of the function execution statistics, but wouldn't continue to trace any requests that are made to external HTTP endpoints or other AWS services. For this, we need to use the AWS X-Ray SDK within our function execution and specifically configure the components we want to trace. There are two SDK method calls that we are interested in for this:

- `XRay.captureHTTPs()`: Wraps our HTTP requests to capture request and response information
- `XRay.captureAWS()`: Wraps calls to AWS services that are made by the AWS SDK

We use these methods to wrap around our normal downstream requests so that they can capture the communication information and ship the metrics off to X-Ray. Let's have a look at how to implement these in a Node.js function:

1. First, we need to install the AWS X-Ray SDK in our development environment:

   ```
   npm install aws-xray-sdk --save
   ```

2. Then, in our function code, we include the SDK:

   ```
   const XRay = require('aws-xray-sdk');
   ```

3. Then, we set the configuration. This wraps our standard HTTP and AWS SDK calls with the capture methods. You can substitute other libraries for your HTTP calls if you wish:

```
const AWS = XRay.captureAWS(require('aws-sdk'));
const http = XRay.captureHTTPs(require('http'));
```

4. Alternatively, we can get more specific trace information from individual AWS services by wrapping the call in a `captureAWSClient()` method. For example, we can use the following code to wrap a DynamoDB call. This would automatically include richer information about the tables that are accessed:

```
const ddb = XRay.captureAWSClient(new AWS.DynamoDB());
```

5. Then, we can simply use the SDK calls that we are used to using to, for example, put an item in a DynamoDB table:

```
ddb.putItem({
  'TableName': tableName,
  'Item': item
}, (err, data) => {
  if (err) { console.log("Error", err); }
  else { console.log("Success", data); }
});
```

These are the most basic steps for enabling tracing in our Lambda function code. There are many more options for tracing using other sources and services. Check the developer guide for a wealth of information; a link to this can be found in the *Further reading* section.

This leads us back to our own development principles and practices. We now know how to run Lambda functions in production, and in the next section, we will look to improve the way we write functions.

Development practices

So, you've been building a few Lambda functions here and there to do some administration, maybe to ship your logs or respond to CloudWatch alarms. Now, you want to take your functions to the next level by using them as the compute mechanisms in a serverless application—maybe the backend of an API or an event-driven integration flow. First, congratulations on your achievement.

Next, you'll need some tips about how to make the most of the execution time you have available and be able to use the execution model to your advantage.

Structuring a function

In Chapter 3, *The Foundations of a Function in AWS*, we learned about the handler of a function and how that was the special entry point that handles the processing of events. We also built our own functions that had logic and did things within the handler function itself. It turns out that's not the optimal way to structure a Lambda function, and here's why.

It's better to approach Lambda development by splitting a function into three main areas of responsibility. These areas are as follows:

- Handler
- Controller
- Service abstraction

Each area forms a physical separation of code and allows you to be smarter about how the code is used. The following is a representation of how each area is logically implemented:

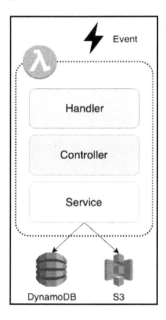

Logical implementation of a Lambda function

In the following subsections, we'll explain these areas in depth.

Handler function

The first area to talk about is the handler function, which we should know fairly intimately by now. The handler's primary responsibility is to process the incoming event that the function was invoked with, and then return with an exit condition and maybe some response data. Basically, it serves as an entry and exit point. It can use that contextual event information to set configurations that change the way the function executes during runtime. The handler code should be very Lambda-specific and wouldn't be portable to other cloud providers or servers. Building on that point, the handler function should never perform any business logic; for example, it should not process or make any decisions on the incoming data.

Controller

The next area of responsibility is the controller. This is where the execution configuration takes place with abstraction behind an interface. It can also be where you perform the setup for dependency injection (or inversion of control) if you're using a language and framework that might require that, and are following that type of design pattern. An example is Java with Spring or Dagger, or injecting mocks for testing. It's worth noting that there is also no business logic that occurs at this layer. This layer is especially good for enabling unit testing because we can inject mocks or use stubs of dependencies.

Before we move on, let's dig into some of the benefits of running dependency injection:

- Decouples the complexities of the execution from the implementation.
- Because it's decoupled, it enables more flexibility, so you can easily change the implementation.
- Greater separation: Each layer or component has its own job to do.
- Increased testability: Can inject stubs or mocks to enable unit testing.

However, watch out for the following:

- Injecting too many dependencies: Heavyweight frameworks such as Spring are not suitable for a Lambda container life cycle. All of your dependencies have to be included in your deployment package, which should be as small as possible.
- Inversion of control doesn't solve things that aren't broken.
- It adds complexity to reduce complexity – there's a balance there somewhere!

Service

The last layer is where the service abstractions are written. For maximum code reuse, these are likely to be libraries that you can reuse in other functions where you need to interact with the same service. For example, you might write a library that interacts with DynamoDB tables in a way that is specific to your problem domain. This is also the place to write bespoke integrations with other systems that the function might interact with, such as a CRM system or SOAP-based service.

 A good idea would be to create Lambda layers from these so that they can be imported with ease when they're needed.

So, where does the business logic go? Well, that really depends on the language you're using, but, as a guide, it can exist anywhere outside of the layers we've talked about here. In Node.js, we might use an exportable function that uses the configuration from the controller and leverages functionality from the service layer. In Java, our implementation would likely be in the form of a class.

 For Python and Node.js, you don't need to include the SDK in your deployment package because it's automatically included.

This section was all about making you aware of the more advanced factors of structuring Lambda functions. This information will be more relevant to you if you are developing serverless applications that are more complex, but there are some good nuggets of best practice to take away.

The next section will explain another characteristic of Lambda functions, that is, container reuse, and how to use this to your advantage.

Reuse and optimization

In this section, we are going to learn how to leverage the execution model to our advantage. We'll also find out about a thing called cold starts, and why we need to be considerate of them.

In the early days of the AWS Lambda service, we could make educated estimates about the underlying implementation of the infrastructure. From this introspection, we were able to postulate that our Lambda code was running within some sort of container. Each time we would trigger a function to be executed, an invisible orchestration service would have to find a physical host with capacity, schedule the container for deployment, download and deploy our .zip package from S3, start the container, and manage it until it was terminated. While the code had stopped executing for that one invocation (it was, in fact, frozen), we found that the underlying container was still available to be reused. Subsequent invocations of the same Lambda functions had a high chance of being scheduled in the existing container environment.

We could infer this from a few factors:

- Any temporary files we had created in our /tmp filesystem were still available in the next invocation.
- Variables that we defined outside of our handler function were still in memory.
- Background processes and callbacks may still not be complete.
- The function executed a whole lot quicker.

In addition to this, we found that the reuse of the same container was not guaranteed. The container would exist for an indeterminately random amount of time until it was either cleaned up by the invisible orchestration service or the invocations of our function reached a point where the Lambda service needed to scale up the number of containers that were deployed.

So, while this gave us developers an opportunity to take advantage of some persistence, we couldn't count on it all the time. This leads us to our first pro tip.

 Declare your database connections outside the scope of the handler function so that they can be (possibly) reused in subsequent invocations, saving the time it takes to establish a connection on every invocation.

This is similar for the /tmp directory. If you had a file you were processing or working on, saving it here would be a good way to enable processing to resume, should the Lambda reach its timeout period.

The amount of time it takes for a new container to be scheduled and readied for your code to be started is called cold starting. In this scenario, you incur a time penalty for every new container. The length of the penalty varies between languages but can be reduced in all examples by making your deployment package as small as possible. This reduces the time that's needed to download the package from S3 and load it into the new container. One other way to avoid this penalty is to always keep your function warm. We know that containers can last anywhere from 5 to 60 minutes before they are cleaned up. This means we just need to invoke our own functions with an event every 5 or so minutes to make it less likely for our end users to be impacted by the penalty.

I did preface at the start that this is what happened in the early days of Lambda. At some time between 2017 and 2018, the Lambda service moved to a new underlying implementation using micro virtual machines, or microVMs. Dubbed as Firecracker, this new virtualization technology is tipped to be the next evolution in how to run massively multi-tenanted functions and serverless workloads on hardware. Firecracker is a virtual machine manager that essentially replaces QEMU to present kernel resources via KVM to microVMs. The benefits of using microVMs over containers are as follows:

- Higher levels of security isolation
- Achieves greater density of VMs to physical resources
- Efficient startup times
- Specifically designed for short-lived transient processes

While this technology is pretty new, we expect the same best practice patterns for Lambda development to still apply.

The next thing to talk about is more focused on optimization once the Lambda is running. Once we have a good baseline for how our function performs and how long it takes to complete execution, we can start playing with the configuration of memory. At the time of writing, you can allocate between 128 MB and 3,008 MB of memory for your function to run with. The Lambda service also allocates CPU proportional to the amount of memory allocated. This means that, if you allocate more memory, you get more CPU to play with as a bonus. More memory also means the cost point is higher per execution, but if your function is executing with more CPU, what if this means the function can complete sooner? There is no silver bullet here, but, I recommend that you thoroughly test your function with different configurations of memory size to find the best setting. You might end up saving heaps on your bill!

This next section is all about using the ecosystem—but what do I mean by this? Let's take a look.

Using the ecosystem

AWS Lambda is just one service out of upwards of 160, each performing its own function for its own use cases. When we develop code for Lambda, there are often other activities that we need to do around that. I'm referring to the authoring, life cycle, and management activities that are necessary as we evolve our service. When we need to add more functionality, we should look to the ecosystem to see what AWS can provide. Using tooling from within the ecosystem can save us setup time and effort in procuring a new tool elsewhere. We can instantly make use of the native integration that the service will naturally provide and know we are covered under our existing support agreement with AWS if anything goes wrong. An additional benefit is that, when we come to declaring all of our infrastructure as code, we can include our extras bundled in the same project structure.

Let's quickly touch on some of the things from the ecosystem that we can use when we develop Lambda functions. When we're authoring, we might be working solo or in distributed teams, following a git branching type of workflow to cut code and merge into the trunk for deployment. We can support this workflow using AWS Cloud9, a browser-based IDE. Developers working on the same function can now be in the same workspace, thus making it easier to collaborate and troubleshoot problems. When you're ready to deploy, the native integration can package and deploy straight to Lambda from the IDE.

In our journey of creating robust enterprise code, we also need a way to enforce versioning and control of deployments. A service such as AWS CloudFormation allows us to declare our cloud and serverless resources as code. You could specify your Lambda functions and any extra resources that are needed, such as S3 buckets or DynamoDB tables in a YAML or JSON template, give the template to CloudFormation, and the resources will be provisioned for you. Any updates to your Lambda function can be deployed by updating and deploying the template again. This allows you to version the surrounding infrastructure, as well as the Lambda code. It also allows you to store your infrastructure definitions right beside your function code, if you're that way inclined, bringing the infrastructure and programming worlds closer together.

Your Lambda function code will most likely need to follow a software development life cycle where code is tested before it is promoted to the next environment, eventually making it to production. AWS CodePipeline can orchestrate and automate the steps for moving the function code through the environments, with AWS CodeBuild running automated tests and deploying to the necessary environments. We'll go into detail about how this works in `Chapter 8`, *CI/CD with the Serverless Framework*.

This section was a brief introduction to make you aware of what can help you when you're developing Lambda functions.

Summary

Congratulations on making it to the end of this chapter! We learned about some of the more advanced topics that will help you take your Lambda functions to the next level. Whether you want to bring your favorite runtime or make better use of code across your function fleet, you now have the knowledge to start. Take these new skills away and experiment before bringing them into your team's development practices. Figure out what works for you and what you might plan to do in the future.

In the next chapter, we'll learn about an application framework that can make our lives even easier by declaring and configuring infrastructure for us, making for an awesome developer experience. Keep reading to find out more!

Questions

1. Which runtime choice allows you to bundle your own binary and run your own language inside a Lambda function?

   A) Python
   B) Go
   C) Java
   D) Custom runtime

2. What's the best way to reuse the same code across multiple Lambda functions?

   A) Shared git repository
   B) Lambda layers
   C) Invoke another Lambda function to use the shared library
   D) You can't reuse code across multiple Lambda functions

3. What is the default maximum number of concurrent Lambda executions per region in an AWS account?

   A) 100
   B) 1,000
   C) 1,000,000
   D) Unlimited

4. Which service would I use if I wanted automated rotation of secrets?

   A) AWS Secrets Manager
   B) AWS Systems Manager Parameter Store
   C) AWS Key Management Service

5. Which part of a Lambda function is responsible for abstracting services and external integrations?

   A) Controller
   B) Environment variables
   C) Handler
   D) Service

6. What will be the response if you synchronously invoke a Lambda function that is being throttled?

   A) HTTP 504 error
   B) HTTP 202 code and the request will be queued
   C) HTTP 429

Further reading

- Runtime API OpenAPI spec: `https://docs.aws.amazon.com/lambda/latest/dg/samples/runtime-api.zip`
- Concurrent Lambda executions: `https://docs.aws.amazon.com/lambda/latest/dg/concurrent-executions.html`
- AWS Cloud9: `https://aws.amazon.com/cloud9/`
- Useful custom runtimes and layers: `https://github.com/mthenw/awesome-layers`
- AWS X-Ray developer guide: `https://docs.aws.amazon.com/xray/latest/devguide/aws-xray.html`

3
Section 3: Development Patterns

This section builds on your foundational knowledge as a step toward creating a production solution in a multi-developer environment.

This section comprises the following chapters:

- Chapter 7, *Serverless Framework*
- Chapter 8, *CI/CD with the Serverless Framework*

7
Serverless Framework

We've reached the part of this book where we get to use what we've learned so far, put our understanding together, and move on to the next level of serverless application development. We've taught you the base knowledge that you need to succeed when you start your first project. In this chapter, we will turn simple lambda function development into full-blown serverless application development. We'll explore an application framework that accelerates our progress and makes it easy to build and deploy.

In this chapter, we'll cover the following topics:

- Understanding the need for a framework
- Exploring the core concepts of the Serverless Framework
- Deploying your first service
- Testing and debugging

Technical requirements

To understand this chapter, you will need prior knowledge of developing lambda functions, either from this book or from real-life experience. You will also need a general understanding of APIs and DevOps.

Understanding the need for a framework

We need to frame the reasons and benefits of introducing a new tool for our development experience. Adopting a new toolset or application framework is not a decision you make lightly, as it will most likely carry through for the entire life cycle of the project. Before jumping straight in, we should understand the pros and cons of the Serverless Framework first. However, we won't spend too long laboring over this point—we want to jump into creating our first project as soon as possible!

When adopting a framework, keep in mind that, if you're using the console to set up serverless components, you're doing it wrong. This statement largely sums up the sentiment behind adopting a framework. Using the management console to create resources, set configurations, perform uploads, and deployments is not a sustainable approach for running serverless applications. The total effort is compounded when multiple developers and testers are contributing to the same project. It's fine for learning and validating how components are connected, but at some point, you are going to want something extra.

A framework gives you the ability to do the following:

- Code and run deployments from your local machine
- Work with multiple developers on the same project
- Version and control changes to assets and resources
- Write test suites and enable development standards across all functions and services
- Share common libraries and utilities
- Focus less on the nuances of the implementation details, for example, how to use IAM to grant the necessary permissions to all the components

Digging more into the reasons for a framework, we will see a real shift toward a developer-focused workflow model. We'll cover this in the next section.

Developer focus

During my experience as a cloud specialist, I've been part of a general movement in the industry for things becoming increasingly codified, which is probably a trend that won't surprise most people in the industry. Things that were manual tasks or sets of implementation instructions are now likely to be cloud resources declared as code and follow some sort of software development life cycle. I'm mostly eluding to the existence of Infrastructure as Code, which is a term that now encompasses a large area. What this means is a general convergence of responsibilities for software developers, engineers, and operators. Because all of our artifacts exist as code, we can now work closely together and share similar toolsets. Did you ever think you would be able to set linting rules on the infrastructure definition of a database server? Or deploy a YAML template for the entire resource stack of an application?

Because our infrastructure is easier to create and operationally manage, we can spend more of our quality time on the business code and on the function that is adding the value. What we care about is primarily the function code, then the event that makes the code run, and then any supporting resources that we might need to facilitate data movement and persistence. What we've learned so far is that we can architect entire applications as functions and events, so what if we could represent and manage that application with one tool?

The following diagram provides an example of the scale of complexities in a serverless project. The 12 components might make up a single solution or application. If you were building this manually using the console, or even the CLI, this could potentially be 12 lots of configuration, infrastructure declaration, and deployment activities. What if there were 100 or 1,000 components?

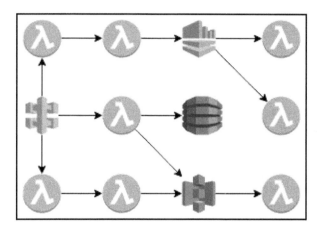

Illustration of a simple serverless application with 12 components

Serverless Framework is an open source application framework that allows you to create serverless applications and manage them throughout their life cycle. When a serverless application grows, it becomes incredibly hard to manage the multiple functions, buckets, security, and permissions for each deployment artifact. The framework provides a new developer experience that reduces the overhead and complexity of managing serverless projects. At the moment, the Serverless Framework is the most popular framework on GitHub and receives improvements from many contributors from the community and from Serverless Inc. as well.

For reference, I've included the following screenshot of the GitHub project, showing the popularity usage statistics:

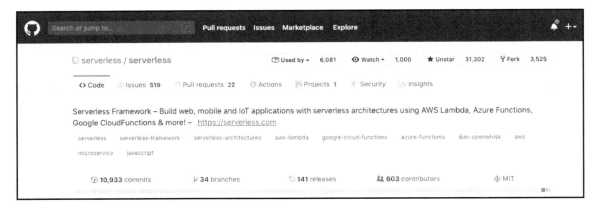

Statistics for the Serverless Framework project on GitHub

The framework is used for developing functions in a supported language and then wiring those functions up to events. How the events are implemented is abstracted away from the developer, so all they have to do is design for reacting to the event data coming into the function. The Serverless Framework is also multi-platform, meaning that you can deploy to multiple different cloud providers from the same developer experience.

 The framework is designed in such a way that the developer doesn't have to worry about the quirks of a function, depending on which platform they are developing against.

It's comforting to know if your organization has a multi-cloud strategy because now you can standardize on one tool across the enterprise. We'll be focusing on Amazon Web Service in all our examples.

The next section introduces you to an approach for managing your Serverless Framework projects.

Managing a serverless project

Serverless applications can quickly get out of hand when the number of functions and their dependencies get too large to fit inside your head space. Due to this, the overhead of packaging and deploying each function one by one becomes tedious.

 A project repository includes all of the function code, libraries, dependencies, tests, and framework configuration files that are required to run the serverless application.

The idea behind using a project structure in the Serverless Framework is that you include all of the functions that contribute to the application architecture in one repository. All of the functions and event mappings can be managed as one unit. As a rule of thumb, you would include functions in the same repository that do the following:

- Are in the same bounded context
- Make up a collection of APIs in the same domain
- Share code in the same bounded context

Now that we know what should be included in each project, let's move on to the next section and find out about the concepts that make up a project in the Serverless Framework.

Exploring the core concepts of the Serverless Framework

Before we can create our first project, we need to know about the bones of the framework, including the terms and definitions that make the experience what it is.

In this section, we'll introduce the terms and point you toward some documentation where you'll find a more complete set of options.

Services

A service is our unit of project. It's our top-level name for the service we are creating and contains all the functions, events, and resources we need for the project. You can build everything you need to in one service, or have multiple services for a single serverless application. It's up to you to define what the delineation is and where the domain boundaries are.

We only need to create the service once, and some boilerplate files are created for us to get going quickly. Using the serverless CLI command, we can run the following code. This will create our service in the directory path we specify:

```
sls create
    --template aws-nodejs
    --path serverless-hello-world
```

At this point, we can choose which language we are writing our functions in using the template option. There are service templates for all of the supported languages.

 Take care when creating the service name because this drives a lot of the naming conventions when things are deployed to AWS.

The files that are created will depend on the template you choose. For Node.js, for example, you get the resulting project structure. The following is a directory structure with our service folder at the top level, followed by two files that were created by the framework:

```
serverless-hello-world
 ├ handler.js
 └ serverless.yml
```

You'll recognize the hander file straight away, but what's this new YAML file for? This is where the service, provider, functions, events, resources, and plugins are all declared and configured. When you go to deploy your new service to your chosen cloud provider, the Serverless Framework uses this file to decide how to assemble the deployment template—in the case of AWS, it is a CloudFormation template and what needs to go into it.

Once we have a service, we can define functions. We'll explore this in the next section.

Functions

A function is our independent unit of deployment and consists of our packaged code, including libraries and dependencies. We're already largely familiar with what a function is, and the Serverless Framework doesn't alter that definition. If we're coding in Node.js, we still have our `handler.js` file, while for Python, we have `handler.py`.

A function declaration is fairly simple—in the declaration block, we specify a function name and handler. There are a lot of other options we can add to customize the configuration as well, such as a timeout period and memory size. If we don't specify the other options, then sensible defaults are applied.

The following snippet goes into the `serverless.yml` file and is the minimum you need to declare a function. You should pick a good name to replace `functionName`—one that describes what your function does:

```
functions:
    functionName:
        handler: handler.functionName
```

You can define as many functions as you like in the `serverless.yml` file. You can also define a function that has a lambda layer attached to it, which we'll cover in the *Layers* section.

We expect our function to have some sort of trigger in the form of an event. We'll explore this in the next section.

Events

Events in the Serverless Framework are what we would expect. Events are anything that can trigger your function so that it's invoked and often includes event data along with it. When we specify an event for a function, the Serverless Framework automatically provisions the infrastructure and wires up the event mapping for us. This is part of what makes the framework awesome—we don't have to spend time building and configuring complex infrastructure; it's all sorted for us at deploy time.

The following snippet expands on our previous example, with an event block being added. This specifies the event that we want to use to trigger the function:

```
functions:
    functionName:
        handler: handler.functionName
        events:
          - http:
              path: hello
              method: get
```

The terms for each event type have been generalized so that the implementation underneath can support multi-cloud deployments. For example, if we assigned an HTTP event to a function like we did in the preceding code, when we deployed this to AWS, we would get an Amazon API Gateway endpoint integrated into trigger our function. In another cloud provider, the equivalent service integration would be created.

You may also want a function to be triggered at regular intervals, and this is where the schedule event is useful. The following function will create a CloudWatch event that fires at the rate you specify, triggering the function:

```
events:
    - schedule: rate(30 minutes)
```

Something that's also supported is the Cron type of schedule if you wanted your function to be triggered at a very specific point in time. The following code would trigger the function so that it's invoked at 11 AM on the first Monday of every month. Cron expressions are very flexible. For more information, check out the *Further reading* section:

```
events:
    - schedule: cron(0 11 ? * 2#1 *)
```

We can define multiple event mappings for each function. The last time we counted, there were 16 event sources that you could define. Head over to the documentation at `https://serverless.com` to check the options for each event type.

Next up are resources and plugins, which help us provide extra functionality. We'll talk about them in the next section.

Resources and plugins

Resources are any infrastructure that may support the functionality we are building with our function. For AWS, CloudFormation template syntax is used to define the resources. An example of this could be an Amazon DynamoDB table to provide a data persistence layer. We can specify the details of the AWS resource configuration in our `serverless.yml` file, and the framework will provision the infrastructure automatically when we deploy it. The following is an example of including a DynamoDB table called `photosMetadata` in the resources section of our `serverless.yml` file:

```
resources:
  Resources:
    photosMetadata
      Type: AWS::DynamoDB::Table
      Properties:
        TableName: photosMetadata
        AttributeDefinitions:
          - AttributeName: id
            AttributeType: N
        KeySchema:
          - AttributeName: id
            AttributeType: HASH
        ProvisionedThroughput:
          ReadCapacityUnits: 1
          WriteCapacityUnits: 1
```

Declaring additional resources is useful because it means we are keeping the other components of our infrastructure stack close to our business logic code. It also means that the infrastructure can be versioned and evolve at the same pace as our functions, all from one location. We can deploy the same definitions of resources, functions, and events to multiple AWS accounts, ensuring each environment is configured the same way.

Plugins are what we use to extend the framework. Everything in the Serverless Framework is made up of plugins, including the deploy CLI command. This makes the framework incredibly modular where we can swap out and replace functionality at any point. Plugins are really good for providing the extra things that are needed to fully implement our software life cycle. For example, you can install a plugin that will allow your functions to be unit tested. The plugin may also come with its own serverless CLI command so that you can build this into your continuous integration pipeline. To enable a plugin (or multiple plugins) after it has been installed locally, we can simply add the following to the plugins section in our `serverless.yml` file:

```
plugins:
  - serverless-kms-secrets
```

We'll explore an example of installing and using a plugin for testing in a *Testing and debugging* section where we learn about unit testing our functions. Plugins can be written by anyone in the community, and there are already heaps available to choose from. Now, we'll take a look at layers.

Layers

Lambda layers are a recent addition to the Lambda feature set and have already been built into the `serverless.yml` syntax. You learned about layers in a previous chapter.

To declare a layer in the Serverless Framework, we use a new top-level block called layers, as shown in the following code. We need to specify the path relative to the function's working directory. This is the directory that lambda will place the extracted files that were bundled in the layer in:

```
layers:
    layerName:
        path: /path/to/layer
```

This declares a layer. Now, we can attach it to a function. Notice that the reference to the layer means that our deploy command will look for that layer in our current serverless service. You'll also note that the framework capitalizes the first letter of our layer name and appends `LambdaLayer`. This could trip you up, so beware!

```
functions:
    functionName:
        handler: handler.functionName
        layers:
          - { Ref: LayerNameLambdaLayer }
```

To add a layer that exists outside of the service, you can simply use the ARN identifier instead of a reference. Just like in the console, you can add up to five layers to a function.

So, that's all we need to learn about in order to understand the terminology of the Serverless Framework. In the next section, we'll put that knowledge into good use and deploy our own service.

Deploying your first service

Alright then, let's get into the bit where we can deploy something ourselves! We have a lot to cover in this section, but, by the end, you will understand how to go from zero to deploying a functional API using the Serverless Framework. Remember that a service is our top-level construct, so, when we're building and deploying a service, this includes all of the functions, events, and resources within the project.

We'll start by installing the framework and explore some of the command-line options that are available. Then, with the help of the framework, we'll create a Hello World API written in Node.js and deploy a real endpoint to our AWS account. After that, we'll dig into some of the underlying details about how deployments work before learning how to run our development locally. We'll also touch on serverless enterprise and the use of the dashboard for an out of the box enterprise experience.

Let's get started by installing the prerequisites.

Installation and the CLI

The Serverless Framework comes with its own CLI so that you can manage and deploy your services. This is also where new functionality can be exposed by installing community plugins. Let's get started:

1. To install the framework, we need to make sure we have Node.js and **node package manager** (**NPM**) installed locally.
2. Then, we can go ahead and run a global installation of serverless. The global option will make the serverless package available to the whole system, instead of just installing it on the current working directory. The installation also sets up a command alias so that you can use the shortened `sls` instead of typing out `serverless` to execute the CLI.

   Run the following command to install the Serverless Framework from the NPM registry:

   ```
   npm install serverless -g
   ```

3. After you have installed the framework, you can run the `--help` command to get a view of all the options that are available:

   ```
   sls --help
   ```

Running the preceding command will give you the following output. Your output could be different from what's shown in the following screenshot, depending on the version and plugins you've installed:

```
Commands
* You can run commands with "serverless" or the shortcut "sls"
* Pass "--verbose" to this command to get in-depth plugin info
* Pass "--no-color" to disable CLI colors
* Pass "--help" after any <command> for contextual help

Framework
* Documentation: http://slss.io/docs

Environment Variables
* Set SLS_DEBUG=* to see debugging logs
* Set SLS_WARNING_DISABLE=* to hide warnings from the output

config ........................ Configure Serverless
config credentials .......... Configures a new provider profile for the Serverless Framework
create ...................... Create new Serverless service
install ..................... Install a Serverless service from GitHub or a plugin from the Serverless registry
package ..................... Packages a Serverless service
deploy ...................... Deploy a Serverless service
deploy function ............. Deploy a single function from the service
deploy list ................. List deployed version of your Serverless Service
deploy list functions ....... List all the deployed functions and their versions
invoke ...................... Invoke a deployed function
invoke local ................ Invoke function locally
info ........................ Display information about the service
logs ........................ Output the logs of a deployed function
metrics ..................... Show metrics for a specific function
print ....................... Print your compiled and resolved config file
remove ...................... Remove Serverless service and all resources
rollback .................... Rollback the Serverless service to a specific deployment
rollback function ........... Rollback the function to the previous version
slstats ..................... Enable or disable stats
plugin ...................... Plugin management for Serverless
plugin install .............. Install and add a plugin to your service
plugin uninstall ............ Uninstall and remove a plugin from your service
plugin list ................. Lists all available plugins
plugin search ............... Search for plugins
login ....................... Login or sign up for Serverless
logout ...................... Logout from Serverless
generate-event .............. Generate event
test ........................ Run HTTP tests
dashboard ................... Open the Serverless dashboard

Plugins
AwsConfigCredentials, Config, Create, Deploy, Info, Install, InteractiveCli, Invoke, Logs, Metrics, Package, Plugin, PluginIns
tall, PluginList, PluginSearch, PluginUninstall, Print, Remove, Rollback, ServerlessEnterprisePlugin, SlStats
```

Commands and plugins available in the Serverless Framework CLI

We'll explore some of these commands in the next section, where we'll create and deploy our own service, but clearly there is a lot of functionality here that is straight out of the box.

The last thing we need to do to be able to interact with and deploy to our AWS account is to set up some credentials for the CLI to use.

4. We need to create an IAM user with an appropriate policy and enable programmatic access. This will give us a new user that doesn't have any permissions to access the console but will create the access key and secret access key that we need to be able to use the AWS CLI. There is a blog from the Serverless Framework that explains all of the permissions that are needed for the framework user in detail. You can find this in the *Further reading* section, at the end of this chapter.

   The serverless CLI will look at the environment variables for your access keys first, but you can also use the AWS CLI's own configuration command or the serverless config credentials command to create a new profile. The details will be stored in a file in your home directory under `.aws/credentials`.

5. In your IAM policy document, grant the user the appropriate permissions for your use case. If you're just starting out and using a fresh lab-type AWS account, then you may want to assign the `AdministratorAccess` policy to minimize the amount of troubleshooting you might run into. If you're developing services that will be deployed to multiple environments, including production, then you should consider creating your own inline IAM policy that follows least-privilege principles.

 Introducing IAM permissions boundaries is also a great idea to minimize the risk of privilege escalation.

Now that we have covered the prerequisites, let's move on! In the next section, we will create and deploy our own service.

Hello World API in 5 minutes

Now, we're ready to get something going. The resources we're going to deploy in this example should be covered by the free tier, and all the services will be of the serverless variety so that the compute doesn't cost when it's sitting idle and not processing responses. Let's get started:

1. The very first thing we need to do after sorting our prerequisites is create the service boilerplate:

   ```
   sls create
       --template aws-nodejs
       --path serverless-hello-world
   ```

   Straight away, we have an example `serverless.yml` configuration file with useful comments in it.

2. Let's simplify this a little bit and remove the comments for now. What we're left with is a very short file that looks as follows:

   ```
   service: serverless-hello-world

   provider:
       name: aws
       runtime: nodejs10.x

   functions:
       hello:
           handler: handler.hello
   ```

   What we're looking at is some provider configuration for AWS and a declaration for a function called hello. The handler is a pointer to the function inside our `handler.js` file. This is the same syntax that we use to represent the handler in a standard lambda configuration.

3. Because we are now working with a Node.js project, we should also initialize the necessary project files. Inside your service directory, run the following command:

   ```
   npm init -y && npm install
   ```

4. We also have a hello world handler function that has been created for us, but let's update it to put our own mark on it. Replace the boilerplate function code with the following:

```
'use strict';

module.exports.hello = async event => {
    return {
        statusCode: 200,
        body: JSON.stringify(
            {
                message: 'Hello World deployed from Serverless
Framework!',
                input: event,
            },
            null,
            2
        ),
    };
};
```

This is cool. If we went to deploy these using the serverless CLI commands, we could, but we haven't specified an event to trigger the function with yet.

5. Let's add an HTTP event so that serverless will create an API Gateway endpoint for us. Update the function declaration in your serverless.yml file to include the event. It should look as follows:

```
functions:
    hello:
        handler: handler.hello
        events:
        - http:
                path: /hello
                method: get
```

Okay, I think we're ready to deploy now!

6. The command to deploy is super easy, and we'll dig into what is happening behind the scenes in the next section. For now, run the following command in your service directory:

```
sls deploy
```

Because I've used a specific AWS CLI profile to set up my new user, I also had to include an option in the command to specify the profile I wanted the CLI to use: --aws-profile <profile name>.

Also, we haven't specified which region to deploy to, so the command line will default to us-east-1. If you want to specify the region, you can add it in the provider declaration or pass it in as an option in the deploy command using `--region switch`.

After running the command, you should see some log output, and when the process is complete, you will see a summary of what has been deployed. From the following output of my deployment, you can see that we have a new service in us-east-1 that includes a function and an HTTP endpoint. This endpoint is now live—we can send a `GET` request using curl and get a response!

```
                          :~/Workspace/serverless-hello-world > sls deploy --aws-profile sa
Serverless: Packaging service...
Serverless: Excluding development dependencies...
Serverless: Creating Stack...
Serverless: Checking Stack create progress...
.....
Serverless: Stack create finished...
Serverless: Uploading CloudFormation file to S3...
Serverless: Uploading artifacts...
Serverless: Uploading service serverless-hello-world.zip file to S3 (789 B)...
Serverless: Validating template...
Serverless: Updating Stack...
Serverless: Checking Stack update progress...
.............................
Serverless: Stack update finished...
Service Information
service: serverless-hello-world
stage: dev
region: us-east-1
stack: serverless-hello-world-dev
resources: 10
api keys:
  None
endpoints:
  GET - https://hqvtsqgiv4.execute-api.us-east-1.amazonaws.com/dev/hello
functions:
  hello: serverless-hello-world-dev-hello
layers:
  None
Serverless: Run the "serverless" command to setup monitoring, troubleshooting and testing.
```

Deployment log output

This was quite a basic example to demonstrate how easy it is to create a project and have a deployed function and RESTful interface in less than 5 minutes. It's important to understand the technical process of what is happening underneath during a deployment, so in the next section, we shall go through this.

Understanding the deployment

So, what actually happens when we run that super easy deploy command? Well, if we use the console output of the service we deployed previously, we can see that there are some log messages.

These log messages show the current deployment progress, which follows the automated steps in the following diagram:

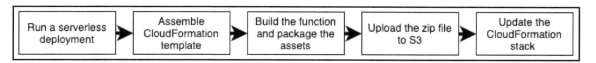

Serverless deployment automated steps

First, the serverless deploy command takes looks at your `serverless.yml` file and figures out what it needs in order to assemble a CloudFormation template. Then, it checks if there is already a CloudFormation stack that has been deployed. If not, serverless will deploy a new stack that only creates an S3 bucket for storing the deployment artifacts (your zipped and packaged code).

If you're using a language that requires some build and compile steps (such as Java with Maven or Gradle), then this will be kicked off now. The output of that process will be our Lambda code, which is then packaged into a `.zip` file and uploaded to our new S3 bucket. The framework will then have an updated CloudFormation template ready with all the events, functions, resources, and additional IAM roles and policies to deploy.

The IAM roles that are created are for the Lambda function to execute with, and you can specify custom policies in your `serverless.yml` file, per service or per function. The existing CloudFormation stack (the one with only the S3 bucket) is then updated with the real deal.

At this point, AWS takes over to complete the creation of the required new resources. The deploy command continuously polls the stack for a completion status and feeds back any errors that occur during the deployment. If there are errors, the framework will roll back the deployment or delete the stack if it was the first deploy.

When you run the deploy command for a second time or any time after that, the Serverless Framework will find the existing CloudFormation stack and update it with the new template. This allows the complexities of handling updates of resources to be shifted to AWS.

It's a good thing that the Serverless Framework leverages the AWS-native method for deploying and connecting resources because, otherwise, it would have to implement and orchestrate all of the AWS API calls itself. This would increase the level of lock of using the framework, which is something we want to avoid. The idea is that if the framework goes away, we can still manage all of our resources through the deployed CloudFormation stack.

Updating CloudFormation stacks can sometimes take longer than we would like. If we're only making updates to our Lambda function code and not the configuration in serverless.yml, then we can use the following command to deploy only the function.

Here's the command to update just the function:

```
serverless deploy function --function hello
```

This process doesn't make updates to the CloudFormation stack at all. Instead, it builds and packages your function, uploads the .zip file in the S3 bucket, and updates the Lambda function directly. This command doesn't create a new version of the lambda; instead, it updates the $LATEST published version. It's important to know this because your CloudFormation stack will still be referring to the version of the Lambda that was published when the serverless deploy command was run. Therefore, it's not recommended to use the serverless deploy function command as a method to update your lambda function in production, but, it is a good way to speed up your deployments during development.

 The serverless CLI defaults to using the us-east-1 region if you haven't specified a region in serverless.yml or your CLI command. It does not respect the default region that's set in your AWS CLI configuration.

Before we move on, I want to introduce the Serverless Framework term called stages. To properly adopt a tool, it has to be able to support deployments to the different environments that you may have or need. Stages are how the framework represents environments or, in other words, the stages in the software development life cycle.

By using a stage, you can separate the deployment into different API endpoints or even different AWS accounts. To specify a stage, you can use the `--stage` option in your deploy CLI command or add it to the provider declaration in `serverless.yml`. The CLI option will always override whatever is in the YAML file, and, if nothing is configured, then the stage defaults to dev.

The framework also uses the stage variable to add a path prefix to the API Gateway endpoint. You will notice that the path of the endpoint we deployed will start with `/dev`, followed by the path we configured for our function. In production, you could use this as a versioning strategy. In the next chapter, where we cover CI/CD with the Serverless Framework, we'll go into this in more detail.

Now, we understand what happens when we deploy our services. Next, we will introduce you to an enterprise feature that allows us to view the details about our deployment in a browser.

The dashboard

The Serverless Framework has recently launched a new SaaS offering for monitoring, testing, and managing deployments for those who enjoy a browser-based UI experience. This means that the framework is no longer just a tool for development and deployment; now, you can extend it to gain insights into your entire development life cycle. The serverless dashboard is part of the serverless enterprise toolset and you need to sign up for an account before you can use it. This crosses over from the open source world into a more enterprise offering with support, so make sure you're aware of the fine print before globally adopting this.

The dashboard introduces a new top-level concept of an app. An app can be made up of multiple services and the app is a way to group those together.

The following is a screenshot of the dashboard showing an example of a serverless-hello-world app:

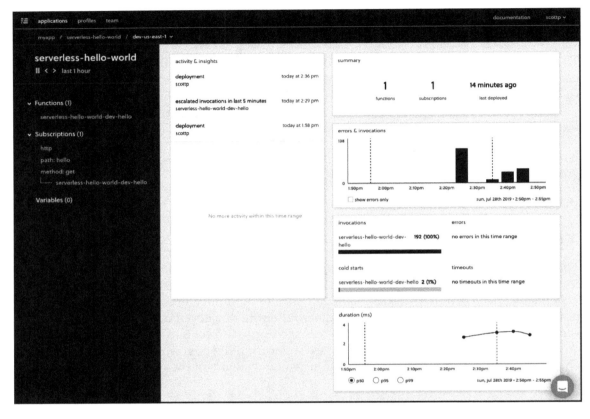

Screenshot of the Serverless Enterprise dashboard showing service insights

To get started using the dashboard, you need to add the following declarations to your existing `serverless.yml` file. The tenant is to match your deployment with your Serverless Enterprise username, while the app is the name of the app:

```
tenant: scottp      #your username in Serverless Enterprise
app: myapp          #the name of your app
```

After saving the file, you need to log into Serverless via the CLI—this will open a browser to complete the signup and authorization process. You will also be able to create your app so that the entity exists when you connect your service up. Use the following command to kick off this process:

```
sls login
```

Finally, run another deploy command. In the output, you will be able to see some new log messages that show that the deployment is now running some standard checks and tests for security. These checks are configurable in the dashboard console. The following is the CLI output when you are deploying with Serverless Enterprise enabled. The output is slightly different here:

```
]                              :~/Workspace/serverless-hello-world > sls deploy --aws-profile sa
Serverless: Packaging service...
Serverless: Excluding development dependencies...
Serverless: Safeguards Processing...
Serverless: Safeguards Results:

  Summary -----------------------------------------------------

  passed - allowed-runtimes
  passed - no-wild-iam-role-statements
  passed - allowed-regions
  passed - no-secret-env-vars
  passed - require-dlq
  passed - allowed-stages
  warned - require-cfn-role
  passed - framework-version

  Details -----------------------------------------------------

  1) Warned - no cfnRole set
     details: http://slss.io/sg-require-cfn-role
     Require the cfnRole option, which specifies a particular role for CloudFormation to assume while deploying.


Serverless: Safeguards Summary: 7 passed, 1 warnings, 0 errors
```

Deployment log output with integrated tests and checks

To get access to the dashboard, you can run the following CLI command, which will launch a new browser tab for the URL of your app:

```
sls dashboard
```

The dashboard follows the same free-tier numbers as lambda, in that you get all the features for up to 1,000,000 invocations per month. After that, you will need to contact the serverless team to explore subscription options. Currently, the dashboard only supports Node.js runtimes.

In the next section, we are going to introduce another way to develop serverless applications using the framework.

Serverless offline (run it locally)

Some developers prefer to do their work locally and make sure everything works on their own machine before deploying to an environment. This is quite hard to do with cloud-native applications because, usually, the services we use are managed services that can't be run ourselves on a server outside of the cloud provider. For example, you can't run the full-blown Amazon S3 service yourself in your own data center or virtual machine.

Some of the benefits that developers are looking for when developing locally are as follows:

- The speed at which new code or changes can be validated and tested. Not every code change requires a deployment to be pushed to a cloud service.
- A better handle on the costs that are incurred if the cloud service pricing model is not easily understood.
- Enabling local debugging can close iteration loops.

Over the years, though, there have been advancements in local development and new options have been created. Now, with AWS, we can run DynamoDB locally, run API Gateway locally using the Serverless Application Model, invoke lambda functions locally, and launch some local endpoints to be able to test applications before deploying them to ECS.

This chapter is about the Serverless Framework specifically, so let's have a look at our options when it comes to running services on our own machines and developing with the framework.

First up, we have the out-of-the-box command to invoke our function locally. After all, functions are only code, so there's not a whole lot to emulate there. The following command shows us the syntax for invoking a function locally using the code we have already developed on our desktops:

```
sls invoke local -f <function-name>
```

The context object is injected with some mock data, the function is invoked, and we should get the output we are expecting. It's a good idea to run this command while you're developing functions before pushing them to AWS, where the code is more integrated into the environment. Any obvious syntax errors that aren't picked up by your IDE's linter are likely to be surfaced here.

When developing locally, there are a couple of plugins that you can install that will make your life easier, as follows:

- Serverless offline plugin
- Serverless DynamoDB Local plugin

If you need a more integrated environment for the Lambda function code to run in, you may turn to the serverless offline plugin (`https://github.com/dherault/serverless-offline`). This is a plugin that adds emulation for API Gateway, as well as the Lambda execution environment. It currently supports Node.js, Python, Ruby, and Go and has a good scope of features that you might need.

Another useful plugin you might need is DynamoDB Local (`https://serverless.com/plugins/serverless-dynamodb-local/`). This will allow you to reference the endpoint of an instance of the DynamoDB service that is running on your own machine.

Let's have a go at installing and configuring the offline plugin and the DynamoDB Local plugin. Remember that these are plugins that developers in the community have written, and they all contribute to the functionality that the framework can provide because of its modular design—awesome.

Let's start by installing these two useful plugins in our project directory. We'll use the `--save-dev` switch in the command so that the packages are included in the development dependencies and not the application dependencies—in other words, these packages aren't needed for the actual function to run in production. Let's get started:

1. Install the plugins from the public node package registry:

```
npm install serverless-offline serverless-dynamodb-local --save-dev
```

2. The next thing we need to do is update our `serverless.yml` file so that we can add a plugins declaration so that the plugins are imported. The best place to add the following block is near the bottom of the `serverless.yml` file.

```
plugins:
    - serverless-offline
    - serverless-dynamodb-local
```

3. Next, we actually need to install the DynamoDB Local service, and we can use the framework to do this for us. The following command will install the necessary files into our project directory, under a hidden directory called `.dynamodb`:

```
sls dynamodb install
```

We should probably add some DynamoDB resources to our `serverless.yml` file while we're at it.

4. Add the following block under the function declaration. Where we can, we'll try to follow the DynamoDB example from `Chapter 5`, *Leveraging AWS Services*, so that we can use this knowledge again. The resources block we are adding will give DynamoDB Local some configuration to start with. When we deploy the same thing to AWS, the Serverless Framework will translate our configuration into CloudFormation to deploy the DynamoDB tables:

```
resources:
  Resources:
    photosMetadataTable:
      Type: AWS::DynamoDB::Table
      Properties:
        TableName: photos-metadata
        AttributeDefinitions:
          ...
        KeySchema:
          - AttributeName: id
            KeyType: HASH
        ProvisionedThroughput:
          ReadCapacityUnits: 1
          WriteCapacityUnits: 1
```

5. We need to add some attribute definitions as well. You can create your own or use my suggested following data points. Substitute the ellipsis in the preceding resource block with some attribute definitions. The reference documentation for attribute definitions can be found at `https://docs.aws.amazon.com/AWSCloudFormation/latest/UserGuide/aws-properties-dynamodb-attributedef.html`:

```
- AttributeName: id
  AttributeType: N
- AttributeName: FILENAME
  AttributeType: S
- AttributeName: FOCAL_LENGTH
  AttributeType: N
- AttributeName: CAMERA_MAKE
  AttributeType: S
- AttributeName: FLASH_FIRED
  AttributeType: BOOL
```

6. We also need to add a customization to the YML file to engage DynamoDB Local. Add the following to the end of our existing file:

```
custom:
    dynamodb:
        stages:
            - dev
```

7. Now, we want to run up the serverless offline system. This starts the local DynamoDB service, which is configured to listen on port 8000. Then, it will start up the endpoint emulator for API Gateway, which will listen on 3000. Use the following command to start the server:

```
sls offline start
```

The node server running serverless offline will stay in the foreground and output any log messages to stdout. Now that we know we have a live local endpoint, we can hit it with some requests!

8. Use the curl command to make a request to your API endpoint running on the local server:

```
curl -X GET http://localhost:3000/hello
```

We can also browse to a useful console for the local DynamoDB instance at http://localhost:8000/shell. This is a web console that makes it easier for us to prepare code to use in our functions. You can execute code snippets directly against your table, with JavaScript only being supported at the moment.

The last thing we should cover is how we can let the function know that it is running locally so that we can update the endpoint for DynamoDB to use our local one. Thankfully, the serverless offline plugin creates a Boolean environment variable called IS_OFFLINE. The plugin sets the variable to true when the function is running locally.

We should be able to use the following function when we set up our client:

```
const dbClient = new AWS.DynamoDB.DocumentClient(
    process.env.IS_OFFLINE ? {region: 'localhost', endpoint:
'http://localhost:8000'} : {}
);
```

It's as easy as that. When we're finished using the serverless offline server, we can hit *Ctrl + C* to kill the node server and stop and clean up the DynamoDB instance that's running.

Next, we are going to learn about testing and how to troubleshoot when things go wrong with a lambda function.

Testing and debugging

Now that we have the tools to be able to quickly create and deploy serverless applications, how do we add our testing practices into the experience to make sure we're covering all bases? We can follow **test-driven development** (**TDD**) in the Serverless Framework, just like we would when developing other applications.

In this section, we'll talk about some of the approaches we can take to make sure our functions are tested properly. We'll start with unit testing, then integration testing, and finish with an overview of logging and monitoring.

Unit testing lambda functions

Unit tests are the fundamental beginnings of making sure our function's functions are behaving the way they're expected to. They are really good to run quickly and often. If you're following TDD, unit tests can even help guide you to only write the functionality you need.

Before launching our options for unit testing plugins, let's not forget the most basic way to test our lambda function using the framework, that is, the `sls invoke` command. We can use the framework to run our function locally, emulating the Lambda environment. The following commands show how we can do this. You can test this on your own function as well:

```
sls invoke local --function hello
```

If we had some input data to inject into the event object, we could use the `--data` switch to specify the data inline with the command or use the `--path` switch to specify a file that holds the JSON or YAML data. We can even view the logs of the function using the `--log` switch.

This is a good way to sanity check that your function runs without error. To take this a step further, after deploying the function to AWS, we can also invoke the function in the same way, but by dropping `local` from the command. This will invoke the deployed function, and I would consider this a semi-integration test given that we're now running in the target environment but not using the full end-to-end functionality.

If you're waiting until the end of your development process to start testing, you might get extremely frustrated with the amount of time it takes to deploy a change to AWS, only to find you have a full stop or space in the wrong place. To shorten the iteration loop, we need to test right from the start of development and test locally. This has the potential to lengthen the time it takes to produce a function but, in the end, you will have higher quality code. Once you get into the routine of writing tests, it actually doesn't take much time at all. I'm skipping over linting here because you should already have one set up in your favorite IDE. If you don't, go set one up now and come back.

We're going to step through the process of creating tests for a Node.js function as an example using the popular Mocha.js test framework with the Serverless Framework. Mocha also uses a really easy-to-use assertion library called Chai.js. There will likely be equivalent testing frameworks for your language of choice, and hopefully, there are already plugins to integrate these into the Serverless Framework workflow. Another alternative in the Node.js world is Jest. There is also a plugin to use this framework instead if you wish.

Here are the steps for creating tests using Mocha.js and the Serverless Framework:

1. The first thing we need to is install the plugin in our project directory. Run the following command to install the plugin. Again, we're going to save it to our development dependencies using `--save-dev` because our function won't need this package to run:

   ```
   npm install serverless-mocha-plugin --save-dev
   ```

2. Then, add the plugin to our `serverless.yml` file using the following declaration block. This tells the Serverless Framework to load the plugin whenever a CLI command is used:

   ```
   plugins:
     - serverless-mocha-plugin
   ```

   Now, the easy part is done. This should give us two new `sls` commands to use:

   - `sls create test`
   - `sls invoke test`

3. Let's create a test for our hello world function with the first command. What this does is create a new boilerplate test file under a directory called `test`. This is where we will write our tests:

   ```
   sls create test --function hello
   ```

Now, we have a new directory in our project called test and, underneath that, we have our first test. The following is the boilerplate test harness that we get:

```
const mochaPlugin = require('serverless-mocha-plugin');
const expect = mochaPlugin.chai.expect;
let wrapped = mochaPlugin.getWrapper('hello', '/handler.js', 'hello');

describe('hello', () => {
    before((done) => {
    done();
});

it('implement tests here', () => {
  return wrapped.run({}).then((response) => {
    expect(response).to.not.be.empty;
  });
 });
});
```

Here, we can see this boilerplate test imports the chai assertion library that was available from the mocha plugin. We specifically use the expect interface here, but you could use the should or assert interface if you favor either of those. Having multiple interfaces gives you a choice about how you represent your tests. We're also getting the handler function of our hello function and using the lambda-wrapper package to emulate the lambda environment, including initializing any specific environment variables we have set in our serverless.yml configuration.

Expect is a useful interface that allows you to write tests that are straightforward to understand since they're human-readable. In the preceding example boilerplate test code, the test expects the response of the lambda invocation to have some content to not be empty. We can add more expect lines to this test as well—we may want to test the length of the response or the data type of a specific value. The it function is a way to group the tests into logical checks, and all the tests in the group need to pass for the group to pass. We can add as many test groups as we like, and this is a good way to build up a good test suite.

We can run our test against our hello function with the following command:

```
sls invoke test --function hello
```

We should get a nice output showing that all tests are passing, like so:

```
hello
  implement tests here

 1 passing (5ms)
```

This is a good way of testing the output of the entire lambda function. We haven't covered dependency injection or mocking to keep this chapter high-level. What I would also encourage you to do is write unit tests for any custom libraries that you have written that will be imported into your function as well.

Integration testing

Now, let's move on to integration testing. This is an important step in the process that allows us to confirm that our code can work when it's deployed into an environment that is connected to all of the supporting infrastructure that the stack needs. This could be the API Gateway, IAM permissions, storage policies, other messaging systems, and databases. We need to make sure our lambda works as expected for our use case.

One way to integration test a Lambda function is to capture the invoking event by deploying the function and writing the event to the logs. You can then find the output in CloudWatch logs and save that to a JSON file. Use this file to invoke your integrated local function using serverless-offline. You can use the same event to invoke the deploy Lambda function as well, which is great for offline/online sanity checking.

However, you can also deploy your stack to an entirely new stage. Your integration testing environment can be exactly the same as the environment you intend to deploy. The workflow would be as follows: deploy a new stage, run automated requests and check the response, terminate the environment, and report on the outcome. In the next chapter, we will learn about how we can build that automation into a continuous integration pipeline.

There's also a new way to run integration tests with the Serverless Framework that turns out to be pretty easy to do. For this, we need to make sure we are logged into our Serverless Enterprise account and that we have our app and tenant declarations set in `serverless.yml`.

Let's go back to the handler function that we have already deployed to AWS.

As a reminder, here's what it should look:

```
module.exports.hello = async event => {
    return {
        statusCode: 200,
        body: JSON.stringify(
            {
                message: 'Hello World deployed from Serverless Framework!',
                input: event,
            },
            null,
```

```
            2
      ),
    };
};
```

Assuming we have the same `serverless.yml` file that we had in the previous examples, we can start a new file called `serverless.test.yml`. In there, we can write some integration tests that give the function some input and check the output. Let's get started:

1. Here are two examples of integrations tests that we can write ourselves:

```
- name: gives us a hello world message
  endpoint: {function: hello}
  response:
    body:
      message: "Hello World deployed from Serverless Framework!"

- name: says hello to alice
  endpoint:
    function: hello
  request:
    body:
      message: "Hello event"
  response:
    body:
      message: "Hello event"
```

2. To run the tests against our function, we can use the new command, which does some magic in the background to interpret the tests we want to run against our `serverless.yml` file and function code. Here's the simple command:

   `sls test`

3. With luck, we will get a bunch of tests passing. Here's what the command-line output may look like for our tests:

```
Serverless Enterprise: Test Results:

    Summary --------------------------------------------

    passed - GET hello - gives us a hello world message
    passed - GET hello - returns hello event

Serverless Enterprise: Test Summary: 3 passed, 0 failed
```

So, you could build this into a CI pipe to test your deployments as you go, but you may as well just fire a real request with a test or real payload.

When things go wrong unexpectedly, we need a way to investigate and identify the errors. In the next section, we will talk about how we can leverage the Serverless Framework's functionality for logging our logs and performance metrics.

Logging and monitoring

Another thing that is great about the Serverless Framework is that you don't have to leave your Terminal that often to find out what's going on. Whether it's creating, testing, or deploying—there's a command for that and you can do it all inside the Terminal. The same goes for trawling the logs or checking your function error rates.

With the serverless logs command, you can go back and see historical logs from CloudWatch logs. You can also subscribe to the log stream, which polls continuously in the background to keep your feed up to date. My favorite command to run after deploying a stack for a serverless API is one that tails the logs. Use the following command to do so:

```
sls logs
     --function hello
     --stage dev
     --startTime 2m
     --tail
```

This command shows you the last 2 minutes of logs and then continues the feed of logs for the lambda function you've chosen to watch—hopefully the one that is currently serving the backend requests for the API. You can even add the `--filter` switch to prefilter the output.

This command could also be useful for a continuous integration, continuous delivery pipeline that had just updated a deployment. The idea would be that it would look for any exceptions or errors (such as internal server errors) that were present in the new logs and then make a decision about whether it should roll back the deployment or call it successful. Combine that with another simple command to roll up the invocation stats for the last 2 minutes:

```
sls metrics
     --function hello
     --stage dev
     --startTime 2m
```

Here, we have a fairly complete suite of tools we can use to do basic monitoring on our functions.

That was a brief overview of two commands that the Serverless Framework offers for logging and monitoring. You probably have your favorite method for troubleshooting, but I hope these will help in your workflow.

Summary

This chapter has been an introduction to how to bring serverless technologies together into the same project space to create richer serverless applications. This knowledge will be enough for you to start building, and there are plenty of more advanced tricks and techniques that you will pick up along the way.

In the next chapter, we're going to integrate our application framework into an AWS-native CI/CD pipeline so that we can take our project and promote it through a software development life cycle.

Questions

1. Lambda functions in the same project structure should do what?

   A) Be spelled similar
   B) Have similar capabilities
   C) Share the same bounded context

2. Which configurations live in a `serverless.yml` file?

   A) Resources
   B) Functions
   C) Events
   D) All of the above

3. What artifact does the Serverless Framework deploy to AWS?

   A) CloudFormation templates
   B) EC2 instances
   C) JAR files
   D) RPM packages

4. You can execute your function code on your own machine.

   A) True
   B) False

5. Which language is the Serverless Framework written in?

   A) Java
   B) Python
   C) Go
   D) Node.js

Further reading

- Node.js installer downloads: `https://nodejs.org/en/download/`
- Setting up credentials for the serverless CLI to use: `https://serverless.com/framework/docs/providers/aws/guide/credentials/`
- Detailed information about serverless and IAM: `https://serverless.com/blog/abcs-of-iam-permissions/`
- Serverless Enterprise testing documentation: `https://github.com/serverless/enterprise/blob/master/docs/testing.md`
- Serverless example projects: `https://github.com/serverless/examples`
- Serverless community plugins: `https://github.com/serverless/plugins`
- Cron schedule expressions in detail: `https://docs.aws.amazon.com/AmazonCloudWatch/latest/events/ScheduledEvents.html#CronExpressions`

8
CI/CD with the Serverless Framework

At this stage, you should have a solid idea of how serverless components in AWS work together to form applications with serverless architectures. In the previous chapter, we introduced a framework that will accelerate iterations of your applications by allowing the developer to be quick. The Serverless Framework gave us a way to reduce the complexities of our deployment environments and focus on writing quality function code that holds the business logic.

The next step is to reduce the burden of testing, deployments, and rollbacks even further by introducing an automated pipeline that can take your projects and promote artifacts through a software development life cycle.

In this chapter, we will cover the following topics:

- Using serverless development pipelines
- Understanding deployment patterns
- Introducing AWS services
- Building a pipeline

Technical requirements

This chapter is focused on DevOps and how we automate some of the manual tasks that developers and testers have to worry about. We will provide a general introduction to the terms, but it would help if you had some idea about the following:

- Continuous integration
- Continuous deployment and delivery

- Git workflow
- The Serverless Framework
- AWS Lambda and Amazon API Gateway

Using serverless development pipelines

Let's start with a question. What is a serverless development pipeline and does it differ from traditional patterns? The answer is yes and no, which means we should probably explore patterns to understand their context.

The idea of pipeline patterns comes from the need to perform source, build, test, and deployment tasks as part of the development life cycle of a piece of software. We use a tool called **Jenkins**, which introduced the idea of creating jobs for each of these stages. From there, we could chain jobs together to create configurable automated pipelines. Jenkins is still widely used today and has strong community support. Thousands of plugins have been developed by the community and support a range of different tasks. Configuration and maintenance are driven through a browser-based user interface, so there is a learning curve when it comes to adopting good configuration practices.

With the move toward configuration and infrastructure being declared as code, we are seeing the same thing happen to pipeline declarations. With the tools and technologies we have available today, it is now easier to define our pipelines (often in a YAML file) alongside the application code and another service can take care of creating, implementing, running, and maintaining the pipeline orchestration.

In this section, we will learn how we can leverage good practices in our DevOps pipeline strategies before we move on to technology options.

Patterns

We're here because we want to know how to deploy a new version of our function code, our infrastructure stack, and all of our configurations. Remembering that these are not different things anymore, we can describe each in code and have an artifact to deploy. Even with the Serverless Framework making life easier when it comes to deploying CloudFormation templates, doing this over and over again for each commit can become arduous and distracting for a developer. Having to validate every deployment in the development environment doesn't scale well, and the problem compounds even more when we're manually promoting a project through testing, staging, and finally production environments.

We need this process to be automated. There are a number of benefits that an automation pipeline provides, as follows:

- The speed of deployment is faster and hands-off, and rollbacks can be automatic.
- We can employ strategies that minimize the impact of deployment to our customers.
- An automated process lets the developers focus on coding instead of releases. From a product perspective, this means that developers can ship new features to production more rapidly, meaning that business value is realized sooner.
- A pipeline that follows a repeatable process reduces the risk of human error.

Before going any further, I need to touch on some definitions that underpin DevOps and shape the way we build automation into code. If you've not heard the term CI/CD before, then listen up. There are also some great resources in the *Further reading* section at the end of this chapter.

The following terms are the core concepts of CI/CD, so you should make sure you understand these as they form the basis of what we are going to be talking about in this chapter.

Continuous integration

Continuous integration is the practice of merging changes into the main or trunk branch as often as possible. This branch is built, deployed, and tested on every commit to a source code repository in an environment that functions similarly to production. The idea is that every piece of code that is checked into the master is tested in a real or mock situation to make sure that the specific change didn't break any functionality. This process helps developers get fast feedback about any failures and enables faster iterations.

Continuous delivery

Continuous delivery involves automating the deployment side of things. The idea behind this is that you should be able to deploy to production at the click of a button, and the deployment will follow a repeatable and zero-touch process. You should be able to deploy to production from the main branch of your repository at any point. This is often scheduled for monthly, weekly, or daily releases.

Continuous deployment

Continuous deployment is the principle of continuously shipping code into production and takes continuous delivery a step further. If all of the automated tests pass during our integration testing, then that piece of code or artifact should be immediately released into a production environment. The premise behind this is that, as soon as our tests pass, then there should be no reason why we can't make that new feature or fix available to our customers.

Often, people will use the continuous deployment and continuous delivery terms interchangeably, but the difference is that continuous delivery often requires manual intervention, for example, an approval step or a task to manually kick off the process.

Let's take a look at serverless pipeline patterns. A traditional CI/CD pipeline would consist of four stages:

Traditional four-stage pipeline

Here, the build is performed and tested, the artifact is created, and then it's deployed. Some additional smoke tests may be performed as well to validate the deployment. For a pipeline that handles serverless projects, we may view the process slightly differently. Because we don't need to pre-provision our infrastructure to deploy to, creating a new environment altogether is relatively stress-free. Our unit of deployment is always infrastructure + configuration + code. This means we might deploy the function code, infrastructure, and configuration all at the same time, test it, and then get rid of it. This may look something like this:

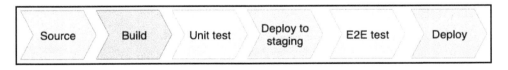

Pipeline for a serverless project

We could also prefix that with a local testing stage and wrap some monitoring around the whole process. What happens in our build stage depends on the language we are using. If we're using a non-precompiled language such as Node.js or Python, then our build step would consist only of installing our dependencies and packaging those up with our function code and Serverless Framework configuration. For a compiled language such as Java, our build environment would need to be able to support a build automation tool such as Maven or Gradle. These tools describe how the application is built and manages all the dependencies that are needed.

The next part of the process is the first testing step and includes basic syntax checking or linting of the function code, checking against any coding standards we might be aligned to, and of course our unit tests. It could also include code security testing if your organization requires it. After our tests pass, we can deploy our serverless project to a new stage.

At this point, you will need to know the strategy for how your organization or team uses stages within the Serverless Framework. These stages are so flexible that you can make use of them how you like, and in the next section, we'll explore some best practices.

When we have a new infrastructure that's been configured correctly and deployed our code, we should be able to run our integration tests to test end-to-end functionality. We may also choose to do some performance benchmarking here as well. If all of these tests pass, then we can terminate the environment and report back on the results.

Then, we can deploy to the stage of our target environment. What I mean by this is that if we are looking to deploy a branch to the development environment, our CI/CD process will create a brand new environment and run through all of the tests. If the testing process was successful, then we can safely deploy our change to the development environment and throw away the other one. If the testing fails, we don't need to run a rollback. In this approach, we are adding extra stability to the development environment because, by the time our change reaches the environment, we are already comfortable that it will deploy okay.

For production, we might not have the luxury of spinning up a similar environment. In this case, we can be confident that our code has been through multiple environments already, so the risk of a deployment failing is lower. If the deployment does fail, a rollback can be performed by either deploying the last known-working artifact again or running the `sls rollback` command (which has the same functionality).

In the next section, we will introduce a mechanism that allows you to move code through the environments in your software development life cycle.

Using serverless stages

In the previous section, we briefly introduced the concept of Serverless Framework stages and how they work. Well, it turns out that stages are a great way to logically and physically separate our environments. Stages are really useful for deploying the same infrastructure, configuration, and code multiple times. Naming a stage is a completely arbitrary endeavor; the framework doesn't care if you call a stage dev instead of scott. This gives you the flexibility to use stages in a way that best suits your team or organization. On the flip side, because stages are so flexible, this means you should probably think about how you also implement governance so that your development standards are being followed.

The framework is also extensible in that you can use the stage you specify as a variable to set other configurations. For example, in your serverless.yml file, you can set variables for where to find the relevant credentials for that stage. The following snippets show some of these options:

```
provider:
  name: aws
  stage: ${opt:stage, 'dev'}

functions:
  hello:
    handler: handler.hello
    environment:
      MY_SECRET: ${ssm:/path/to/service/mySecret}-${self:provider.stage}
```

The preceding example takes the stage you provide on the command line using the --stage option. If you don't specify this option, then it defaults to using dev. In the function declaration, we are setting an environment variable called MY_SECRET for the function called hello. The value of the secret will be pulled from the Systems Manager and it will be a different secret depending on the stage.

Let's talk about best practices. In my experiences, it has been valuable to use stages as part of the production API versioning strategy. Name your stages so that they align with non-production environments, for example, dev, uat, and so on, so that entirely new CloudFormation stacks are deployed for each environment. When it comes to production, this is where you would want to name stages so that they align with the current major version of the interface specification, for example, v1, v2, and so on. By doing this, we can still maintain our agility when we need to move clients between versions. We're not forcing our consumers to update their implementation of our API all the time, and we're also not requiring our developers to release things that are always backward-compatible.

So far, we have learned about CI/CD patterns and how we can implement them with features from the Serverless Framework. In the next chapter, we will explore the various options for rolling out code, and see which method might work best for our own deployments.

Understanding deployment patterns

There are a lot of different ways you can release your code into your environments. They range from deploying all your assets at once to the more risk-averse canary release with traffic shifting. There are a lot of considerations when choosing your deployment strategy.

In this section, we will go over some of the more common options and how they can be implemented in your Serverless Framework workflow.

Deploying all at once

The first and most basic method is to deploy everything at once. This includes the infrastructure (such as Lambda, API Gateway, and DynamoDB), the function code, and any configuration that's required. This is the pattern we have been using throughout all the examples in this book.

The good thing about the Serverless Framework is that, if you already have a whole stack deployed, the framework will update the deployed CloudFormation stack instead of deploying an entirely new environment, provided you are deploying to the same stage. CloudFormation can then make a decision about which parts of the template have changed and update the resources accordingly. It also knows how to handle updates for each service, for example, if the change to the resource needs a whole redeploy or an in-place update.

The key thing to get right in this and all the other patterns is to make sure rollbacks work. Test your rollback strategy from time to time to make sure the process goes to plan. But how do you know when you need to do a rollback? It would be an obvious case for a roll back if a deployment doesn't make it all the way to the end, but crucially what we're looking for here is a key metric that will prompt us to fail a deployment. Your deploy process might have made it all the way to the end, only to find out that the error rates for logins to your product are significantly increasing. This could be a sign that the version you deployed is adversely affecting another service, so you should use this as a trigger to fail and roll back your deployment.

In this case, we need to add a monitor component to our diagram:

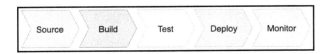

Adding a monitor stage to our CI/CD pipeline

It's a good idea to use your application performance monitoring tool to watch application-level metrics. This will provide additional confidence of a successful deployment above the usual infrastructure and log monitoring capabilities.

As we mentioned previously, if a deployment goes wrong for any reason, there could be a redeploy process, which may involve an outage to a service while it takes place.

A less risky method is to make sure our entire environment deploys properly by testing it out of band and then switching to it.

Blue/green environment switching

These type of deployments follow a phased approach where a whole new environment is deployed alongside an existing live environment. You can perform an end-to-end test on the new environment before deciding whether to cut the traffic over, sending all of the traffic to the new live environment, and sending none to the old (previously live) one. There is a higher-level piece of infrastructure or routing logic that needs to be present to enable the traffic switching:

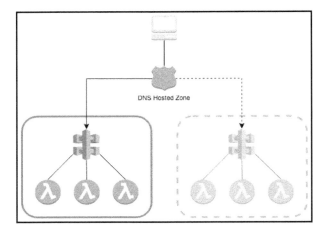

Blue/green deployment using Route 53 for cutover

Careful attention should be given to your key monitoring metrics after the switch. A rollback in this method is a complete cutover back to the previous environment. For deployment and subsequent cutovers, this is deemed successful since the old environment isn't needed anymore and can be terminated.

To make this process easier, the new environment usually uses the same data store as the live environment. This reduces the complexity (and inherent risk) of creating new data stores and keeping them in synchronization.

Amazon CloudFront and Route 53 are two options that can help direct traffic to your chosen environment. Implementing the blue/green strategy using CloudFront can be achieved by having two origins in your distribution: one for the live environment and one for the new environment. The switchover is then a change in the behavior for the default path pattern. The time it takes for the configuration to propagate to all of the edge locations can be restrictive if your environments are simple.

For these more simple environments, it's better to use Route 53 and run a DNS-based cutover by changing the CNAME or ALIAS records. For this method, we are only restricted by the TTL we have set for our zone. We're also relying on our clients respecting the TTL and not caching the DNS address for longer than specified.

It's a good idea to run a blue/green or canary strategy (explained in the next section) when releasing changes to production because it gives you a chance to verify that the new environment has been created correctly before serving real traffic. Rollbacks are also much more simple and less error-prone because we are failing back whole environments, instead of partial environments in an unknown state.

 If you have messaging systems such as an Amazon SQS queue in your solution, you will need to think about how to gracefully quiesce messages before cutting over environments.

In the Serverless Framework, blue/green deployments are not easily accomplished out of the box. It would be possible to employ a higher-level piece of infrastructure to perform a switchover, but it would be better to manage this outside the project. Let's look at another way of dealing with this.

Canary or traffic shifting

Canary deployments, also known as linear or traffic shifting, have similarities to the blue/green approach. We also deploy a new environment alongside our live environment but, instead of a traffic cutover event, we configure a small amount of traffic to be served from the new environment. We monitor closely, and when we gain more confidence that the change we have introduced has not adversely affected our service, we can gradually increase the amount of traffic that's served out of the new environment until the previous environment is no longer active.

The idea behind this is that by introducing a change slowly, and to a small subset of users, we can greatly reduce the impact should something go wrong. All going well, a deployment should be transparent to any clients or users. A rollback here immediately shifts the traffic back to the last environment by setting the traffic shifting weight to zero or deleting the canary altogether:

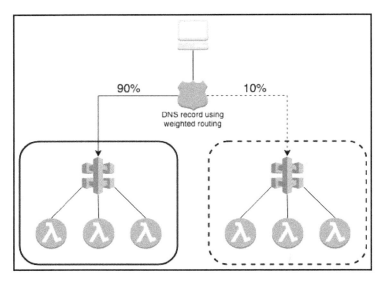

Canary deployment using weighted routing in Route 53

It's also really important to identify the key metric or metrics that you want in order to trigger a failed deployment. These could be error rate-related at the infrastructure or application level, for example, measuring the number of application exceptions over a certain time period. Alternatively, they could be product-related; for example, are my users still clicking on a particular button? Has the experience changed for my users? Only you will be able to select the best metric for your trigger, so it's a good idea to canvas different stakeholder groups to make sure you choose the right thing.

How we enable a variation of this method in the Serverless Framework is by using a plugin that was developed by David Garcia, aptly called **Serverless Plugin Canary Deployments**. This utilizes the traffic shifting capability in Lambda as well as AWS CodeDeploy to automatically update Lambda alias weights:

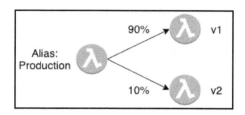

Traffic shifting with lambda aliases

The plugin supports everything that you will need to run your own canary deployments, including various shifting schemes, alarms to trigger deployment rollbacks, and process hooks to run your own customization or integration tests using lambdas and the CodeDeploy SDK. Hats off to this plugin—it takes care of some complex Lambda automation to make the configuration straightforward to understand.

So far, we've learned about some of the methods we can use to deploy our stacks. Some have less risk than others, and we can apply this lens to our own environments. The next chapter will introduce some of the services that are involved in implementing the patterns we have talked about here. They are all serverless and native to AWS.

Introducing AWS services

So far, we've learned about a lot about pipeline and deployment patterns that are available to us, and hopefully you can take this knowledge away and make a decision about which fits your team or organization the best.

The next logical step is to introduce some AWS-native technologies that we can implement in the architecture pattern before we look at an example.

AWS CodePipeline

The first service we need to introduce is CodePipeline, which is the orchestrator service for the pipeline process. It provides a workflow capability to implement a CI/CD automation pipeline by managing the inputs and outputs of other AWS services. It also provides a way to visualize the entire release process and status with its own management console. The console also does a great job of pulling together all of the resources that are used in the pipeline, such as CodeBuild projects and CodeCommit repositories:

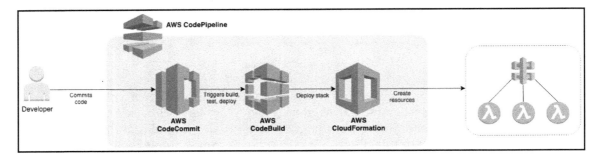

CI/CD pipeline for a serverless project

CodePipeline pipelines can be triggered by supported source control systems or uploads to S3. A trigger will kick off the process for building, testing, and deploying if you have configured your pipeline to do that. An added feature is that you can also include approval gates in the process, which will send an email out to the person who approves it, prompting them to approve or decline the next stage. This means you can add a manual intervention step, which will help you change management when deploying to production.

Within a pipeline, we need to be able to run some compute tasks. We will cover this in the next section.

AWS CodeBuild

AWS CodeBuild provides compute resources that allow you to build, test, and package your software to create artifacts. It runs the continuous integration part of the puzzle by supplying managed build environments. These are pre-built Docker containers, and there's a whole range of containers for the language and versions that you're building for. You can also supply your own build container. When a build is run, your containers can scale so that you have multiple builds running in parallel. This means no more waiting in the build queue!

Creating a build project is easy:

- Pick your build container
- Add some basic configuration
- Tell CodeBuild where the project instructions are

These instructions are specified along with your code source in a file called `buildspec.yml`. In this file, you can include all of the commands that you want to run inside the container to build, test, or package your source. Within this file, you can specify various phases as well:

- `Install`: This is used for installing the necessary development packages that your build might need.
- `Pre_build`: This command is run before the actual build.
- `Build`: Here, you would include your build command sequence.
- `Post_build`: This is used to package up any artifacts that the build might have created.

These phases give you quite a lot of flexibility for implementing your custom build process. It's also a good idea to add an echo statement to each of these phases to explain the process that is happening. `Stdout` will be viewable in the logs that are created.

When using CodeBuild with Serverless Framework projects, we can run the entire build, package, deployment, and test from one CodeBuild job. If you wanted, you can also split the testing into a separate CodeBuild project as well. The types of testing you might do here include linting to check for syntax errors, any checks on coding standards, unit tests, and even functional end-to-end tests.

For building Node.js and Python services, you would use `npm install` to source all of the libraries and dependencies that are needed. All the dependencies must live in a folder called `node_modules` at the project root level.

For Java, a good way to source dependencies would be to use Maven or Gradle. Compiled classes and other resources should live at the root level and any other .jars that are required should be in a `/lib` directory. The packaged ZIP file can contain the function code and dependencies or a standalone .jar.

For C#, we should use NuGet, which is the package manager for .NET applications. Again, all of the assemblies should live at the root level and the ZIP package can hold either the function code and dependencies or a standalone `.dll` file.

A good pipeline always starts with a source code repository. Next, we will introduce one that is native to AWS.

AWS CodeCommit

CodeCommit is a managed Git repository that gives you a place to commit and store code. It's integrated with IAM, so the permissions model is similar to other services in AWS. It also has some extra native functionality that makes it a really useful tool in the AWS ecosystem:

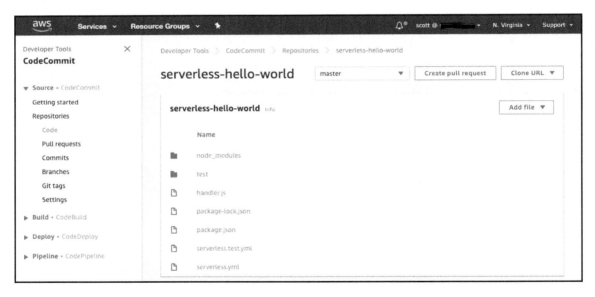

CodeCommit console showing files in a Git repository

CodeCommit is a supported trigger for CodePipeline, meaning that you can configure your pipelines so that they kick off based on a commit to a particular branch. It also has the ability to trigger Lambda functions when certain actions happen in your repository, such as creating or deleting a branch. This is great because you can run a Lambda function to dynamically create a pipeline when a new release branch is created.

In the next section, we will put all of these services together to create our own pipeline that we can use to deploy our Serverless Framework projects.

Building a pipeline

Now that we've learned about patterns and technologies, we're going to create our own pipeline so that we can get our serverless projects into production. The examples we will run through in this section are specific to Serverless Framework projects. CodePipeline and other services are so flexible that they can be configured and used for other types of project as well.

In this section, we'll learn how to create a pipeline and then go further and learn how we can create a pipeline that deploys itself.

Creating the pipeline in production

We're going to run through an example of deploying a serverless project to a pre-production environment, running some tests, and then deploying to production via an approval gate. We are using the "all at once" method of deployment and will be using the same account for all of our environments. The environments will be separated by using different CloudFormation stacks and different API Gateway stages and endpoints.

For a real production environment, you would want to have entirely separate AWS accounts for development, pre-production or staging, and production. This allows for a greater separation of IAM permissions and duties. It also means that if any account resource limits are reached because of a bug or testing in one environment, the other environments aren't impacted.

Let's crack on, then. The first thing we will need is an S3 bucket that CodePipeline can use to store any artifacts that it produces. We also need a CodeCommit repository with our Hello world source code in it. Let's get started:

1. Go ahead and create an S3 bucket and a CodeCommit repository. Then, jump over to the CodePipeline console and create a pipeline. The following is the first screen in the process of creating a pipeline:

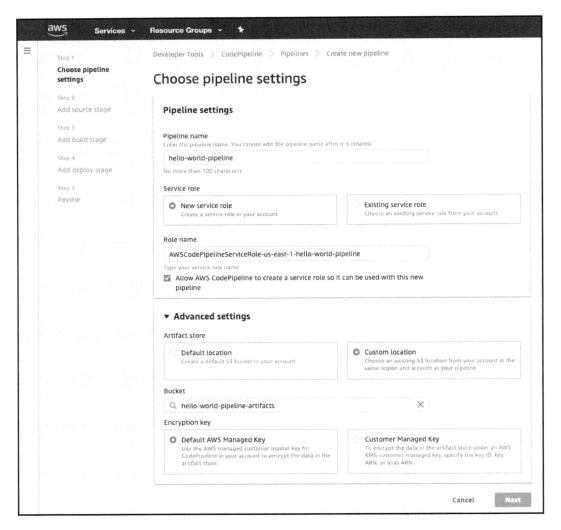

Creating a new pipeline in the CodePipeline console

Here, we have a choice between creating a new IAM role and specifying our bucket. For this example, we are going to let CodePipeline create its own service role, which will include a policy that allows access to the other services we need. For your real production environment, you may want to give this extra thought and make sure you are following the principle of least-privilege.

The next step is creating the stages we need for our pipeline. First is the source stage; so, where do we get our source code from? This is where you can connect to GitHub, CodeCommit, ECR, or S3.

2. Choose a CodeCommit repository and branch and click **Next**. The following screenshot shows the configurations for the source stage:

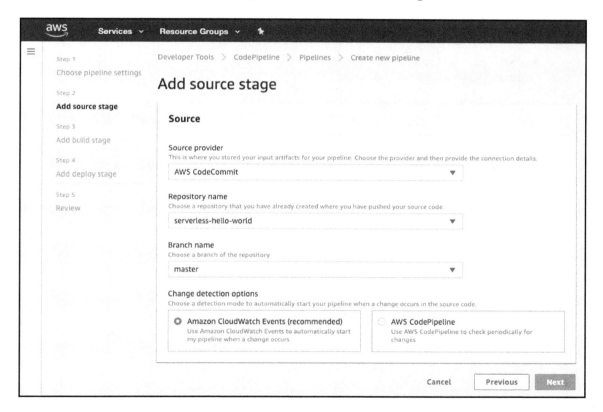

Adding stages to a pipeline in the CodePipeline console

Next, we get to specify our build stage. CodePipeline can reach out to your own Jenkins server to run the builds. For this example, we are going to create our own build project using a managed build environment—CodeBuild.

3. Select the **CodeBuild** option and then **Create project**. This will open a new window with the CodeBuild console. What we want to do here is pick our build environment and add our build specification.

   For the environment, we'll use the following:

   - **OS**: **Ubuntu** is the OS that the underlying container will run on.
   - **Runtime**: **Standard** is the option that will include all of the runtimes you may need to access.
   - **Image**: `aws/codebuild/standard:2.0` is the latest version.

4. We'll also let CodeBuild create a new IAM role for us, so select the **New service role** option and give it a name.

   If you have used CodeBuild before, you may have noticed that you no longer have to pick a build container that exactly matches the runtime of your code. That's because all of the common runtimes are now included in one image.

 Make sure the role you assign to CodeBuild has access to your artifacts bucket.

5. For the buildspec, we would normally save a YAML file with the information alongside our code in our source repository. This is so that buildspec can be versioned and maintained as code. For this example, let's use the inbuilt editor and input directly into the project. You can use the following snippet to create yours. The following code specifies the commands we want CodeBuild to run at each phase of the build:

```
version: 0.2
phases:
  install:
    commands:
      - npm install -g serverless
      - npm install --only=dev
  pre_build:
    commands:
      - mkdir -p pkg/pp
      - mkdir pkg/prod
  build:
    commands:
      - sls invoke test -f hello
      - sls package -v --package pkg/pp --stage pp
      - sls package -v --package pkg/prod --stage prod
```

6. At the bottom of the file, we also need to specify the artifacts we want this process to create. Add the following to the bottom of the buildspec file. This will pass several files onto the next stage:

```
artifacts:
  files:
    - serverless.yml
    - package.json
    - pkg/**/*
```

What this phased build process is doing is installing the dependencies that are needed, creating new directories for the outputs, running our mocha unit tests, and creating some artifacts that are ready to be deployed to **pre-production (pp)** and **production (prod)**. We'll create build projects to run the deployment soon. If we were using a language that needed to be compiled, such as Java, then we would also run our build commands in the build phase.

7. Let's skip the deployment stage, complete our CodePipeline setup, and see what we've got. This will likely kick off the pipeline, and it should be able to run all the way through successfully. The following screenshot shows the pipeline with the **Source** and **Build** stages:

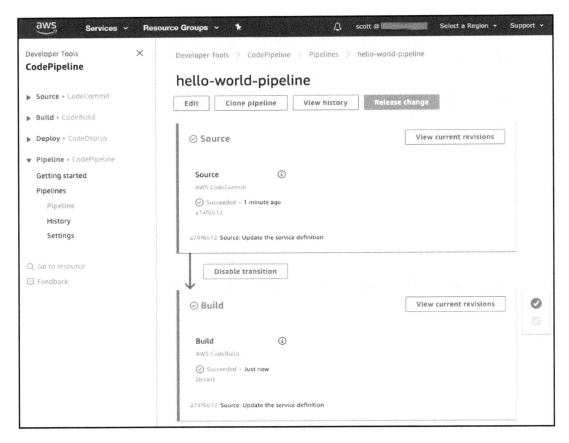

Overview of a two-stage pipeline

Now that our source and build stages are done, we need to be able to deploy to our environments.

8. We need to edit the pipeline (by clicking the **Edit** button) and add another stage for deploying to pre-production. The following screenshot shows where you will find the button for adding a new stage to the pipeline:

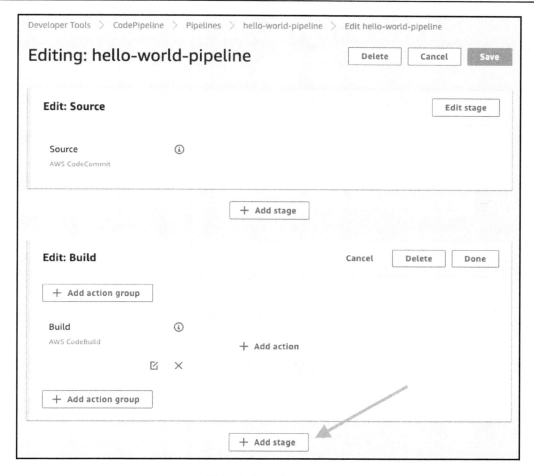

Editing a pipeline to add another stage

You can call the stage whatever you like—I've called mine `DeployToPreProd`.

9. Next, we need to add an action for our new CodeBuild build project. Follow the same steps to create a new project, but this time use the `hello-world-deploy-pre-prod` name and use the existing IAM role.

10. We also need to expand the **Advanced configuration** options and add an environment variable. The following variable signals to the deploy stage that the environment we are deploying into is pp:

Environment variables			
Name	Value	Type	
ENV	pp	Plaintext ▼	Remove

Snippet of the CodeBuild project configuration options, showing where to add environment variables

We're doing this so that our buildspec knows how to deploy our environment.

11. Create a new buildspec that's similar to the following. This file tells CodeBuild about the commands we want to run at each phase. We start by installing the Serverless Framework package, add the dev dependencies, and then finish by running the serverless deploy command in our chosen environment:

```
version: 0.2

phases:
  install:
    runtime-versions:
      nodejs: 10
  commands:
    - npm install -g serverless
    - npm install --only=dev

build:
  commands:
    - sls deploy -v --stage $ENV --package pkg/$ENV
```

Save the project. This will take us back to the pipeline configuration, where we need to do one last thing: set the input artifact for the deploy action to the output artifact from the build stage (in my case, it's called `BuildArtifact`). This will pass the .zip files from the build stage to our deploy stage so that we have something to deploy.

The `$ENV` in the buildspec denotes an environment variable where we set which serverless environment we want to deploy. Soon we'll create pretty much the same build project again for production.

12. Save the pipeline and run it again to check if all the lights are green. If it fails, check the logs for error messages—it's likely that you'll need to tweak your permissions.

    Before we can add the production deployment stage, we need to add a gate so that our changes can be checked by a human and validated before going any further. If you were following pure continuous deployment to create this pipeline, then you probably wouldn't have this step.

13. We need to edit the pipeline once again and add a stage and an action. Our action provider should be manual approval. We also need an SNS topic so that CodePipeline can publish an approval notification. If you don't have one of those, head over to the Amazon SNS console, create a topic, and add your email address as a subscription.

    While we're still editing the pipeline, let's create another stage to deploy to production.

14. Follow the same steps you took for the pre-production build project but, for the environment variable, use `ENV:prod`. We can even use the same buildspec because we have written it so that it is generic for all kinds of environments—nice.

15. Save the pipeline and kick off a release!

You should have all green lights. Now, you can follow the CodeBuild logs to see what was deployed or check out the stacks in the CloudFormation pipeline. Check out the following screenshot of a pipeline that successfully completed a full execution:

The new stages added to our pipeline

So there we have it—we've been able to use AWS services to build an entire CI/CD pipeline. We built it so that it's flexible for use in multiple environments and can support multiple runtimes with minimal changes.

In the next section, we'll go a step further and explore a self-deploying pipeline.

A pipeline that deploys itself

This section is pipeline inception. Wouldn't it be good if the pipeline only existed when we needed it? This would save costs and make our environments simpler. Often, we will have a branch for a particular build or release candidate that we need to run tests on before merging it into the trunk branch. If you're following the GitFlow versioning and release strategy, release candidate branches have a limited lifetime and can be deleted once a release has been tagged and the branch has been merged. It would be great if we could set up some automation to do that process for us when we need it.

The following is our GitFlow example for a **release candidate** (**RC**) branch that splits from the master and is then merged back after a few commits:

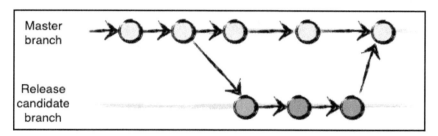

GitFlow release candidate branching strategy

We can create a dynamic branch pipeline by using the awesome trigger features of CodeCommit. This feature allows us to add an SNS topic or lambda function for a particular action within a repository. This would allow the repository to notify a subscriber to an event or run some code to add value to a process in response to an event. In our case, we want a Lambda function to be invoked when a new release candidate branch is created so that we can deploy a CloudFormation that describes a pipeline. We also want to trigger the function when the branch is deleted so that we can then clean up our resources.

The following screenshot shows where we would set that up—the following screenshot shows the settings page of the CodeCommit console. In **Triggers**, we can see that two triggers have already been created:

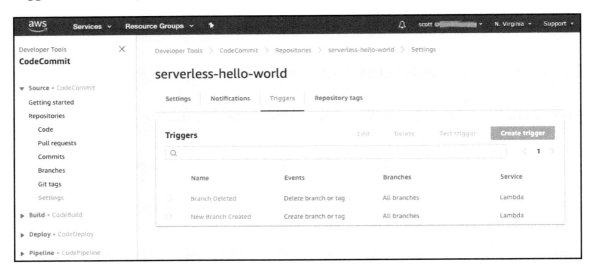

CodeCommit console showing where to set up triggers on a repository

The invoked lambda function could pull a CloudFormation template from source control and then deploy a new stack for a CI/CD pipeline with the correct configuration, so that it can link up to the release candidate branch. When the release branch is deleted, the same lambda will find the stack based on a predetermined naming convention and remove it. Pretty neat!

Here's what the process would look like. A developer pushes a new release candidate branch to CodeCommit, which triggers a lambda function. The function takes some input (such as the repository's details) and deploys a CloudFormation stack representing our pipeline:

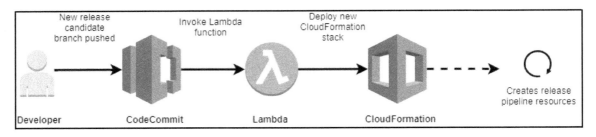

Triggering deployment of a new pipeline

The new pipeline would pull the code, build it (if required), package it, deploy it to a new stage or environment, test it, push a test report to storage, and then remove the environment altogether:

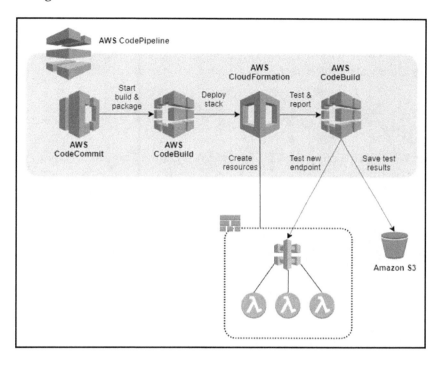

Pipeline process for building and testing a release candidate. Not shown is the resource stack removal.

The process finishes when the developer merges the RC branch back into the master and deletes the branch. The pipeline is no longer needed. Because of the delete event, a CodeCommit trigger invokes a lambda function and passes the repository information. The function finds our temporary release pipeline and deletes the CloudFormation stack:

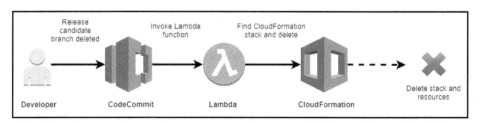

Triggering a pipeline to be deleted

So there we have it—a pipeline that manages its own life cycle. I really like this example because the pipeline only exists for the time it is required. In addition to making better use of resources, you don't have to worry about the state or queued jobs, which you might have to with a shared pipeline.

In this section, we have learned how to build a CI/CD pipeline that takes care of our serverless projects. Then, we learned about a more advanced approach that allows the pipeline to deploy and remove itself.

Summary

We've covered a lot in this chapter. CI/CD pipelines can be complex and we need to be able to use tools and technologies that will allow us to be flexible enough to build complexity where we need it. The native AWS services do a great job at that without being too opinionated.

The deployment patterns we learned about in this chapter will be helpful when we move our Serverless Framework projects into production and we need to start thinking about reducing any potential impacts on real consumers.

The next chapter provides some tips about how we can use serverless services to automate some of the security and operational tasks we face when running in AWS.

Questions

1. What is the best way to separate environments when using the Serverless Framework?

   A) Deploying multiple times
   B) Using multiple service definitions
   C) Using stages
   D) It's not possible

2. Which deployment strategy has the least risk of impact for a release to production?

   A) All at once
   B) Canary
   C) Manual
   D) Blue/green

3. AWS CodeCommit provides which stage of a pipeline?

   A) Source
   B) Deployment
   C) Build
   D) Test
   E) Orchestration

4. Why would we be interested in separating deployment environments at the AWS account level?

   A) Separation of IAM permissions
   B) Reducing the impact of reaching service limits
   C) Greater segregation of duties
   D) All of the above

5. What is a likely reason for why my CodeBuild project is failing to download the source?

   A) CodeBuild doesn't have access to the CodeCommit repository
   B) The bandwidth limit has been reached
   C) The source files are too large to download
   D) The IAM role running the build doesn't have access to the artifact bucket

6. What should I consider when using Route 53 to enable a blue/green cutover?

   A) Time To Live (TTL) value on the DNS record
   B) Updating the load balancer routes
   C) DNS outages during the cutover
   D) Terminating the blue environment straight after the cutover

Further reading

- Continuous integration: `https://martinfowler.com/articles/continuousIntegration.html`
- *Continuous Delivery* by Jez Humble and David Farley: `https://www.amazon.com/gp/product/0321601912`
- AWS CodeBuild build specification reference: `https://docs.aws.amazon.com/codebuild/latest/userguide/build-spec-ref.html`
- Serverless plugin for canary deployments: `https://github.com/davidgf/serverless-plugin-canary-deployments`

Section 4: Architectures and Use Cases

The objective of this section is to create awareness of some common examples of serverless architectures and apply the knowledge you've preciously gained.

This section comprises the following chapters:

- Chapter 9, *Data Processing*
- Chapter 10, *AWS Automation*
- Chapter 11, *Creating Chatbots*
- Chapter 12, *Hosting Single-Page Web Applications*
- Chapter 13, *GraphQL APIs*

9
Data Processing

Ingesting, processing, normalizing, extracting, transforming, and loading are all activities we do with raw data. Each of our organizations has a wealth of raw data of different types and classifications. To be able to make sense and draw greater meaning from this data, we need to be able to store, process, and identify patterns on a huge scale. The services provided by AWS make it easier for us to process data by taking away the undifferentiated heavy lifting of building and operating enterprise-scale data management solutions.

The focus of this chapter is to give you an introduction to how to process data using serverless services in AWS. As you can imagine, it would be impossible to cover all the aspects of data processing in one chapter, or even in a whole book for that matter. We'll cover the basics for each type of processing and then dig into a real example. By the end, you will be able to describe and use the available toolset of serverless AWS services, without having to spin up and manage your own EC2 instances.

We'll cover the following topics:

- Types of data processing
- Building a batch processing workload—a real example
- Data analytics and transformation

Technical requirements

This chapter is all about how we can use serverless to process data. It would be handy if you had a potential use case from your own organization—something that you could experiment with after following the example. You will need the following:

- A good understanding of AWS
- Knowledge about how the services are secured with IAM

Getting across the processing types

Because data processing is such a vast subject, you will find different definitions and opinions across the internet about how it can be categorized. For learning purposes and to keep it as simple as possible, I'll talk about the three main types of processing we usually find in real life data-related projects. We'll have a quick look at what they are in the following sections.

Batch

Batch processing is by far the most common type of data processing. If you consider, for example, traditional business intelligence and data warehouse workloads, usually there's a fixed schedule that defines when an **Extraction, Transformation, and Load** (**ETL**) will happen. Often, this implies taking action on a relatively large amount of data at once. The batch model is also the most cost-effective of all of the processing types and will generally be efficient enough for most of the business use cases out there.

 Ideally, you should only consider micro-batch or streaming when you are sure the batch method is not good enough for your solution.

The next two processing types will increase complexity and costs as well. The most popular batch data processing tool on AWS at the moment is AWS Glue, a managed ETL service based on Apache Spark. AWS Glue has a few capabilities other than running batch jobs, such as crawlers, data classification, and data cataloging.

We will use some of those later in this chapter when we build our own ETL process using Glue in the *Building a batch data processing workload* section. The next model takes the batch model and adds a new approach to make it more flexible.

Micro-batch

The use cases for micro-batch data processing can be similar to traditional batch processing. The main differences are that the data will be processed more often and in smaller volumes. When designing a micro-batch process, there are two ways to approach the scheduling model. It can be based on the following:

- Time interval-based: This is when you process data on a predefined schedule, for example, every 5 minutes.
- Event-based: This is when you choose to process data when the amount of data that's available or queued for processing reaches a defined threshold, for example, every 2 MB or every 1,000 records.

Apache Spark is one of the most popular open source tools for micro-batch workloads—AWS Glue is also based on Apache Spark. However, the most suitable service for a micro-batch type of workload in AWS is Amazon EMR (Elastic MapReduce). Glue is designed for batch processing and is not the most suitable for micro-batch.

Moving on from batch, the next processing type is all about continuous streaming from data sources into our processing pipelines.

Streaming

Streaming data is data that is generated continuously by one or multiple data sources. These sources typically generate large volumes of data records simultaneously and in small sizes (order of bytes or kilobytes). Streaming data includes a wide variety of data, such as log files generated by customers using mobile applications or web applications, e-commerce purchases, in-game player activity, information from social networks, financial trading floors, geospatial services, and telemetry from connected devices or instrumentation in data centers.

Usually, streaming use cases require low latency processing—second or sub-second order—due to the near-real-time or real-time nature of the application. AWS offers a few options to deal with streaming workloads in a serverless manner:

- Amazon Kinesis Streams: This enables a high level of control and customization of streams and workloads.
- Amazon Kinesis Firehose: This adds an extra layer of abstraction to Kinesis Streams requiring less customization, allowing the streams to run as a fully managed service.

- Amazon EMR running the Apache Spark Streaming API: This is similar to the micro-batch use case, except it makes use of the Streaming API embedded into Apache Spark.
- Amazon Managed Streaming for Apache Kafka (Amazon MSK): This is a managed Kafka cluster service. One of the main complaints against Apache Kafka is not its efficiency, but how complex it can be to maintain a cluster. The AWS service offering takes that overhead out of our hands.

In the next section, we'll go through an in-depth example of how to build a process using the batch data processing model, combined with using serverless AWS services.

Building a batch data processing workload

It's hard to know just where to start when you approach building your first data processing workload. The data you are working with is not the same as the data other people are working with, so the examples are sometimes challenging to apply.

In this section, we'll go through a real example to learn how to use AWS Glue to process some data. After finishing this section, you will have a grasp of the high-level methodology and be able to apply the same steps to the dataset that you are looking to process.

Where do I start?

Start with batch processing. Always start with batch! To build our first batch workload, we will use a combination of the services mentioned here:

- **S3**: To be able to process data in batch mode, we need to have our raw data stored in a place where data can be easily accessible by the services we are going to use. For example, the transformation tool, Glue, must be able to pick up the raw files and write them back once transformations are done.
- **Glue**: This is the batch transformation tool we will use to create the transformation scripts, schedule the job, and catalog the dataset we are going to create. We also need to create crawlers that will scan the files in S3 and identify the schema—columns and data types—the files contain.
- **Athena**: To query the datasets we store in S3 and catalog on Glue, we can use AWS Athena, a serverless query tool that allows you to query files using SQL, even though the data is not stored in a relational database. Athena leverages the data catalog that's created and populated by Glue. We'll explore this in the next section once we have our data catalog.

For this example, we will use some files containing meteorology data in JSON format. The sample data was collected from the `https://openweathermap.org/` website, which makes weather data openly available. There are a plethora of websites, such as `https://www.kaggle.com/` and `https://www.data.govt.nz/about/open-data-nz/`, that offer hundreds of open datasets if you want to explore other options. Once we have the files in an S3 bucket, we need to understand the structure and content of the data.

Now that we know how to approach building our first workload, let's have a look at what we will build at a high level.

The ETL blueprint

AWS Glue allows you to implement an extract, transform, and load process from start to finish. This pattern is a common methodology for processing large amounts of data. In the coming sections, we're going to step through an example using sample weather data.

To get an understanding about what we are about to build from a high level, study the following diagram:

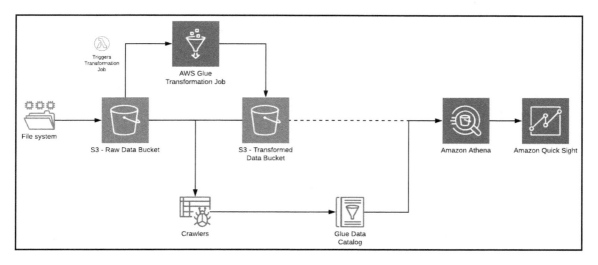

ETL process showing components and high-level data flows

As you can see in the blueprint diagram, our data source will be a filesystem that holds the weather data files to be processed. In this case, the filesystem is your local machine.

You can download the sample data files from the following public S3 bucket: `s3://weather-data-inbox/raw/`.

This is a JSON dataset that's curated from Open Weather. If the preceding S3 location is unavailable, you can always find your own dataset by searching for JSON open weather data.

Once you have downloaded the dataset, we need to place the files in a location that has been allocated for storing our raw (pre-transformed and pre-curated) data. S3 is a great storage system for data objects, so let's move on to the next section to find out the best way to get the data into our raw bucket.

Data storage using S3

Loading the files into S3 is a task that can be achieved in multiple ways—you can get creative depending on the requirements, data volume, file update frequency, and other variables. A few possible ways are as follows:

- A custom shell script (or a set of scripts) that runs AWS CLI commands to send the files to an S3 bucket
- The AWS SDK for your favorite language
- AWS DataSync
- AWS Storage Gateway

We're going to use the AWS CLI directly from the command line to sync a local folder with a newly created bucket:

1. Let's create a bucket that will receive our raw data. As you already know, S3 bucket names must be unique, so update the following command accordingly and choose your unique bucket name. This will create the bucket to store our raw data:

```
aws s3 mb s3://[raw-data-bucket-name]/
```

2. Now that the bucket is ready, let's send the file from the local machine to S3 using your chosen upload method. We want to copy the weather-dataset.json file in to our raw data bucket. Here's an AWS CLI command that will get the job done:

```
aws s3 sync ~/[path-to-downloaded-file]/weather-dataset.json
s3://[raw-data-bucket-name]/
```

With the data file in S3, we can move on to AWS Glue and start the data processing step. The first topic to cover with Glue is how to create the data catalog, so let's find out what that is in the next section.

Data cataloging – Glue

Welcome to what might be a new AWS service to you—AWS Glue. Glue is meant to simplify the ETL process by discovering your data and learning information about it. The idea is that we first need to define our own data classifiers and crawlers. We can then register our data sources and Glue will start to build the data catalog. After that, we can get creative in the way we map and transform the data. Then, we can configure regular ETL jobs for batch processing.

To build our data catalog, the first thing we need is to create a classifier. We'll take you through the steps in the next section.

Custom classifiers

Head over to the **Glue** console. In this section, we'll be using the components under the **Data Catalog** group.

The first component of our data catalog that we need to create is a classifier. As you can observe in the JSON file structure of our sample data, we have a nested dataset of the file that contains *structs* and *arrays*. This means we need to tell Glue how to read the file by specifying a *JSON path*; otherwise, each entry of the file will be loaded as a single line, which is not very useful for analysis. Later on, we will see we can *unnest* the records using Athena as well, but we want to avoid unnecessary work.

For files that don't contain nested structures, this step is not necessary as the default JSON classifier embedded in Glue will be perfectly fine.

If you're not following along yourself, here's a snapshot of the dataset file so that you can get an idea:

```json
1  {
2      "cod": "200",
3      "message": 0.0149,
4      "cnt": 40,
5      "list": [
6          {
7              "dt": 1567868400,
8              "main": {
9                  "temp": 9.26,
10                 "temp_min": 9.26,
11                 "temp_max": 10.05,
12                 "pressure": 1004.63,
13                 "sea_level": 1004.63,
14                 "grnd_level": 995.68,
15                 "humidity": 85,
16                 "temp_kf": -0.79
17             },
18             "weather": [
19                 {
20                     "id": 804,
21                     "main": "Clouds",
22                     "description": "overcast clouds",
23                     "icon": "04n"
24                 }
25             ],
26             "clouds": {
27                 "all": 99
28             },
29             "wind": {
30                 "speed": 4.74,
31                 "deg": 46.154
32             },
33             "sys": {
34                 "pod": "n"
35             },
36             "dt_txt": "2019-09-07 15:00:00"
37         },
```

Screenshot of a JSON file viewed in Visual Studio Code

Let's follow an example so that we can create a classifier in AWS Glue:

1. To create a classifier, go to the **Glue** console, click on **Classifiers** under **Crawlers**, and hit the **Add classifier** button. Complete the definition by using the information shown in the following screenshot. This will create a new custom classifier for our data:

Adding a classifier

The $ [*] pattern tells Glue to look at all the structs in the JSON schema and convert them into columns.

Now, you should see your newly created classifier, which is highlighted in the red box, as shown in the following screenshot:

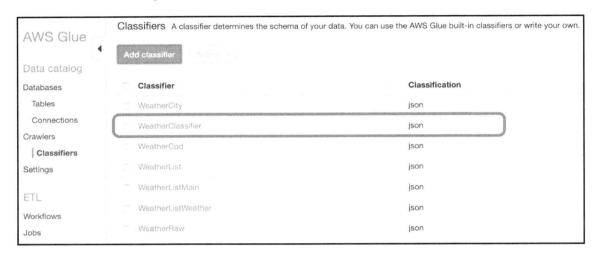

List of available classifiers

You can find more information about Glue classifiers in the *Further reading* section of this chapter.

In the next section, we will create a database for our data catalog and find out exactly what Glue defines as a database. It's not what you might expect!

Databases

In the Glue data catalog context, a database is a logical abstraction that allows you to group the metadata tables for organization. It helps you set boundaries around grouping files in a bucket, for example, or logically group data that should be seen as a single dataset. Let's get started:

1. Click on **Database** and then click on the **Add database** button.

2. Choose a database name, `weather`, add an optional description like the following, and hit **Create**. This will create a database for our tables:

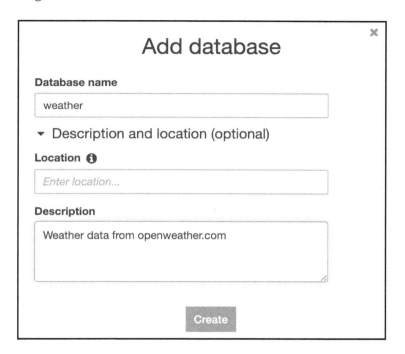

Adding a database

Your database has been created but it's empty; if you click on the database name and then click on **Tables in weather**, you will see no tables, but there will be a button offering you the option to **Add tables using a crawler**.

So, that's what we will do in the next section: add a crawler. This will analyze our sample data file and find all of the characteristics and attributes.

Crawlers

Now, things start to get exciting because we are going to read the real file and the crawler will map the schema for the data in the file—that's the structs, arrays, columns, and data types. Sounds good! The following screenshot shows that we don't have any data in our tables yet:

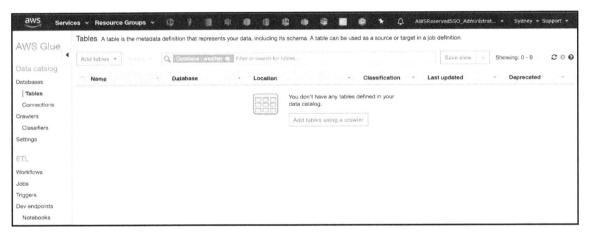

Tables in our new database

We need to add a crawler to populate that for us:

1. To do so, click on **Add tables using a crawler**. The Glue console will launch a wizard that will guide you through the process of creating a crawler.
2. Enter the crawler name—I've chosen `rawDataWeatherCrawler`—and expand the **Tags, description, security configuration, and classifiers (optional)** section.
3. We also want to make sure we add the appropriate classifier that we created in an earlier section (*Custom classifiers*) so that the JSON schema is interpreted correctly. You will see the recently created classifier on the left column; click **Add** to send it to the right column so that, every time this crawler runs, the custom classifier will be prioritized. If Glue is unable to find the specified JSON path defined in the custom classifier, the default classifier will be used instead. The following screenshot shows where you can find the classifier and what it looks like when you have added our `WeatherClassifier`:

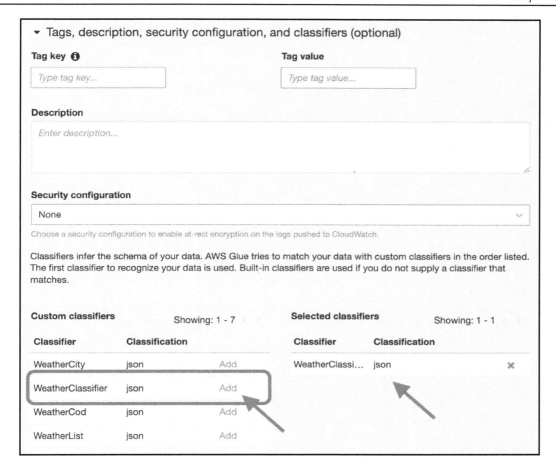

Adding tables to the database

You can also add tags and descriptions, which is highly recommended, especially for production workloads.

4. Click **Next** and specify the source type. The following screen shows the options for source types:

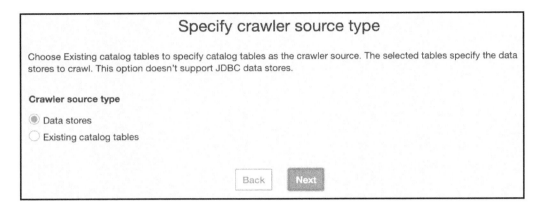

Selecting a crawler source type

5. We are creating a new data catalog, so we are going to select the default option, that is, **Data Stores**. Click **Next**.

   For our data store, we are going to select S3. The other options are DynamoDB, which is a native AWS service integration to allow you to connect directly, or JDBC, in case you have set up a JDBC connection previously. Setting up a JDBC connection means you can connect other databases, for example, a remote Oracle instance, and let the crawler scan the Oracle schema for you. We are selecting S3 because that's where our file is.

   We also want to point the crawler to an S3 bucket in our own account. If you have multiple accounts or need to consume data from a third-party account, you can also point the crawler to an S3 bucket in another AWS account, provided you have sufficient privileges to access the bucket.

6. Now, we need to tell the crawler exactly where the file is stored; you can type in the path or click on the folder icon on the right-hand side of the field and select your S3 bucket/path. In our case, we are providing the bucket name and the `raw` folder—you can be more specific and specify any S3 path. This is useful when you store different datasets with different schemas in the same bucket but in different paths.

7. Finally, we have the **Exclude patterns** field, which is where you can define which folders in the bucket the crawler should not scan. We don't need to specify this field because we want to scan everything in the bucket. The following screenshot shows an example configuration of the data store:

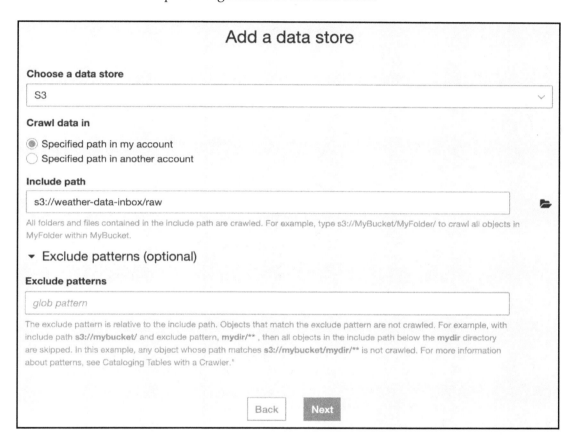

Adding a data store

8. Click **Next** twice as we don't want to add another data source at this point.

Just like pretty much any other AWS service, Glue also requires an IAM role to run; in this case, the crawler requires a role to be able to read the files in S3. I already have a role for that, so I'm reusing it.

9. You can create a role while creating the crawler or you can go to the IAM console and do it from there. For our example, we're going to click **Next** on the following screen to accept our existing role choice:

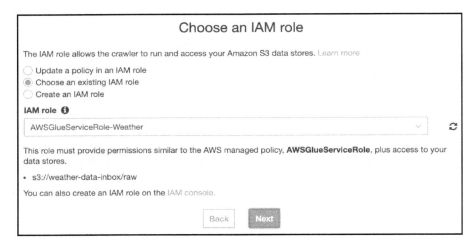

Creating a service-linked IAM role for AWS Glue

You need to think of when you need to run a crawler in a real application. If you are updating your datasets once a day, you only need to run the crawler once a day, but notice that even if the JSON schema doesn't change, you need to rerun the crawler when you add more data to your dataset.

 Make sure you schedule your crawlers to run at a satisfactory rate as you don't want to have new data sitting in your S3 bucket that's not accessible by your analytics tools.

10. For now, we'll keep the schedule option as **Run on demand**. If you select other options, such as **Choose Days**, the scheduling setup will change accordingly. The following screenshot shows us the simple screen with our choice:

Crawler schedule

11. Now, we select which database will hold the metadata that will be scanned by the crawler. We have created our `weather` database already, so let's select that one. In case you didn't, you can also create it on this page.
12. Leave everything else as default for now and click **Next**.
13. Finally, we can review our settings and hit **Finish** to create our crawler. Make sure you are happy with the configuration and go ahead. The following is what my review screen looks like:

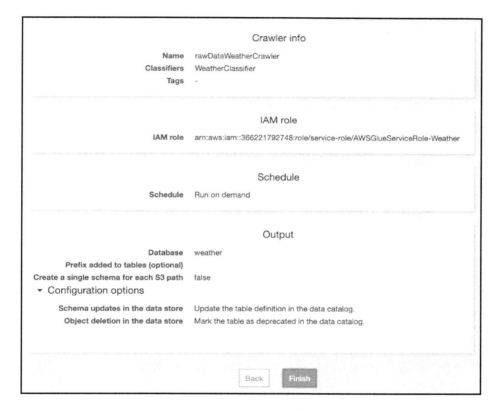

Review screen for creating a crawler

Now, after going through that whole process, you are probably thinking: that's a lot of steps just to create a simple crawler, right? Right—a much better way to do this is using the AWS CLI. We can create exactly the same crawler with the following CLI command:

```
aws glue create-crawler
    --name rawDataWeatherCrawler
```

```
--role service-role/AWSGlueServiceRole-Weather
--database-name weather
--description rawDataWeatherCrawler
--classifiers "WeatherClassifier"
--targets '{"S3Targets": [{"Path": "weather-data-inbox/raw"}]}'
--region us-east-1
```

Feel free to use the preceding command by updating with the appropriate parameter values; for example, your S3 bucket will definitely have a different name.

Glue is quite comprehensively supported in the AWS CLI and AWS CloudFormation. All of the step-by-step processes we go through here are for learning purposes; it's always good to keep in mind that one of the characteristics of great software engineers is that they should be lazy enough to automate everything that can possibly be automated.

To run the crawler you just created, you can use the following CLI command. Make sure you adjust the options so that they match your environment:

```
aws glue start-crawler
    --name rawDataWeatherCrawler
    --region us-east-1
```

14. Go back to the **Glue** console and, on the **Crawlers** page, check the status and wait for it to finish running. Observe the number of tables your crawler has created and updated.

That concludes the steps to create our data catalog. Now, we have given Glue all of the information it needs about the raw dataset that we have in storage. In the next section, we are going to give Glue some instructions to process or transform our data into a format that we specify. This is an important step because we get to define what the final format of our data will be before we move into analytics.

Data transformation – Glue

Data transformation is the process of taking our raw data from one format and mapping it to a new structure or format that we choose. This process is a fundamental part of all data processing and usually requires a lot of storage space, as well as large-scale computations. We can speed up the transformation process by parallelizing the processing, which is something that Glue can do for us out of the box.

In this section, we are going to create our own transformation process using Glue. We will take the existing knowledge about our data, which can be found in our data catalog, and create a target structure. It will be clear which fields we want to map to our new structure, and we'll also learn a tip about a file format that will increase the efficiency of our analytics queries in the future.

Creating a Glue job

Okay—it's time to create our first Glue job:

1. On the AWS console, go to the **Glue** console and on the left-hand side menu, under **ETL**, click on **Jobs**.
2. Then, hit the **Add Job** button. The **Add Job** step-by-step configuration process will start and you can set up the ETL process. Ideally, you will give it a name that describes what the job will do. In this case, I'll call it `TransformWeatherData` and will use the same IAM role I've used for the crawler—make sure yours has the necessary permissions for the new location. The following screenshot shows an example of my configuration, but yours will have different S3 locations:

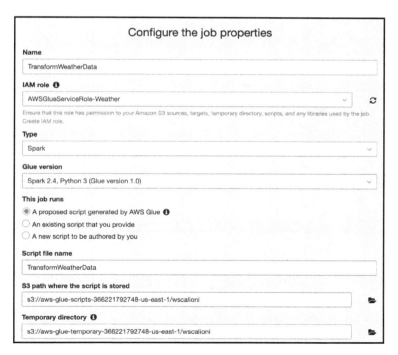

Creating a Glue job

3. Leave the other fields with default values, including **A proposed script generated by AWS Glue**, which will give us a baseline script so that we can customize transformations if required, or move data from one dataset to another.

4. Expand the **Security configuration, script libraries, and job parameters (optional)** option and under **Maximum Capacity**, change the default value from **10** to **2** and set the **Job timeout** to 10 minutes. We are processing a small amount of data, so that should be more than enough. The following is a sensible configuration for our job parameters:

Glue job properties

AWS Glue uses **Data Processing Units (DPUs)** that are allocated when a job starts. The more DPUs a job uses, the more parallelism will be applied and potentially, the faster the job will run. Each ETL job must be evaluated and optimized accordingly to run as fast as possible with the minimum incurring costs as possible.

Allocating DPUs costs money. When you run a Glue job, you pay for the amount of allocated DPUs and for the amount of time the job runs at a minimum of 10 minutes, and at 1-minute increments after that. This means that if your job runs under 10 minutes anyway, ideally, you should allocate the minimum amount of DPUs as possible. Glue requires at least 2 DPUs to run any given job.

5. Hit **Next**.
6. Choose your data source. We currently have our raw data in an S3 bucket; what we want to do is read raw data, apply some transformation, and write to another bucket—one that will hold transformed data. In our example, we want to select `raw` as the data source and click **Next**. See the following screenshot, which is highlighting our raw data source:

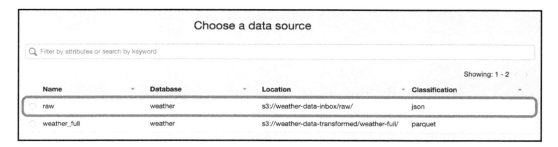

Choosing a data source

7. Choose a transform type. Select the **Change schema** option as we are moving data from one schema to another and click **Next**. The following screenshot shows the options that are available:

Adding transformation options

8. Choose a data target. We need to choose where the data will be written after it's been transformed by Glue. Since we don't have an existing target database, such as an RDS Aurora or a Redshift database, we are going to create a new dataset on S3 when the job runs. The next time we run the same job, the data will be appended unless you explicitly delete the target dataset on your transformation script.

9. Select **Amazon S3** from the **Data store** drop-down menu and the output **Format** as **Parquet**, given we want this dataset to be optimized for analytical queries. Other columnar data formats are also supported such as ORC and Avro, as you can see in the **Format** drop-down menu. Common formats such as CSV and JSON are not ideal for analytics workloads—we will see more of this when we work with queries on AWS Athena. The following screenshot shows the options that are available, including where to select our target file format:

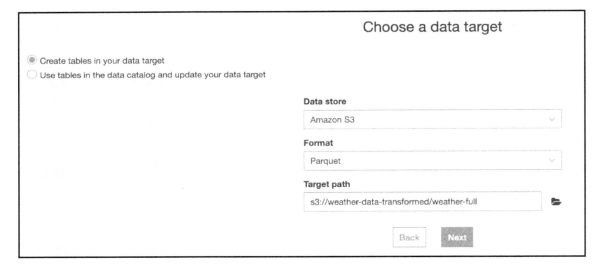

Choosing a data target

10. Now, we need to map the source columns to target columns. As you can observe on the source side (left), we have a few different data types coming from our JSON file. We have one `string`, one `double`, and one `int` column, all of which are clearly defined. We also have one `array` and one `struct`, which are more complex data types, given they have nested objects within them. The following screenshot shows the fields from my raw data—yours might be different if you are using a different dataset:

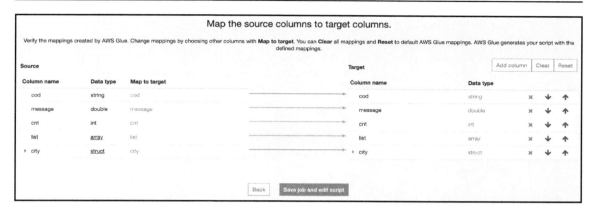

Raw data structure against the target structure

When we expand `city`, we can see there's another struct level called `coord`, which finally has the latitude and longitude (of the double type) of the city. Have a look at the following screenshot to see what I mean:

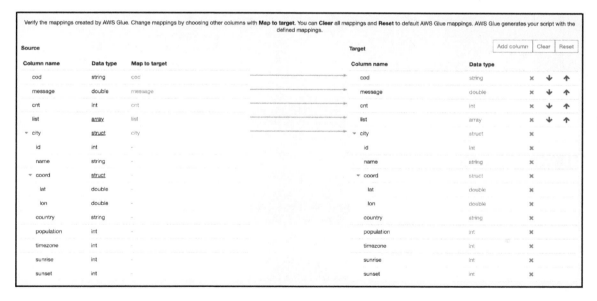

Nested structures in our raw data

The nested structures under `city` are not mapped by default on the **Glue** console. This means that if we leave the mapping as is, `city` data will be loaded to the target as a nested structure just like the source, but that will make our queries more verbose and it will make it slightly harder to work with our dataset. Because of that annoyance, we will flatten out the structure of the city data and only select the fields that will be useful to our analysis, not all of them.

11. To do that, we need to remove the mapping for the `city` field by clicking on the **x** next to the **Data type** on the **Target** side (right) for all the columns under `city` (inclusive) until your mapping looks as follows:

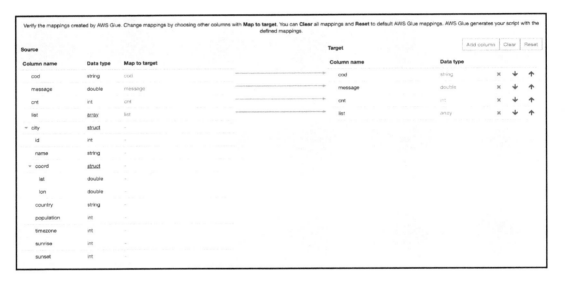

Changes to the target data structure

12. Now, we need to map the data as per our requirements. Click on **Add Column** at the top-right corner and create a new column on the target called `cityid` of the `int` type.

13. Go to the `id` column under `city` in the source and click on the row. A drop-down menu will allow you to select which column will receive the value of the `id` column. Choose the one you just created, `cityid`, and hit **Save**. The following screenshot shows you what to expect when you click the drop-down menu:

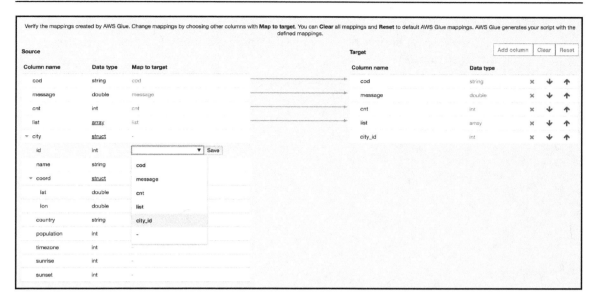

Selecting the mapping between raw and target fields

A new arrow from the **Source** column to the **Target** column will appear and the ID of the city will be loaded to the target as a column by itself rather than as part of a nested structure.

14. Repeat this process by adding the columns listed here and their appropriate mapping. Don't panic if these fields aren't the same as yours—follow your nose to map yours to the right fields:

```
cityname
country
population
sunset
sunrise
latitude
longitude
```

Once you've finished the mapping configuration, it should look something like this. The following shows how we are mapping a bunch of nested structures to a flat target structure:

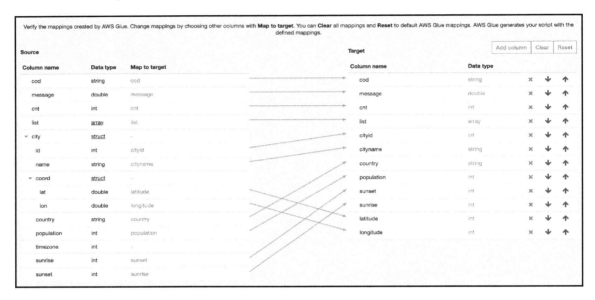

Our targeted structure for transformation

15. Now, you can click on **Save Job** and **Edit Script**. The script editor will show you the generated code that you can now customize.

16. For now, we won't change the content of the script—all we want to do is flatten out the city data structure that we configured in the previous step.

If you want to see where that transformation is implemented on the script, it's usually done with the `ApplyMapping` class. In this case, that's line 25 of our auto-generated transformation script. If you do some side-scrolling, you will find the mapping of the columns that are coming from the `city` struct. Close the script editor by clicking on the **x** at the top-right corner of the editor:

AWS Glue script editor

> **TIP**
>
> As you will see when creating a Glue job, Glue scripts are stored on S3 buckets. That means you have all of the flexibility of S3 and can use any IDE to create and develop your transformation scripts in Python or Scala and upload them to S3. Also, setting up a CI/CD pipeline and automating the testing of your scripts is highly recommended.

Once you are happy with the transformation script and all of the settings of the job that has just been created, feel free to go ahead and jump to the next section to learn how you can run your newly created Glue job.

Running a Glue job

So far, we have created a job that knows about our data. We've specified which fields are extracted, which structures we want to be transformed, and where to load the data to. Now, we are ready to run the Glue job, so let's learn how to do that by following these steps:

1. Select your job by clicking on the checkbox next to it. Then, hit **Action | Run job**:

Actions in the job screen in the Glue console

2. While your job is running, select the checkbox next to the job name again if not already selected. On the detail panel below, you will see your job running.
3. Click on the Run ID to get job details. You can also check the logs that are being generated and if you have errors, click on **Error Logs** to go into CloudWatch and see what happened.

Instead of using the console, you can also run the job by using the following CLI command:

```
aws glue start-job-run
    --job-name TransformWeatherData
    --timeout 10
    --max-capacity 2
```

The CLI will output the Job Run ID as per the following if your CLI configuration is set to return responses in JSON format. You can compare that with the Glue console:

```
{
    "JobRunId":
```

```
"jr_cd30b15f97551e83e69484ecda992dc1f9562ea44b53a5b0f77ebb3b3a50602
2"
}
```

My job took 5 minutes to run, as shown in the following screenshot. You should see the **Run Status** update to **Succeeded**:

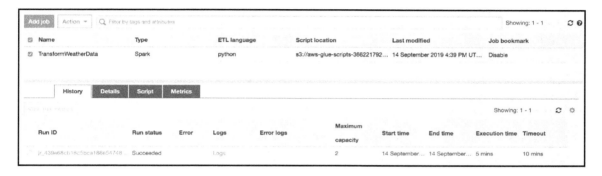

Job screen showing the progress of a running job

Just to confirm that some data was generated on S3, let's have a look at the bucket where the Glue job has written the data.

4. Head over to the S3 console and look at the target location in your S3 bucket:

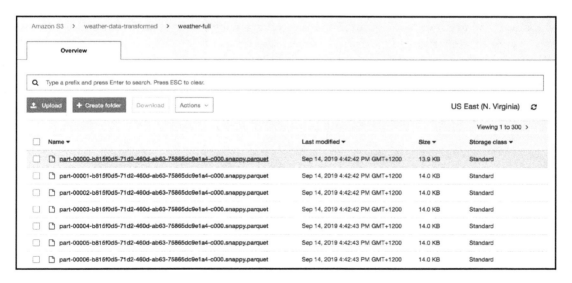

The listing of our S3 bucket with the transformed parquet objects

Hundreds of Parquet files were generated and written to our bucket. If you try to download one of these files and open it on a text editor, it won't work as Parquet files are binary; what we need is a piece of technology such as AWS Athena to be able to read them and run some analytical queries.

But before we move on, to enable Athena to read the schema and content of the Parquet files in our bucket, we need to update our Data Catalog again. This is so that the new dataset that contains transformed data is included. You have already learned how to create a crawler, so go ahead and create a new one called `tfdDataWeather`. You can also either create a new database on the data catalog or you can use the same `weather` database. As the path for the raw dataset and transformed dataset are different, separate tables will be created so that there's no problem in using the same database as the one that's used for the raw data. Once the new crawler is created, don't forget to run it.

Excellent—so what we have done in this section is learn how to create and run an entire ETL process using AWS Glue. That's pretty awesome.

Now that we have some newly transformed data, let's go and analyze it. Move on to the next section when you're ready.

Data analytics and transformation

Okay, so now, we have some extracted raw weather data that we transformed to our liking and loaded into another location in S3. This is where we get to start using the data and really dive into the structure, perform queries, and draw insights. For this, we are going to use Amazon Athena, a serverless query service that we can use to access our transformed data directly in S3, without loading it into another data store, such as a relational database.

Let's kick off by learning how to use Athena to query data in S3.

Querying data in S3 with Athena

At this point, we know we need something else to read the data that was collected, transformed, and cataloged by Glue. You can see tables and schemas on Glue but you cannot see the content of the files, that is, the actual data. For that, we need to use Athena:

1. Go to the **Console** and open up the Athena console. If it's the first time you are doing this, the **Get Started** page will show up. Hit **Get started** and have a look at the interface:

Query editor in the Athena console

The query editor is where the action happens: you can write SQL queries to interact with files directly. This means you don't have to set up expensive instances and relational databases before you can run some simple queries and aggregations on your data. Athena uses Presto to give you ANSI SQL functionality and supports several file formats.

On the left, you will see the database, which is exactly the list of databases you have on the Glue data catalog. Glue and Athena are strongly coupled and share the catalog. When you add databases and tables to Glue, they are also made available straight away in Athena.

2. With the `weather` database selected in the Athena console, you can see the two tables we created: `raw` for the raw data and `weather_full` for the transformed data.

3. Expand the **2** tables to see their structure by clicking on the small arrow next to their names:

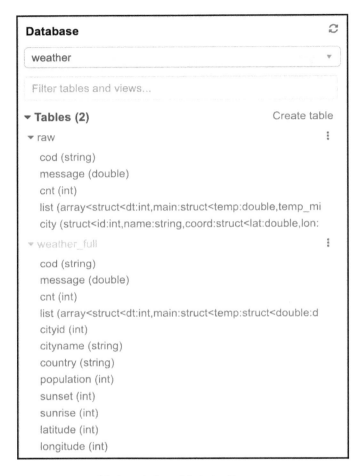

Selecting our database and viewing the table structure

Our raw table has fewer columns because it has nested structures. Our `weather_full` table holds the flattened out structure that we created during our transformation process. Notice we still have an array (list) in our transformed data; we will play with that soon.

4. Click on the three stacked dots next to the `weather_full` table name and select **Preview table** from the menu:

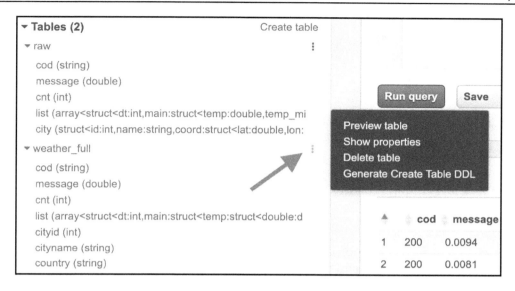

The table view in the Athena console, showing the stacked dots options button

A new query was created for you, limiting the results to 10 records:

```
SELECT * FROM "weather"."weather_full" limit 10;
```

Also, Athena gives you the amount of time the query took to run and the amount of scanned data. The reason for this is because Athena pricing is based on the amount of data your queries scan. When stored, Parquet files are smaller in size than JSON files for the same amount of data. Query efficiency for both cost and performance are the main reasons why we converted the JSON files into Parquet files for consumption. It would work if the transformed files were in JSON format as well, but for larger volumes of data, the performance would not be ideal and the amount of scanned data would be higher, meaning our overall cost would be higher as well.

Athena will scan data on S3 based on partitions. Normally, what goes into the WHERE clause in a SQL query tends to be a good candidate for a partitioning strategy. Certainly, every dataset may have different partitioning requirements that will be driven by business requirements but, for example, if most of the queries that are executed on an S3 dataset have a date filter, it is likely that the partitioning strategy will suggest data on S3 to be organized as something like the following:

```
bucket-name/2019/01/01/part-00960-b815f0d5-71d2-460d-ab63-75865dc9e1a4-
c000.snappy.parquet
bucket-name/2019/01/01/part-00961-b815f0d5-71d2-460d-ab63-75865dc9e1a4-
c000.snappy.parquet
```

```
. . .
bucket-name/2019/01/02/part-00958-b815f0d5-71d2-460d-ab63-75865dc9e1a4-
c000.snappy.parquet
bucket-name/2019/01/02/part-00958-b815f0d5-71d2-460d-ab63-75865dc9e1a4-
c000.snappy.parquet
. . .
```

By using that type of partitioning strategy, `-bucket-name/YYYY/MM/DD/[data-files]`, when a business analyst runs a query that only retrieves data from the 1 Jan, 2019 (that is, `WHERE date = '2019-01-01'`), Athena will only scan data on the `bucket-name/2019/01/01/` path instead of scanning the entire bucket, optimizing the query's performance and running costs.

The following query shows how you can access the data inside an array (the `list` column in our dataset) in a catalog table. You can take care of this in your transformation script and load a completely flat and denormalized dataset to be used on your queries, or you can access data within arrays by using the UNNEST operator, as per the following example:

```
SELECT
    full_list.dt_txt as ReadingTimeStamp,
    city.name as CityName,
    full_list.main.temp.double as Temperature,
    . . .
    full_list.main.temp_kf.double as TemperatureKF,
    full_weather.main as WeatherMain,
    full_weather.description as WeatherDescription,
    full_list.wind.speed.double as WindSpeed,
    full_list.wind.deg.double as WindDeg
FROM
    "weather"."weather_full"
CROSS JOIN
    UNNEST(list) as t(full_list), UNNEST(full_list.weather) as
s(full_weather)
LIMIT 10;
```

That concludes our introduction to Athena. Now, you can run and experiment with SQL queries in the console.

Have a go at ingesting some other open datasets and using different transformation strategies. As a stretch goal, have a look at Amazon QuickSight for ways to turn your data and queries into visualizations.

Summary

When it comes to data processing workloads, the possibilities are almost endless. The options that can be leveraged with the native integration between AWS services allow us to collect data at pretty much any point of any cloud application in a serverless manner. Using S3, Glue, Athena, and QuickSight is a very cost-effective way to process large volumes of data in a secure and fast way without having to commit to expensive hardware or upfront costs. This solution can be extended as much as required by adding tools such as EMR, Lambda, RDS, Redshift, DynamoDB, or API Gateway. S3 is an extremely reliable storage service and is used at enterprise scale as a foundational Data Lake solution. What's also important to point out is that a solid data management layer is key when implementing a successful data workload on the cloud. On top of that, data governance, data quality, data catalog, and other capabilities are equally key to enable a secure, useful, and reliable data platform.

I hope you have come away with some new knowledge about how to process your data. Get ready for the next use case for serverless in `Chapter 12`, *Hosting Single-Page Web Applications*.

Questions

1. Given a data processing workload that extracts data from an on-premise ERP (source) and loads into S3 (target), what is the LEAST cost-effective type of data processing—assuming business analysts don't require real-time analysis since they access the financial reports once a day?

   A) Batch
   B) Micro-batch
   C) Streaming

2. One of the situations where Glue custom classifiers are required is when data sources contain nested data structures. When data structures are flat on the source, the default classifiers are sufficient for standard data ingestion processing.

   A) True
   B) False

3. When is it necessary to run a crawler?

A) When the schema of the crawled dataset has changed
B) When data was added to a previously crawled dataset but the schema hasn't changed
C) When the dataset was moved to a different S3 bucket
D) Both A and B

4. Which file format is best to use to optimize query performance in Athena?

A) CSV
B) JSON
C) Parquet
D) DOCX

5. When authoring a custom Glue script, which native Glue classes can be used to help with the transformation tasks that need to be applied on a dataset? (Choose three)

A) ApplyMapping
B) Relationalize
C) Deduplicate
D) ResolveChoice

6. To run Glue workloads efficiently from a cost and performance perspective, some of the variables that need to be evaluated are as follows: (Choose two)

A) The maximum number of CPUs allocated to a job
B) The number of parameters a job requires
C) The maximum number of DPUs allocated to a job
D) How long the job takes to run, which is highly impacted by the volume of the data to be processed
E) The definition of the micro-batch threshold in records or megabytes

Further reading

- AWS Glue documentation: `https://docs.aws.amazon.com/en_pv/glue/latest/dg/how-it-works.html`
- Apache Parquet project: `https://parquet.apache.org/`
- AWS Athena: `https://docs.aws.amazon.com/en_pv/athena/latest/ug/glue-athena.html`
- Example sample data:
    - OpenWeather—subscribe to their API and make direct calls to it. `https://openweathermap.org/`
    - JSON dataset curated from OpenWeather: `s3://weather-data-inbox/raw/`

10
AWS Automation

The change to a serverless mindset brings with it a renewed focus on automation and agility as key factors. Practically any task you might want to do in the AWS ecosystem can be automated, making administration and operations easier than before. With the serverless services themselves, there are fewer components in our scope of responsibility, which further reduces our operational burden. We should definitely put these new serverless components to good use when developing solutions—whether legacy or cloud-native.

In this chapter, we are going to explore some uses for serverless technologies in enabling automation. We'll cover the following topics in this chapter:

- Continuous compliance
- Resource tagging
- Running scheduled tasks

Technical requirements

This chapter has no specific technical requirements, but it would help if you had a background in an operations or support type of role.

Embedded security

If it's true that we can now automate more than ever, then it's also true that we can monitor, test, and release our code more often. To keep our agility and speed of release, we must be able to prove that we are making changes in a secure fashion, and not introducing new vulnerabilities. That means our security compliance game needs to step up in parity with the speed of release. This is what SecDevOps is all about.

To reach the pace of innovation our organizations strive for, we must automate security compliance with scanning tools and testing strategies, and apply guard rails. With the tools and capabilities we have now, we can embed these things into our automation processes so we are far more on top of security at all layers.

Enforcement via tagging

Somewhat of a prerequisite for automating things in AWS is the ability to add tags to resources. Tags are a key/value pair that you can add to supported resources. They allow you to create an arbitrary piece of data that is attached to a resource, such as an EC2 instance, a security group, or a Lambda function. There's a long list of resources you can tag, so check the AWS documentation for further details.

The reason you would want to add a tag to a resource is that tags are returned when you request information about the resource. For example, the `describe-instances` operation for EC2 API returns any tags associated with an EC2 instance. You can also filter the query down to display just the tags for a given instance ID:

```
aws ec2 describe-instances
    --instance-id i-123456780
    --query "Reservations[*].Instances[*].[Tags[*]]"
```

A few examples of a tag could be as follows:

- `owner: Scott`
- `cost-center: Technology`
- `backup: true`

You can use this contextual information to drive the logic in your automation. You might want to assign an owner to a machine so you know who is responsible for it, or attribute the usage cost to a particular billing center, or flag that the instance should be added to the standard backup policy.

Tags are easy to add. Here's an example of tagging Lambda functions:

- This is how you tag using the Lambda management console:

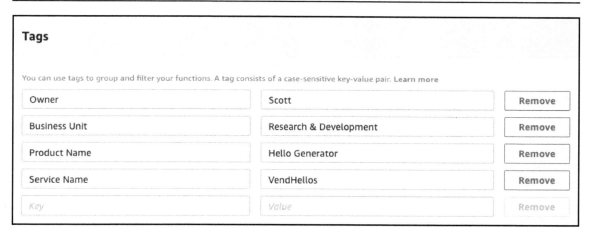

Snippet of a function configuration in the Lambda console

- Now for tagging using the AWS CLI.

  When creating a new function, you can use the `--tags` option. You can include multiple tags separated by a comma.

  ```
  aws lambda create-function
      --function-name hello-world
      --handler index.py
      --runtime python3.6
      --role
  arn:aws:iam::123456789012:role/lambda_basic_execution
      --tags "Owner=Scott,Environment=UAT"
  ```

  Alternatively, you can achieve the same result by adding tags to an existing function using the `tag-resource` action of the Lambda CLI, as follows:

  ```
  aws lambda tag-resource
      --resource arn:aws:lambda:us-
  east-1:123456789012:function:hello-world
      --tags "Business Unit=Research & Development"
  ```

- Adding tags to a CloudFormation template is also possible by specifying the `Tags` property in a function declaration. See the following for an example:

```
HelloFunction:
  Type: "AWS::Lambda::Function"
  Properties:
    Handler: "index.handler"
    Code:
      S3Bucket: "lambda-functions"
      S3Key: "function.zip"
    Runtime: "java8"
    Tags:
    - Key: "Owner"
      Value: "Scott"
    - Key: "DeployedByPipeline"
      Value: "serverless-hello-world-pipeline"
```

- When adding tags to your resources in the Serverless Framework, you can add tags just to the functions that you create:

```
functions:
  hello:
    handler: handler.hello
    tags:
      DeployedBy: Serverless
```

- Or—and this is extremely useful—you can add tags that attach to *every* resource that gets created by deploying the CloudFormation stack as part of a serverless deployment. This declaration is made at the provider level:

```
provider:
  name: aws
  runtime: nodejs10.x
  stackTags:
    DeployedBy: Serverless
```

Okay; let's move on to a reason where we may be able to leverage tags, and then move on to an example.

Automatic detection and remediation with AWS Config

When developing and deploying solutions for your organization, you will most likely be governed by a framework or set of principles or processes that must be followed. The principles will clearly define both what is not acceptable from a risk perspective and the security controls that must be put in place to prohibit the action. The process might describe the path you need to take through the organization to gain approval to make a change.

An example here could be that users of an AWS account shouldn't be able to deploy resources into a **Virtual Private Cloud** (**VPC**) that has direct access from the internet. There are various components that would need to be put in place to make sure this couldn't happen, such as IAM policies, service control policies, network access control lists, and security groups. Such security controls could be spread across multiple locations and services to mitigate the risk of users creating public resources. Responsibility for maintaining these controls could be spread across different teams as well—as in having an identity team and a network team. This is stacking up to be a complex challenge, so how do we make sure the configuration of these distributed controls is adhered to?

This is where a combination of resource tagging, Lambda functions, and AWS Config can help. With Config, we can set up security rules and guard rails that we can then manage as code. We still need to configure the IAM policies as a first defense (for example, denying the `AllocateAddress` API action), but then we should create a custom rule in AWS Config to check whether we have any elastic IPs attached to an instance. If we find one attached, then we may want to first detach the address and notify the owner of the instance (which would hopefully be found in the tag). This is a real example of security defense in depth, where we trust that something won't happen but then verify and check it nonetheless.

AWS Config works by continuously recording changes in configurations against the resources that the service has discovered and added to the inventory. The service can then use this information to check against the various rules that have been enabled. Rules can be AWS-built or custom-made using a Lambda integration. A rule evaluates a configuration and determines the compliance state of a resource, which could be either:

- `COMPLIANT`: The resource meets the criteria set by the rule.
- `NON_COMPLIANT`: The resource doesn't comply with the rule.
- `NOT_APPLICABLE`: Can occur if the resource was deleted or removed from the rule's scope.

- `INSUFFICIENT_DATA`: If AWS Config has not received an evaluation for the resource or rule.

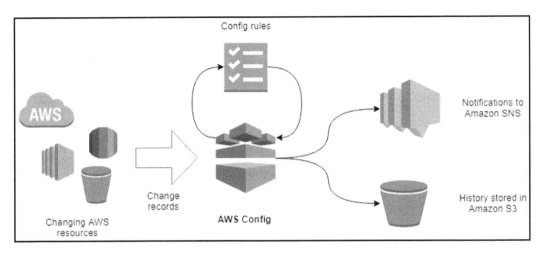

AWS Config ingesting change records and making evaluations

If a rule determines that a resource is out of compliance, then AWS Config can send notifications to a **Simple Notification Service** (**SNS**) topic. This is where you can integrate a remediation workflow in your chosen technology. A good idea would be to use Lambda for this.

In creating rules that trigger automatic remediation activities, what we're actually doing is achieving continuous compliance with the governance requirements set by our organization. Moving into the next section, we will go through an example of how to implement this.

Implementing continuous compliance

Okay; as we have understood what is possible, let's see it all in action and create our own custom Config rule. Our example organization has an internal policy that states that every production server must be backed up daily. Being awesome AWS engineers, we are using the AWS Backups service and have created a backup plan that takes a daily snapshot of **Elastic Block Store** (**EBS**) volumes that have been assigned to the plan. The backup plan looks for a resource tag called `Backup` with the value of `Daily` and automatically adds those to the plan:

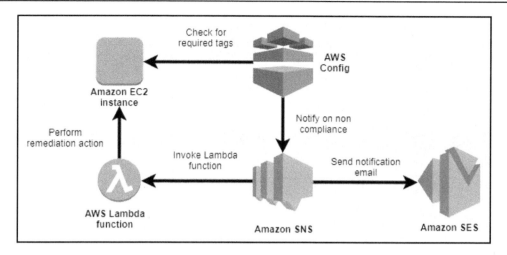

AWS Config triggering remediation action on non-compliant resource

Now that it would be easy to comply with our company policy by creating the tag when the instance is built, we could use a Lambda function to listen for `CreateInstance` actions in CloudTrail and check that the tag is present as well. However, what if something happened to the tag after the instance was built? It could have been removed or the value could have been changed, causing the instance to drop out of the backup plan. This is where an AWS Config rule is perfect, because the service is continually monitoring the configuration of our resources. If a tag on an instance is removed or updated, we can trigger a Lambda function to run to check that the resource is still complying with our policy.

So, let's go and create that Config rule. But first, we need to create the Lambda function to implement the remediation logic. I've chosen to use a blueprint to start with, the one called **config-rule-change-triggered**. This will include some scaffolding that we can use to get started faster. Take some time to familiarize yourself with the functions that are in there, because they will help you to do your checks and run your configuration evaluations. Whatever logic you choose to implement, you need to assemble and return a payload to the `PutEvaluations` action of the Config API. The structure of the payload is an array with evaluations. Here's an example of one evaluation:

```
[
    {
        ComplianceResourceType: configurationItem.resourceType,
        ComplianceResourceId: configurationItem.resourceId,
        ComplianceType: compliance,
        OrderingTimestamp: configurationItem.configurationItemCaptureTime,
    }
]
```

Okay; so, now we have a function that can receive an event if triggered. Now, we need to create a new trigger in Config. Head over to the **AWS Config** console. If this is the first time you have used the service, you will need to set up some initial configurations. This includes creating an S3 bucket to store all of the configuration records and an IAM role for Config to use. We're then presented with a rather blank-looking dashboard, which will be populated when Config completes the discovery of the inventory:

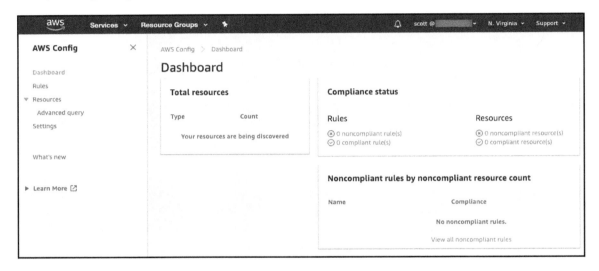

AWS Config console

Next, we need to create our custom rule. First, click the **Rules** option on the left-hand side menu and then click the **Add rule** button. I'm going to call my rule `prod-backup-compliance-rule` and drop in the **Amazon Resource Name** (**ARN**) of the Lambda function that it will trigger. The rest of the details are easy to follow as well:

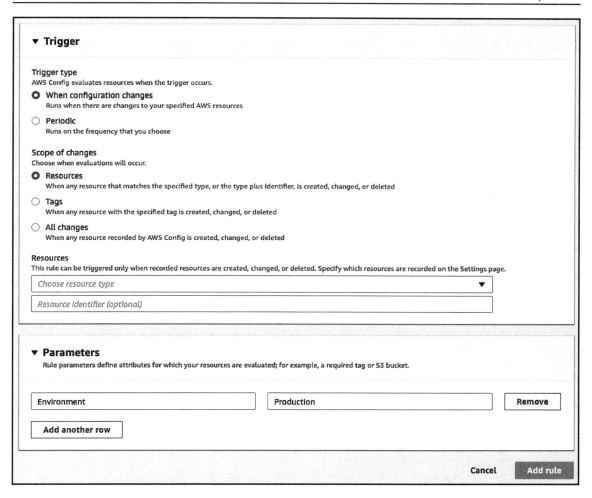

Configuration options when creating a Config rule

We want our rule to fire when it notices changes to the configuration, specifically changes to EC2 instances. There's also a space at the bottom for us to add some arbitrary parameters that the Lambda can use during execution. I've passed in the tag that we will be interested in. Externalizing this value is a good idea because it means we don't have to hardcode it into the function code, so we can write the function to be reusable for other environment tags should we need to.

After we create the rule, that's all we need to do. The trigger is set up and enabled and will trigger the Lambda function to execute whenever a change to an EC2 instance is made.

This is a great example of how you can enforce your security compliance policies using only serverless services.

Running scheduled tasks

Another component that can benefit from using serverless resources is automated tasks that run on a regular schedule. Externalizing configuration and processing from a server allows more of the allocated compute resources of the server to contribute to running the workload. In some cases, it may even mean that the size of the server can be reduced after moving the processor-hungry scheduled task into a Lambda function. Additionally, centralizing the automation as code allows you to keep track of the processes that are deployed and manage changes more easily.

Replacing server-based local schedulers

It really is down to your imagination as to what tasks could be moved into a Lambda function or other serverless compute services. The services that will be really useful in this area are listed here:

- AWS Lambda—for running the compute tasks where extra processing is needed
- AWS Step Functions—when a higher level of coordination is needed to run the process
- Amazon DynamoDB—to keep track of state or progress of tasks
- Amazon SNS—to fire off completion notifications or error messages to subscribers
- Amazon CloudWatch Events—to run the schedule and trigger a process to start
- Amazon Systems Manager—for running commands on instances

To help piece these together, I'm going to suggest three common examples for scheduled processes that can happen externally to a server.

The first is quite simple when you think about it. In your organization, you will probably have multiple environments' worth of servers that aren't used for any live workloads—the non-production environments such as dev, test, and staging. These environments are only in use when developers and testers are working, so how about we turn them off outside of business hours?

Running this process will often halve your EC2 usage bill, and it's simple to do. What we need is a CloudWatch Events rule that fires at the end of the day (at, say, 6 P.M.):

```
aws events put-rule
    --schedule-expression "cron(0 18 ? * MON-FRI *)"
    --name end-of-day-event
```

And we need one that fires at the start of the day:

```
aws events put-rule
    --schedule-expression "cron(0 8 ? * MON-FRI *)"
    --name start-of-day-event
```

Then we can link them up to simple Lambda functions that query the running instances, look for the appropriate tags that denote the environment, and then take the appropriate action. If there are errors when waking an instance up again, we might want to send an email to the owner of the server—a server that we have hopefully tagged with an owner and their email address!

The next tip is a bit more advanced, but is a good thing to have in your toolbox because it allows you to create your own completely custom scaling process for servers. I'm talking about using the lifecycle hooks in Auto Scaling to trigger functions to perform custom actions. In an EC2 Auto Scaling group, you can add a lifecycle hook to the launch or termination events. This will attach the group to a notification target (such as an SNS topic or CloudWatch Event) that you can use to trigger a Lambda function on the scale events. The lifecycle transition will go into a wait state until Auto Scaling receives a callback to proceed. You can also do this when using spot instances, making it possible to delay an unexpected termination until you have quiesced a task or gracefully removed the server from a cluster.

Here's an overview of what happens:

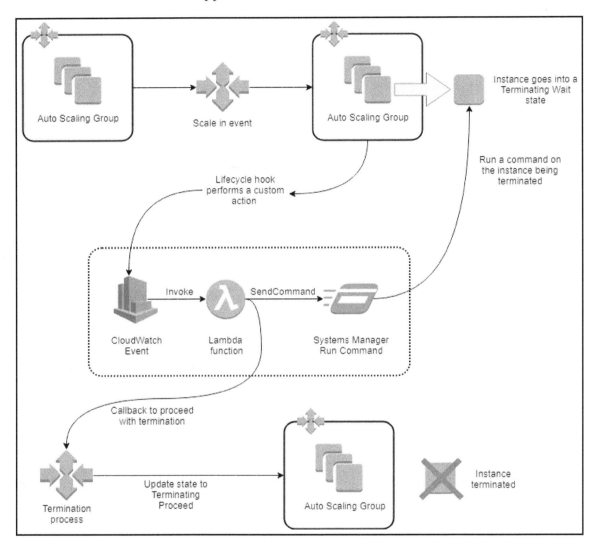

Using serverless to automate server lifecycles

The custom action, in this case, uses CloudWatch Events as a notification target. This event triggers a Lambda function, which makes a decision about what command it would need to run on the instance. The function then issues the command using the Systems Manager Run Command feature. You can read more about how to execute remote commands using Systems Manager Run Command in the *Further reading* section at the end of this chapter.

This next example is worth mentioning because it takes away the need for a manual operational process that was previously an operational burden. Keeping your base operating system image up to date used to be an arduous task that wouldn't go away. Well, today, using some cracking AWS services, we can spin up a new EC2 instance, patch it to our hearts' content, bake it into a new **Amazon Machine Image** (**AMI**), then terminate it. All without logging in to it! I'm calling out one of the most useful automation documents available in AWS Systems Manager—AWS-UpdateLinuxAmi and AWS-UpdateWindowsAmi.

To run one of the automation documents and create a new patched AMI, all you need to do is run the following command. This will start an automation execution against an AMI using the AWS-UpdateLinuxAmi document:

```
aws ssm start-automation-execution
    --document-name "AWS-UpdateLinuxAmi"
    --parameters
        "SourceAmiId=ami-1234567890abcdefg,
        IamInstanceProfileName=MyInstanceProfileRole,
AutomationAssumeRole='arn:aws:iam::123456789012:role/AutomationServiceRole'
"
```

To make this process even better, you could create your own CloudWatch event to invoke a Lambda function at scheduled intervals. This function could then run the function to kick off the automated patching for you. Awesome!

Auditing and reporting

Following the theme of continuous compliance, we also need to provide our stakeholders with some assurance. This usually comes in various flavors of reporting, whether that be security event reporting, cost trend analysis, or patch currency reports. Reports are, for the most part, a point-in-time snapshot of a particular set of metrics. These metrics are likely to be tracked closely by risk or governance teams, so they must be accurate. It would be great if we could automate this, so we can have the results in a timely manner with minimal input from ourselves.

One of the compliance frameworks your organization might be aligning to and reporting against is the CIS Controls and Benchmarks. This is a standard that encompasses many industry best practices and methodologies for securing IT solutions, including servers. As AWS engineers, if we are running in an environment with hundreds or thousands of servers, how do we make sure we are benchmarking our systems against the controls? How do we do this in a repeatable and automated way by building it into our DevOps practices?

Thankfully, there is a serverless service called Amazon Inspector that does this for us. Inspector can automate the security assessments, identify security issues, and compile a report of the findings. It uses an agent installed on each server to collect the data. You can kick off an assessment through the console, using the CLI, or I suggest running it on a scheduled basis and continuously feed the actionable findings to the responsible teams.

A good idea would be to run Inspector on all newly built AMIs. That way, you can identify if the new build introduces any vulnerabilities so you can address them before creating any instances. You could get your AMI build pipeline to produce the AMIs, then run a Lambda function when done. The function would launch a new instance with restricted network access and then trigger Inspector to run an assessment on that instance.

It might look something like this:

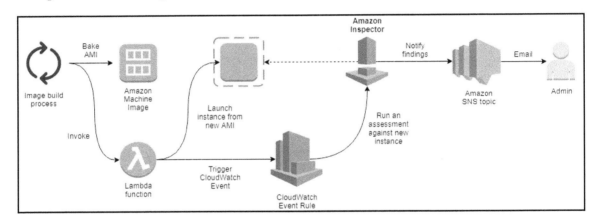

Using Inspector to scan newly created AMIs

If there were any new findings, an admin could be notified by email. Better still, SNS could post directly into a Slack channel.

This was an overview of some of the auditing and reporting components we might think about when building automation into our environments.

Summary

This chapter has given us an idea about some of the things we can achieve by automating common tasks. It's highlighted that automating the ecosystem is really driven by the tags you use to describe your resources. Your Lambda functions will make decisions based on these tags that might affect the way they are handled. From reading this chapter, you will be able to take the examples away to apply them in your own organizational context, but don't stop there. Find more areas where tagging could be useful, to really strengthen your automation capabilities!

In the next chapter, we are going to learn how serverless has changed the way we process data in the cloud.

Questions

1. What is a good thing to have before implementing continuous compliance?

    A) Lots of time
    B) Server-based infrastructure
    C) Backup strategy
    D) Resource tagging

2. Which AWS service continually monitors changes to your resources?

    A) AWS CloudTrail
    B) Amazon CloudWatch
    C) AWS Config
    D) AWS Lambda

3. What is not a valid compliance type for AWS Config evaluations?

    A) COMPLIANT
    B) NOT_APPLICABLE
    C) NON_COMPLIANT
    D) NOT_COMPLIANT
    E) INSUFFICIENT_DATA

4. Why are lifecycle hooks useful in Auto Scaling groups?

A) To run a custom action on an instance before it progresses to the next state
B) To cancel a lifecycle transition
C) To deploy a new version of an application

Further reading

- CIS Benchmarks: `https://www.cisecurity.org/cis-benchmarks/`
- Systems Manager Run Command: `https://docs.aws.amazon.com/systems-manager/latest/userguide/execute-remote-commands.html`

11
Creating Chatbots

Chatbots have become a new digital channel with which customers can engage with a product or service team. They are a form of self-service automation that uses natural language processing to help an organization scale operations and save cost. Chatbots present themselves on social media or other platforms in the same way as you'd send an instant message or interact with a real person. The goal of a chatbot is to understand what you are asking and perform actions that don't require human intervention.

AWS offers an artificial intelligence service called Amazon Lex where you can create and publish your own conversational bots. These bots can send events to AWS Lambda so that you can add business logic and integrations into your own systems.

Some common use cases for chatbots include customer service, IT operations, helpdesks, travel, and finance.

Chapter explores how to create a chatbot with native AWS services and then explores how to wrap a different chatbot into a project using the Serverless Framework.

In this chapter, we'll cover the following topics:

- Building a chatbot with Amazon Lex
- Building a Slackbot using Serverless Framework

Technical requirements

This chapter will introduce another AWS service and also build on the knowledge we acquired in Chapter 7, *Serverless Framework*. It would be helpful if you had experience using the following:

- The AWS console and CLI
- Slack (you will need admin access)
- Serverless Framework (this needs to be installed)

Building a chatbot with Amazon Lex

Amazon Lex is a fully managed service that uses artificial intelligence and natural language understanding to enable a conversational experience for users. Its text and speech understanding uses the same underlying technology that powers Amazon Alexa, while Amazon Polly provides the functionality for text-to-speech.

In the Lex console, you can configure your inputs in the language model to build your bots and then deploy them to multiple platforms, including mobile applications and social media platforms such as Facebook. Lex scales automatically behind the scenes and can handle many concurrent conversations. What's even better is that, over time, Lex learns how your users are interacting with the bot and can continuously improve the machine learning model to provide a better experience.

We're going to learn about language model concepts that are used by Amazon Lex in order to build, test, and publish a chatbot. Then, we will put our new knowledge into practice and build our own Lex chatbot!

Let's start by understanding the language model.

Understanding the language model

Instead of a programming model, in Lex we have a language model. This is a set of concepts and constructs that allows a user to program a conversational bot to react to requests, gather data, and respond with a meaningful answer.

We're about to run through three of these concepts to get a better understanding before we start building our own:

- Intents
- Utterances
- Responses

Intents

The bot that we create will have one or more intents. An intent is an interaction that you want to perform with the bot and is something that you want to do or make happen. You would expect the bot to respond to an intent by performing an action or providing some form of useful information.

When you're thinking about which intents to create for your bot, you should think about all of the actions on each of the entities that the user expects to interact with. For example, if you were creating a bot for an airline customer service desk, a caller would typically want to book a flight, update or cancel an existing flight, add bags, or check their air miles points balance. Therefore, you would want to give clear names to intents – `BookFlight`, `UpdateFlight`, `CancelFlight`, `AddBags`, and `CheckPointsBalance`. Intent names can't be changed later, so put some thought into your entity relationships upfront.

For each intent, we add a number of utterances and slots, which we will find out about next.

Utterances

Utterances are a list of sample phrases that the bot's user might say in order to invoke an intent. Within each intent, we add these utterances to help the bot map a user's request to the intent. These phrases help train the underlying machine learning model to make the bot smarter.

The smarter the model, the more effectively Lex will be able to match the phrase to an intent and the less likely it is you'll have to tell the user that you didn't understand the request. People coming from different backgrounds with different language characteristics and cultures will ask for things differently. It's good to add as many sample utterances as possible to cover the possibilities.

The following are some examples of sample utterances for our airline chatbot:

- `Book a flight for Tuesday`
- `Check the balance of my air miles points`
- `Add bags to my flight booking`
- `Check for available flights to Wellington on March 17`th

Slots can help extend utterances by creating variables that are populated by user inputs. We'll look at slots in the next subsection.

Slots

You may have noticed that in the preceding example utterances included some dates and a location. It would be great not to have to list every possible utterance for every location we want to fly to and every possible date combination. For this, we can use slots, which are parameters or variables that can be input by the user.

In the preceding examples, we can add new slots for the following variables:

- `Book a flight for {Date}`
- `Check for available flights to {City} on {Date}`

If we use those variables, then we can reuse our utterances for whatever the user chooses to input. With any variable, it's often a good idea to limit the number of valid answers or provide extra validation against an expected format. The purpose of this is to limit possible options to valid items, for example, valid cities. To achieve this, we can use slot types. Every slot has a slot type that can be a built-in or a custom type.

 Check the documentation for a current list of built-in slot types.

With the `City` and `Date` slots we have identified, we might pick the `AMAZON.City` and `AMAZON.DATE` built-in slot types. Each slot type has a different behavior for how the phrase logically maps to a value. For example, if we used the phrase `Book a flight for today`, the `Date` slot would map to `2019-10-31`, which is today's date (at the time of writing). This value would be passed on to our application logic in our fulfillment step (covered in the *Fulfillment* section).

So, if slots define the values that we need from the user, then we need a method to elicit any missing values that the user is going to provide. This is where prompts are helpful.

Prompts

Prompts are when the bot puts questions to the user in order to populate fields and parameters in slots. This information is required to complete the action asked in the intent. Prompts are really useful when it's not obvious to the user exactly what information needs to be provided. As we've learned already, an utterance may have a number of slots that need to be filled, and a prompt is a way of asking the user for those values.

In our airline example, if you ask `Can I book a flight?`, the bot doesn't magically know all of your travel intentions—more information is needed. In this example, a prompt back to the user for this intent might be as follows:

- `Where would you like to fly to?`
- `Which day would you like to fly on?`

Your bot may also include a prompt to confirm that the information the user has provided was actually what they intended to provide. This serves to sum up all the details you have provided during the conversation to make sure you are okay with the action that is about to take place. The following is an example of a confirmation prompt:

- `Okay, so you want to book a flight from Wellington to Auckland on November 4th at 7:30 am?`

When you respond with `yes`, that's when the language model hands over control to the application logic.

The application or business logic is also known as the fulfillment. This is the stage where the action from the intent is carried out. It's often a complex stage, so let's find out more about it.

Fulfillment

The fulfillment stage of the model is where we add integration to our own application logic. Activities in this stage might include further validation of the intent and then performing the action to fulfill or carry out the intent. Using our airline example again, when booking a flight, the fulfillment stage might include some of the following tasks:

- Check that the user is a valid traveler in the CRM system
- Update the flight booking ERP system
- Debit the user's credit card
- Send a confirmation email

Of course, the real-life process is much more complicated than this, but you get the idea.

We have a couple of options for the implementation of the fulfillment stage. These options are as follows:

- Return the intent response data to the client application for fulfillment
- Use a code hook to invoke a Lambda function

When Lex passes control to the Lambda fulfillment function, the function you specify is invoked with an event. This event is a JSON object that contains some contextual details about the conversation.

The following is a stripped-down example event that Lex uses to invoke the fulfillment function:

```
{
  "currentIntent": {
    "name": "BookFlight",
    "slots": {
      "originatingAirport": "Wellington",
      "destinationAirport": "Auckland"
    },
    "confirmationStatus": "None"
  },
  "bot": {
    "name": "AirlineChatbot",
    ...
  },
  "userId": "spatterson",
  "inputTranscript": "Text extract from the conversation",
  "invocationSource": "FulfillmentCodeHook"
}
```

You can see that it includes an object with the values of the slots. The confirmation status will be set if we have enabled that particular prompt, and additional valid values for that are Denied or Confirmed.

Lex also expects a callback with a particular response format so that it can update the conversation to let the user know the outcome of the fulfillment. We can reasonably expect a couple of scenarios from the fulfillment:

- Maybe all is well; the flight was booked successfully, so we should respond appropriately.
- There may have been an error during the fulfillment and we need to prompt for more information.

In both cases, we need to assemble a JSON object to respond with. This will tell Lex how to handle the next part of the conversation.

The basic structure of the response object begins as follows:

```
{
    "sessionAttributes": { ... },
    "recentIntentSummaryView": [{ ... }],
    "dialogAction": {
        "type": "ElicitIntent" | "ElicitSlot" | "ConfirmIntent" |
"Delegate" | "Close",
        ...
    }
}
```

The first two keys are optional and help maintain the conversation's context if needed. The third key, dialogAction, is required. This is a specific instruction to respond back to Lex with, and each different type has a specific object structure.

You can check the documentation for the exact structure, but I wanted to at least supply an explanation of each dialog type because it is important. The following are possible options for types of dialogAction:

- ElicitIntent: This prompts the user to say a phrase or use an utterance that includes an intent. I want to book a flight is not the same as I'm going on holiday, so we need to ask what the user would like to do.
- ElicitSlot: This tells Lex that there is a slot that we need a value for. With the I want to book a flight to Auckland utterance, the booking system needs a time or a date to make a valid booking, so we have to go back to the user for more information.
- ConfirmIntent: When you are looking for a yes or no confirmation from the user.
- Delegate: This is when you delegate the responsibility for what happens next in the conversation back to Lex.
- Close: This is the closing statement for the conversation and often confirm that the fulfillment was successful. It also tells Lex not to expect another response from the user. An example message would be: Thank you, your flight to Auckland has been booked.

This has given you a high-level introduction to the concepts involved. Next, we're going to build our own chatbot using Lex with Lambda as our fulfillment integration.

Building and testing your bot

In this section, we are going to create a simple bot that uses Lambda as a code hook integration. We'll continue with our airline customer service desk example and make a bot that can book a flight:

1. Jump into the Lex console, making sure you're in a supported region. If you haven't created a chatbot before, you will be presented with a welcome page.
2. Click **Get Started** and select **Custom bot**.
3. We're going to create the airline example we've been using throughout this section. Create the bot using the values shown in the following screenshot:

Creating a new bot

When you click **Create**, a service-linked IAM role is created for you with enough permissions to get you going. You're then presented with a screen with not much going on. A chatbot isn't much without at least one intent, so let's create one.

4. Click **Create Intent** and add one called `BookFlight`. Now, we have a blank form where we need to add our utterances, slots, and fulfillment integrations.

5. Let's start with the slots because we'll need them when we write our sample phrases. Use the following slots in your intent. I've used the `AMAZON.US_CITY` slot type for the locations and the `AMAZON.DATE` slot type for the time of the flight:

Slot configuration for an intent

You can also create your own custom slot type and populate it with valid cities, but we're not going to go into that in this example. For the prompts, you can optionally configure more prompts by clicking the **Settings** button on each slot. It is good to add a bit of variation into the conversation.

6. It's usually a good idea to ask for confirmation when we're doing something as important as booking a flight. Therefore, we should enable the **Confirmation prompt**. This is also where we get to use variables for our slots. Notice in the following screenshot that I have used the slot names as placeholders. The syntax for this uses curly braces around the slot name:

Enabling a confirmation prompt for an intent

7. You can keep Fulfillment set to **Return parameters to client** for now. We're going to go back later and connect it up to our Lambda function once we create it.

8. We're not finished yet, though. Let's circle back and add some sample utterances to our intent so that the bot understands more about which intent to match a phrase to. Notice that I've used slot placeholders here as well, and this time they automatically color-code themselves to make it easier for us to see them. I've gone with a range of phrases in order to cover each level of detail that we expect our airline users to include:

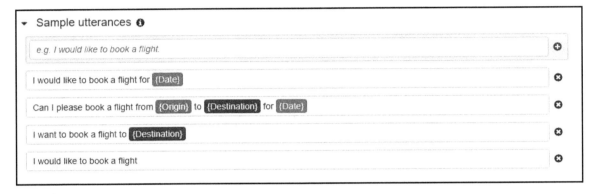

Adding utterances to an intent

We're almost ready to rock. The last thing we need to do is save the intent so that we can come back to the Lex console later to connect our Lambda function.

9. Hit **Save Intent** at the bottom of the page and then jump over to the Lambda console.

What we're going to do now is create a simple Lambda function that will respond to a fulfillment event generated by Lex. To keep it simple, all our function will do is respond with a Close fulfillment type. In a real chatbot, this is where you would include all the logic and integrations to book a flight in the airline's system. Let's get started:

1. Create a new function using a Node.js runtime.

2. Update the function code to the following. This code takes the slot values that were passed in the event during the invocation from Lex and sets them as session attributes. This is an optional step and we will find out more about session management later on in this chapter. `dialogAction` is where we create the response format that Lex will be looking for. Here, you can see we have used the `Close` type, which will let Lex know that the conversation has come to an end:

```
exports.handler = async (event) => {
  let res = {
    "sessionAttributes": {
      "destination": event.currentIntent.slots.Destination,
      "origin": event.currentIntent.slots.Origin,
      "date": event.currentIntent.slots.Date
    },
    "dialogAction": {
      "type": "Close",
      "fulfillmentState": "Fulfilled",
      "message": {
        "contentType": "PlainText",
        "content": "We have booked your flight from " +
event.currentIntent.slots.Origin+ " to " +
event.currentIntent.slots.Destination+ " on " +
event.currentIntent.slots.Date
}}} return res;  };
```

3. Once you've saved this function, head back to the Lex console and find your `AmazonianAirways` chatbot. Now, we need to add our new function as a fulfillment integration for the `BookFlight` intent:

Connecting the fulfillment stage to a Lambda function

4. Now that everything has been connected, go ahead and click **Build** on the top right of the console. This will build the model behind the scenes and also initialize the chatbot in the same console screen so that we can test it.

5. It will take a few moments to build. Let's test it using the dialog box that pops up from the right-hand side of the screen:

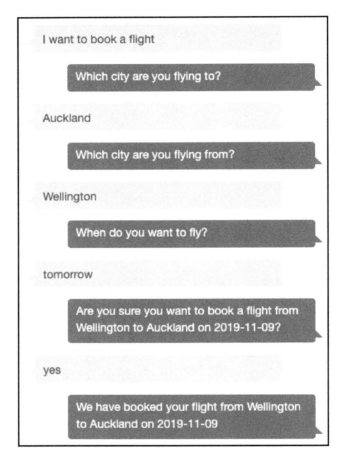

Testing the bot using the Lex console

Our bot works! If we wanted to improve our experience even more, we could respond with a more readable date. So, now that you know how to create a conversational bot, can you think of a use for one?

In the next section, I will introduce a different type of bot that can help automate operational tasks just like another member of your team.

Building a Slackbot using Serverless Framework

In the previous section, we learned how to create a very basic chatbot for an airline. In this section, we will explore a different sort of use case where a chatbot would be extremely useful – and this time, we're not going to use Lex.

ChatOps is a term that's used when operational tasks are driven from a conversational platform. It is focused on people collaborating around a particular workflow or process, and a bot can often streamline the automation that's involved. Introducing a bot to the platform that you're collaborating on means that you don't have to break out of your working environment and disrupt your thought process to go and gather facts. This means the team can be much more efficient in investigating and resolving the incident at hand.

If development and support teams are centralizing all of their conversations within a particular chat channel, then it makes sense for a bot to exist as just another team member. For all intents and purposes, a bot looks like another use in a chat channel. The bot can be silent until it is asked a question or asked to carry out a task. Alternatively, it can regularly ping the channel with notifications.

An example could be when a site reliability engineering team is working on a networking issue. They are troubleshooting, gathering facts, and investigating the incident, all while going back to their collaboration platform to share findings. In this situation, you might ask a bot, `What are the open ports on instance i-123456789abcdef0?`. The bot would go away and query security groups attached to that instance and then respond with the open ports. Alternatively, it could ask for more information, such as clarifying whether the user wanted ingress or egress ports, or both.

A popular Software-as-a-Service collaboration platform used by many teams across the world is Slack. Collaboration spaces are divided into channels that hold users, files, conversations, and other things. Slack is very extensible, so it's possible to connect other tools to complement the work you are doing. There's already a large number of tools and services that integrate with Slack.

What we will be learning in this section is how to pull together tools we know about—Serverless Framework, API Gateway, and Lambda—to create a new integration for Slack. We'll create a bot that can perform optional tasks right from a chat channel.

First and foremost, we need to understand what we're gearing up for, which will be covered in the next section.

Understanding the architecture

Because Lex is not involved in this architecture, we won't have the luxury of natural language understanding, so we will need to be quite particular about how we ask things from our bot. This makes our bot follow a rule-based response model, where inputs are mapped to outputs. Using Lex would give you more artificial intelligence—inputs are mapped to intents instead of a predefined response. It's important to be aware of the difference and use the method that's most suitable for your use case.

In the following architecture diagram, you can see we are making use of the Event and Web APIs from Slack. Events are posted to our API Gateway, which invokes a Lambda function. The function performs the bot application logic and posts the response back to the Slack Web API:

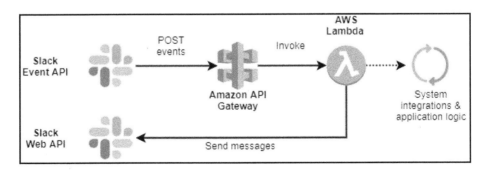

High-level architecture

Now that we understand what we are about to build, we'll go through the steps in the next section.

Deploying a Slackbot

To write and deploy our Slackbot, we are going to use Serverless Framework. This is quite suitable because, as you saw in the architecture diagram, we're essentially only building an API that has a different use case. We'll also need to create some integration points for our chatbot service that will be triggered and respond to Slack, so let's do that first.

When asked, our bot's brain is going to respond with a list of ingress ports that are open on a given EC2 instance. For this to work, the brain needs to check the security groups connected to the instance, assemble a list of open ingress ports, and respond appropriately.

Registering a new Slack app

In order to connect up our intended service to Slack, we need to register a bot app.

 An app is a construct in Slack whereby you can extend its standard functionality and incorporate your own logic.

To register an app, we need to use the developer console that Slack provides. We're doing this so that we can set up triggers within our Slack group that will create events for our bot to respond to. Let's get started:

1. Head over to `https://api.slack.com/` and create a new app. If you're new to Slack, you will need to create a workspace first. I've created a bot called `ConfigBot` that will be used to query for configuration items in the AWS accounts that our fake team manages.
2. After creating our first app, we need to add a bot user. This will generate some credentials for our service so that it can authenticate users. Take note of these because we will need them later.
3. Next, we need to install the app into our Slack workspace; you can find the **Install** button on the dashboard of the app page. Take note of the Bot User OAuth Access Token value because we'll need that later as well.

4. Finally, we need to add an event that this app is subscribed to. We are going to choose `app_mention event` so that our app can respond accordingly. Here's where you can find the event subscription settings:

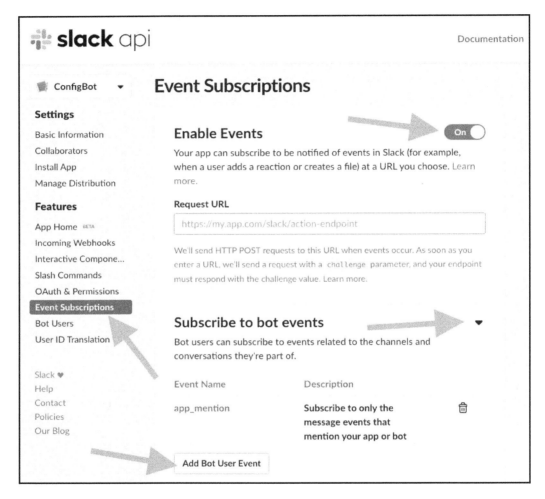

Adding an event subscription to our bot app in the Slack API console (https://api.slack.com)

That's all for now. We'll come back to these settings to complete the setup process after we've created our bot service in the next section.

Crafting the bot's brain

To build the AWS components for this service, we will use the Serverless Framework. Let's fire up our `sls` commands and get into it:

1. First, create the service. For this example, we will use Node.js, but feel free to use another runtime if you prefer:

   ```
   sls create
       --template aws-nodejs
       --path serverless-configbot
   ```

2. Then, we need to get our `serverless.yml` file into shape. All we need for now is a function with an endpoint that Slack can make API calls to using the POST method:

   ```
   service: serverless-configbot

   provider:
     name: aws
     runtime: nodejs10.x

   functions:
     configbot-brain:
       handler: handler.configbotbrain
       events:
         - http:
             path: events
             method: post
   ```

Next, we need to create the brain for configbot. Our `sls` command has already created a `handler.js` file with some boilerplate code in it, so let's reuse that to add our functionality. In this example, instead of giving you the complete Lambda function to use, I'm going to give you snippets that you might want to add. I'll leave it up to you to find the best way to piece those together, but just be aware that these snippets won't work independently.

The first thing our Lambda should do is find out the identifiers of the security groups that are attached to our given instance. We can do this quite simply with the following function. This returns a resolved promise with the output of the `describeInstances` method from the EC2 API:

```
const getInstance = (instance) => {

  return new Promise(resolve => {
    let params = {
```

```
        InstanceIds: [ instance ]
    }

    ec2.describeInstances(params, (e, data) => {
      if(e) console.log(e, e.stack);
      else resolve(data)
    })
  });
};
```

Then, we need to query the rules within the attached security group. For simplicity, my code assumes there is only one security group attached to the instance, but you can easily extend the example code in the future. The ports that are specified in each rule within the security group are added to an array and returned as a resolved promise. This function uses the describeSecurityGroups method from the EC2 API:

```
const getPorts = (securitygroups) => {
  return new Promise(resolve => {
    let params = { GroupIds: [ securitygroups ] };
    ec2.describeSecurityGroups(params, (e, data) => {
      if(e) console.log(e, e.stack);
      else {
        let rules = data.SecurityGroups[0].IpPermissions;
        let ports = [];
        rules.forEach(rule => {
          if(rule.FromPort == rule.ToPort) ports.push(rule.FromPort)
          else {
            let range = rule.FromPort + "-" + rule.ToPort;
            ports.push(range)
          }
      }); resolve(ports) } }) });
```

Awesome – so that completes our custom logic part of the brain. Now, we need to add some functionality so that we can communicate with our Slack app.

Remember those credentials that we created in the Slack console earlier? Now, we're going to build a validation step in to our function code so that Slack knows we're a trusted party.

Connecting our bot to Slack

Back in the Slack console, under the **Event Subscriptions** page, we will add the endpoint of our chatbot API to the **Request URL** field. In the following, you can see we are receiving a 500 error:

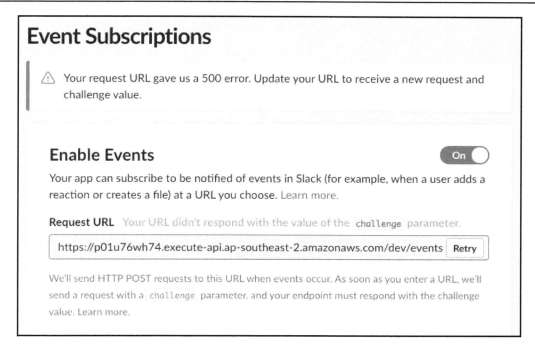

Adding a request URL resulting in an error

This happens because, when we subscribe to events, Slack will send a URL verification object to the request URL. Our code doesn't cater for this yet, so we need to add that as a feature. The object that Slack sends for verification looks like this:

```
{
    "token":"GveYU40cwJ3NPGNM4MnVYHEe",
    "challenge":"Bo0A0QRp5Z7lUILCWfIA284rCQ32cyAkfADRyVNQRopVb2HIutgv",
    "type":"url_verification"
}
```

What our function code needs to do is respond with the plaintext value of the challenge key. The key changes every time you retry the validation, so you shouldn't need to store this anywhere. The idea of this challenge is to provide the other side of our handshake so that Slack knows that our endpoint is legitimate. You can find more details on this in the link in the *Further reading* section.

Once you've responded to the URL verification handshake, you can continue to subscribe to events. The one we are interested in is the `app_mention` event. This will trigger an event to be sent to our API method with all of the details of the mention.

A mention in Slack is when you address someone directly using @, followed by their username.

What we want our bot to do is respond to a question such as `Hey @configbot, what are the open ports fori-06dd90c34b8f87d76?`. Every time we use the @ mention, our endpoint will receive an event with contextual information about the mention (who it was from, what the text was, when the time was, and so on).

Once we've got the details coming in, we can pull out the requested instance ID to look up security groups and find the open ports. Then, we need to send those details by making a request to the Slack Web API.

To make it easier to do this, Slack has a nice Node.js SDK that we can use. Import it at the top of your function using the following command:

```
const Slack = require('slack');
```

You'll also need to install the package in your working directory using the Node Package Manager:

```
npm install @slack/web-api
```

To use SDK to post a new chat message, use the following function:

```
const sendSlackMessage = (channel, message) => {
    let params = {
        token: process.env.BOT_TOKEN,
        channel: channel,
        text: messgage
    }

    return Slack.chat.postMessage(params);
}
```

In the params object in the preceding function, you will notice that the token key has a value of `process.env.BOT_TOKEN`. This means that the function will look for the value of this in the `BOT_TOKEN` environment variable. We need to provide our bot user's OAuth token as a parameter for the `postMessage` function to authenticate properly.

This value should be kept secret, so where should we store it? I've chosen to store mine in the Amazon Systems Manager Parameter store under a parameter I named `slack_bot_token`. Now, we can add a reference to this in our `serverless.yml` file so that we don't have to store secrets directly in source control. Add the following to your function configuration in `serverless.yml`. At deploy time, the Serverless Framework will pull this parameter and add it as an environment variable for our Lambda function to use:

```
environment:
    BOT_TOKEN: ${ssm:slack_bot_token}
```

Remember to run another deployment after you make this change.

Let's test this out in Slack. I've created a new channel called `#application-support` and invited our old friend `@configbot`. When I ask the question, I get a response right away, and I can see the open ports on my instance. Nice!

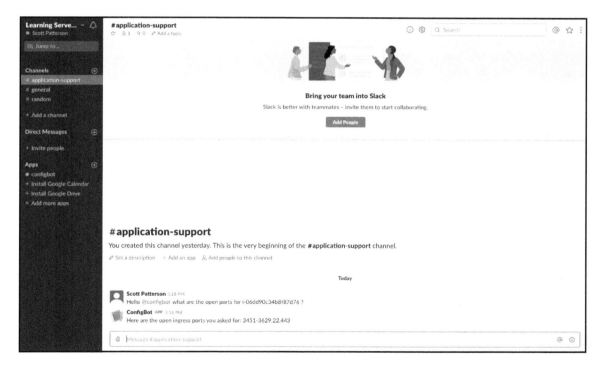

Testing configbot in a channel in Slack

Now that we have the brain as a base, we can extend our configbot so that it's smarter and can respond to more things.

That concludes this section, where we learned about what a rules-based bot can do and how they can be used to assist operations activities. We also learned how to create an integration with Slack. We will be able to use this knowledge to build new functionality in our chat channels.

Summary

This concludes our chapter on chatbots, where we learned about two common use cases. In the first use case, we created a bot using Amazon Lex, which uses artificial intelligence to provide natural language understanding. This experience was very conversational and with the comprehensive dialog model, it was easy to see just how extensible the Lex platform is.

The second use case showed us how we can automate command-type tasks using a bot to gather facts or perform actions. Integrating this type of bot into our current ways of working is really useful but does require more programming to get right.

In the next chapter, we will explore another set of serverless components that have redefined how we host static web applications.

Questions

1. Which service provides natural language understanding using artificial intelligence?

   A) Amazon Polly
   B) AWS Lambda
   C) Amazon Rekognition
   D) Amazon Lex

2. In a Lex-based bot, what are we attempting to match a user's question to?

   A) Another question
   B) An intent
   C) A wish
   D) A prompt

3. Which dialog action type do we use when we need more information?

    A) ElicitSlot
    B) Close
    C) Delegate
    D) ElicitIntent
    E) ConfirmIntent

4. Amazon Lex can invoke Lambda functions for fulfillment.

    A) True
    B) False

5. What type of bot is a Slackbot?

    A) AI bot
    B) Rule-based bot
    C) Command bot

6. Which type of authentication mechanism does Slack use for bots?

    A) SAML
    B) Basic
    C) Kerberos
    D) OAuth

Further reading

- Built-in slot types for Lex utterances: `https://docs.aws.amazon.com/lex/latest/dg/howitworks-builtins-slots.html`
- Lambda input events and response types: `https://docs.aws.amazon.com/lex/latest/dg/lambda-input-response-format.html`
- Responding with the Slack challenge value: `https://api.slack.com/events/url_verification`
- A detailed guide on bot users: `https://api.slack.com/bot-users`

12
Hosting Single-Page Web Applications

We've made it this far through this book, and we know the basics and some useful tips. Let's look at a real-life use case for serverless. In this chapter, we'll introduce a modern way to build and host web applications using serverless architectures components. Ease of deployment, limitless scalability, and cost-efficiency are just a few of the benefits you can expect from adopting this pattern. Keep reading to find out how to deploy a basic example.

We'll cover the following topics:

- Understanding serverless **Single-Page Applications** (**SPAs**) on AWS
- Building SPAs with Serverless Framework

Technical requirements

This chapter will follow a high-level architecture of a single-page web application, so it would be prudent if you had a good understanding of frontend and backend web development and how the tiers relate to each other. You should also be putting your architect hat on to understand the bigger picture and how this pattern might fit into the context of your organization.

Understanding serverless SPAs on AWS

Serverless SPAs are the new 3-tier architecture for websites. If you've already had experience with them, then you'll know how easy they are to deploy and release changes to. If you're a frontend developer, then you can finally take control of the infrastructure, and have the website code sitting in the same repository existing as one stack. If you haven't yet needed to use a serverless SPA, this is an introduction to the components involved.

We'll first cover the architecture pattern in order to understand it from a high level, then have a deeper look into the components involved. We'll finish by learning how to build an SPA using Serverless Framework.

The architecture

A SPA is a client application that runs entirely in the browser. The web apps load into a single HTML file (or fragments of it), which loads JavaScript and CSS to enable a reactive experience. The browser can then use Ajax to send and receive data from the server and update the view without reloading.

Here's an example of how a client application and server interact through Ajax:

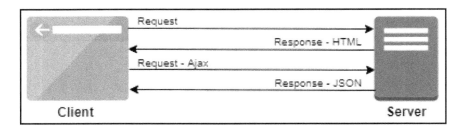

Client/server communication with Ajax

The benefit here is that, without the constant reloading, we get better performance, making for a better overall user experience.

In the serverless world, we split out the traditional server component into two main components:

- The **hosting** components provide our static HTML through a distribution network, backed by S3 storage.
- The **API** component provides the dynamic content through a RESTful interface.

Splitting the components allows us to logically separate the code base as well. Now, there is a clear definition between the frontend code and the backend code. The deployment of new frontend code is simply a copy into the S3 bucket that is storing the HTML, and potentially a cache invalidation request sent to CloudFront.

The following is a high-level diagram of how we represent the frontend and backend components using serverless services:

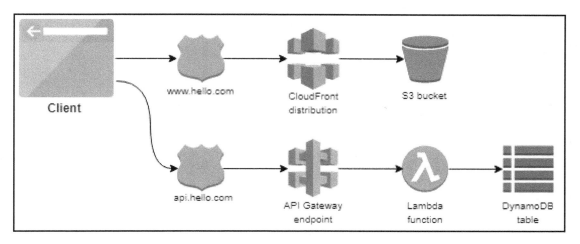

A web application using serverless components

By using API Gateway and Lambda as the backend for our SPA, we can obviate the need for a server altogether. If we need to save some state or add persistence, we can use Amazon DynamoDB as well. Because these services are serverless, we're only paying for them when our website is in use and so the cost of development can dramatically reduce.

Okay, so there are some circumstances where you would need to add some server infrastructure to your solution, such as if you were serving up specific dynamic content or performing server-side rendering of the fully structured HTML. If you find yourself in that situation, the SPA pattern does support being extended by adding a traditional server tier. We can add an application load balancer fronting an EC2 auto scaling group, and add the routes accordingly using our CloudFront distribution. The root path still makes its way to the S3 bucket, while everything under /traditional is routed to the load balancer fronting the server components and relational database.

The following is our new route (`/traditional`), which is required to provide some specific dynamic content that can't be delivered by API Gateway. The backend application is running on EC2 instances in an auto scaling group, and they all have access to data stored in an **Relational Database Service** (**RDS**) database:

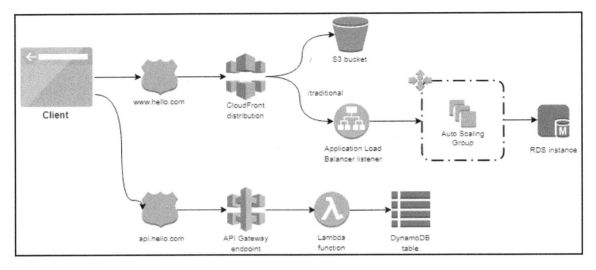

Combining traditional web application patterns with serverless components

So, now we've seen a high-level overview of the architecture, let's drill into some of the components and see what considerations we need to give for each.

The components

It's really easy to set up an SPA using serverless components on AWS. We've already learned about how to set up a serverless API backend, so let's go over the frontend components to find out the function that they are performing.

By understanding each component independently, we'll then be able to introduce a framework that takes care of setting up all of the things. Let's start by learning about the components in the next sections.

Amazon S3

First up is Amazon S3. This is where we store all of the static content, including the images, web pages, style sheets, JavaScript files, and any other content such as PDFs. Website hosting is a feature that you can enable in an S3 bucket, so this component replaces the need to run something such as Apache HTTPD or NGINX on web servers combined with a load balancer.

To enable static hosting, you can run this command on an existing bucket. This will enable the website hosting feature and configure S3 to load a particular HTML file for the index and error pages:

```
aws s3 website s3://hello-website/
    --index-document index.html
    --error-document error.html
```

Alternatively, you can find the options to enable website hosting in the properties of the bucket in the console. The following screenshot shows the different options to configure the index and error document locations in the console:

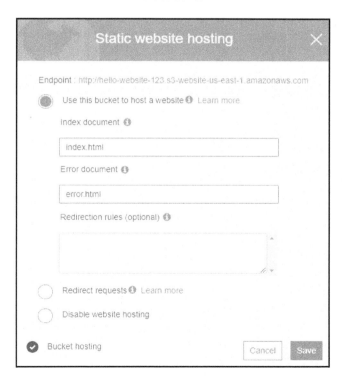

S3 website hosting configuration

All we need to do is indicate which file is served up by default (the index document). We also need to open up public access to the bucket and add a bucket policy.

The key to a performant web application is the content delivery network. We need to add one of these in front of our S3 bucket to enable caching at edge locations and provide extra functionality for management and routing. In AWS, the best component to use would be Amazon CloudFront, which we will cover next.

Amazon CloudFront

Let's move on to Amazon CloudFront now. This is our content distribution network and edge caching layer. We use this to publish the web app to the internet, and additionally to provide a higher level of routing flexibility. What we need here is a web distribution that routes to our S3 bucket. This is where we might add a route to a traditional hosting pattern if we needed one of those. It would look something like the following, with the /alternative path routing to an origin that is backed by a load balancer.

The following is a screenshot from the CloudFront console showing two routes, one that is the default route going to our S3 bucket, and the other is routing to an application load balancer. The second is only needed if we're building in a traditional server stack to the pattern:

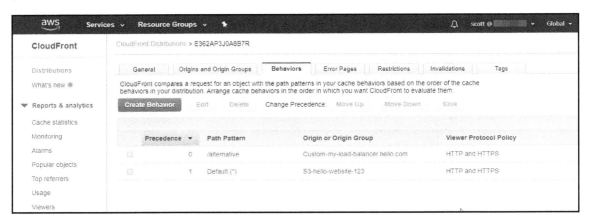

CloudFront distribution routing behaviors

When creating your distribution, it can take around 15 minutes to deploy to all of the CloudFront edge locations. If you make any subsequent changes, these also need to propagate to the edge locations.

It's important to note here that you should use the S3 web hosting URL in the **Origin Domain Name** field. The console will attempt to auto complete to the bucket name, but you don't want that.

It's a good idea to use object versioning in your S3 bucket location if you are often deploying changes to existing objects. This will inform CloudFront to update the copy in the cache and replicate around to the edge locations. If you're not using object versioning, you can also force cache invalidation manually using the following command:

```
aws cloudfront create-invalidation
    --distribution E3HCM3F21RZ42L
    --paths "/*"
```

There are some specific limits around how many files you can invalidate at once. You also get 1,000 manual invalidation requests for free and, after that, you pay per 1,000 requests.

Once we have the frontend set up, there are some more requirements that our client needs to render the website. Let's explore the backend options next.

Backend services

For our backend, we've chosen to go with a RESTful interface using API Gateway, Lambda, and DynamoDB. We're already familiar with deploying these services from earlier in Chapter 4, *Adding Amazon API Gateway*, and Chapter 5, *Leveraging AWS Services*. What we also need here is to add Route 53 so that we have a public DNS record that matches our domain.

We could also add some identity functionality with Cognito—if we had data related specifically to a user, we might want to protect that endpoint to validate the identity of the requestor. This would be set up as an authorizer for API Gateway to match a valid **JSON Web Token (JWT)** with a user, and to implement login and sign up flow.

For DynamoDB, if our request load was significant and consistently hitting a particular table or tables, we could investigate using **DynamoDB Accelerator (DAX)**. This is a caching layer for DynamoDB that can reduce the latency of our queries—in some cases, down to the microsecond.

And that's all we need to get going. The components here will allow us how to scale to millions of users without any significant input from administrators. There are also now more options than ever to represent these components as code, in a single framework. We'll have a look at one option from a high level.

Building SPAs with Serverless Framework

As well as building and maintaining the resources and configurations with CloudFormation, the CLI, or in the console directly, we can also manage the components in the Serverless Framework. To make it even easier, we can leverage the serverless SPA plugin:

1. To install it, this time, we're going to use the serverless `install` command to create the new service. That's because this command has an option to input a URL, and we're going to input a URL that contains a boilerplate structure for an SPA project. Have a look at the following command:

```
sls install
    --url
https://github.com/serverless/examples/tree/master/aws-node-single-
page-app-via-cloudfront
    --name hello-website
```

   What this command does is seed our service with the configuration we need to get started.

2. After running the command, have a look at the `serverless.yml` file to view all of the resources that will be created.
3. The minimum configuration you need to do is update the S3 bucket key with your bucket name.
4. When you deploy the service using the `sls deploy` command, it might take 15 minutes or so for the CloudFront distribution to replicate around the edge locations.

The plugin also comes with a useful command to upload your files to the S3 bucket. You can use this command to sync the directory called `app` in your project space to S3.

Once you have deployed your SPA service, try the following command to push your content to S3. This simple process can be used as a content deployment mechanism, and there are no other services that need to be configured or restarted for the deployment to take effect:

```
sls syncToS3
```

You can use this command any time you need to deploy new or updated content into your bucket.

It's as easy as that! In this section, we learned the basics of creating an SPA project with Serverless Framework. There aren't many steps to it, so it should be clear how easy it is to get started building your own SPA on AWS.

Summary

This chapter was a quick introduction into a use case for how to use serverless components to host a single-page web application. There are a lot of configurations and options for hosting your own serverless SPA, and it's great that we can again use Serverless Framework to consolidate our technology stacks into one project.

In the next chapter, we're going to introduce an emerging type of API that can help with making API calls from the frontend easier.

Questions

1. What does S3 replace in a modern serverless SPA architecture?

   A) Databases
   B) Web servers
   C) Application servers
   D) Cache

2. Traditional server-based solutions can still be used in this architecture:

   A) True
   B) False

3. API Gateway and Lambda are used to provide what to the client?

   A) Static content
   B) Connectivity to a database
   C) Dynamic content
   D) System integration

Further reading

- *Mastering JavaScript Single Page Application Development*: https://www.packtpub.com/web-development/mastering-javascript-single-page-application-development

13
GraphQL APIs

For website frontends and mobile applications, RESTful APIs have long been the method of implementing the presentation tier to serve up dynamic content. This layer, often referred to by developers as the experience layer, relies heavily on reliable and low latency endpoints and adherence to strict interface specifications. REST is doing a great job at providing these services but it is not without challenges.

Now there is a new technology called GraphQL, which was originally developed by Facebook. Since a public launch in 2015, there has been wide adoption from several large organizations such as GitHub, Airbnb, and Twitter. GraphQL is a type and query specification that is optimized for fetching and manipulating data. It was designed to provide exactly the right amount of data and in the format that the client requested. The technology exposes a single endpoint to query and interact with data instead of the verb words defined in REST.

In this chapter, we will touch on the basics of GraphQL and introduce a managed serverless service. You should come away with an understanding of what GraphQL is and be ready to start experimenting with your own APIs.

We'll cover the following topics:

- The core concepts of GraphQL
- Two approaches to building a GraphQL API

Technical requirements

This chapter is focused on APIs specifically made for frontend clients. You should have an understanding of the following:

- You should know about web development or experience layer APIs.
- It would also help if you have developed RESTful APIs before and are looking to expand your options.

Introduction to GraphQL

GraphQL is the new way of developing APIs intended for use with web applications and mobile needing low latency communication to data sources. To clear up a common confusion, when we are talking about GraphQL, we are talking about the query language and communication protocol and not referring to graph databases.

Let's quickly run through some of the concepts and benefits before moving on.

Core concepts

GraphQL is not a database, nor a library. Simply put, it is a runtime combined with a language for querying and accessing the backend data. We use it mostly to implement experience layer APIs where the response can match only the data that is needed by the client. It's really good when you need the data to drive the user interface, like when you have a data structure that multiple users are making changes to and you need to make updates to the view in real time.

The client sends queries that are evaluated against a predefined schema, which is a type system created and designed by ourselves. This defines what is possible for users to query, similar to an interface specification. It's here where you define all of the fields and data types available.

Here's an example of a simple schema. The schema shows two object types defined—Hello and User:

```
type Hello {
    user: User
}

type User {
    id: ID
    name: String
    age: Int
}
```

A schema defines the relationships between types. In the preceding example, every Hello object has User. There are five categories of types in a GraphQL schema:

- **Scalar**: This is a primitive type such as an integer or a Boolean.
- **Object**: This is a collection of fields that can be either a scalar type or another object type.

- **Query**: This defines the possible read queries that a client can perform against the data.
- **Mutation**: This defines the possible write queries that a client can perform against the data.
- **Input**: This is a special type that allows you to pass arguments, parameters, or other objects to queries and mutations.

The schema itself is an abstraction from the underlying infrastructure implementation so it does not define where or how the data is stored.

The schema also supports native versioning and that is another big benefit over REST. Instead of versioning the endpoint, it's more focused on managing individual fields. You can add fields with no impact on the consumers, but you still need to be careful about maintaining backward compatibility. There's a @deprecated directive that can mark fields that are no longer used, which is cool.

With an inherent filtering function in the queries, you can just ask for what you want in your request. This cuts down the over- or under-fetching tendency that you get with REST. A query is a read operation and allows a client to ask for the exact data it needs, in the structure that it wants. Here's an example query following the preceding schema.

The (very basic) query language shown in the following code is passed during the request and is querying for the name field within the User object that the Hello object has a relationship with:

```
{
    hello {
        name
    }
}
```

The preceding could return some JSON like this:

```
{
  "hello": {
    "name": "Scott Patterson"
  }
}
```

The runtime or engine behind the query language parses your query into a graph, and then uses each node in the graph to run resolvers to fetch the data from the source. Resolvers are functions and templates that interface with data sources. Each resolver represents one field of the data, and the resolver function knows how to retrieve that field from each data source. An example of a data source could be a database table, a cache, or even a RESTful API.

We've covered reading data, but how about writing? A mutation is a GraphQL write operation, much like PUT, POST, or DELETE. They are the things that a user can do with your data.

An example using our schema could look like the following. It's almost the same as a query, but this time we've added an input type to simplify the syntax:

```
type Mutation {
    createUser(data: CreateUserInput): User!
}

input CreateUserInput {
    name: String
    age: Int
}
```

And to run that in the query language would be as follows:

```
mutation makeAHelloUser {
    createUser(
        name: "Scott Patterson"
        age: 10000
    ) {
        name
        age
    }
}
```

So, there are the basic concepts of the query language, queries, mutations, and the schema. Next, we're going to move on and introduce a managed GraphQL service that we can use to create our own APIs.

Building GraphQL APIs

This chapter wouldn't be complete without first exploring what our options are for implementing a GraphQL API in AWS. GraphQL fits perfectly with serverless components, so we're going to see a birds-eye view of implementing GraphQL with Lambda, and then introduce a fully managed GraphQL service.

By the end of this section, you'll have a better understanding of what an implementation looks like and be ready to get started on your own development tutorials.

Lambda-backed endpoint

You can actually use a combination of API Gateway and Lambda to implement a GraphQL API. Within API Gateway, create a proxy endpoint with one route: `/graphql`. The following diagram shows that it looks much the same as the API Gateway and Lambda combination that we're already used to:

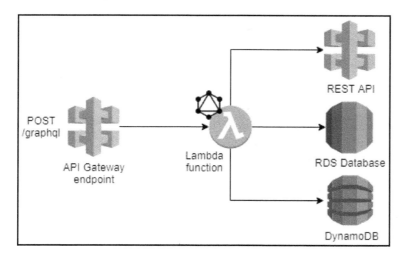

Non-REST-compliant API that exposes an endpoint with a /graphql route

This endpoint will send requests with the POST verb to the backend lambda for processing. Queries and mutations will be parsed and converted into the data source's native query language—whether that be SQL or an AWS SDK request.

In Node.js, there's a package called graphql that will be crucial to implementing the Lambda. In Python, there is a library called Graphene. And in Java, there is GraphQL Java. As usual, there's also a plugin for the Serverless Framework with a heap of features supported.

It's a lot of work to implement this by yourself in Lambda, even with the frameworks available. You need to write your own resolver and interfaces to your data sources. Luckily, there's an easier way.

Next, we will introduce you to a managed service that will streamline your graph implementation.

Using an AWS-managed service

This chapter is really about introducing you to AWS AppSync, the fully managed serverless GraphQL service. By all means, you can implement your own graphql runtime using Lambda compute, but why would you when there is one built and maintained for you? Using AppSync allows you to focus more on building the application, rather than the infrastructure.

AppSync provides one controlled API endpoint that you POST your operations to. It's a little different from the resource-based URLs that you might be used to in REST. The endpoint is reliable and scalable and supports WebSockets for real-time event-driven APIs.

The following diagram shows how the new implementation looks when using AppSync. You can see that our API Gateway endpoint and backing Lambda have been replaced by AWS AppSync:

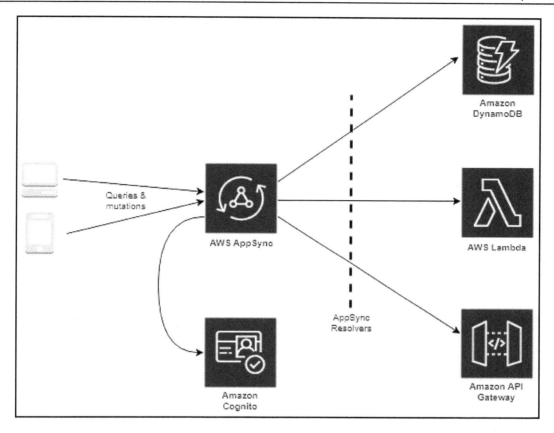

Implementation of a GraphQL API using AppSync

AppSync comes with managed resolvers that can natively communicate with several AWS services and other REST endpoints. As a GraphQL developer, you provide templates written in **VTL** (short for **Velocity Templating Language**) that map the requests and responses to the appropriate fields. These mapping templates are actually powerful enough that you can implement custom business logic to transform the fields during the mapping.

AppSync, of course, gives you a place to create your own schema, or import an existing one. Also, don't forget your security. AppSync integrates with Cognito User Pools (or any OpenID Connect provider) so you can use `jwt` tokens with your requests. You can even go one step further and define in your schema which groups of users in Cognito are allowed to run each query or mutation. So, that brings native authentication and authorization into your GraphQL schema—that's cool.

Once set up, the basic flow of data looks like this:

- The frontend makes an HTTP POST request to our AppSync API endpoint.
- AppSync uses our GraphQL schema to validate the request.
- AppSync uses our request mapping template to map the request to our data source.
- Data is fetched from the data source.
- AppSync uses our response mapping template to map the response from our data source to fields in the API.
- The frontend receives an HTTP response from our AppSync API.

The AppSync service was designed to simplify the setup required for a frontend developer needing backend infrastructure. Where the service shines is the amount of time it takes to spin up a streamlined CRUD API for backend data sources such as DynamoDB.

That was a brief introduction to AppSync; hopefully, it is clear that it is much simpler to use a managed service to implement your GraphQL runtime.

Check out the *Further reading* section for getting started tutorials.

Summary

In this chapter, we learned about another form of API that we can use for developing mobile applications and web application frontends. We reviewed two methods of implementation, both with varying degrees of flexibility and management. After reading this chapter, you should now have the knowledge to get started experimenting or following a tutorial that steps you through the setup process.

Thank you for reading this book through to the final chapter! I hope you have learned many new skills using serverless and that your brain is so full that you can't wait to start implementing some of your ideas. Here is an overview of what we have covered throughout the chapters:

- Understanding the evolution of compute and how the function came about
- Introduction to the event-driven mindset behind serverless and cloud computing
- Learning about how functions as a service work in AWS using Lambda, including a deep dive into the more advanced topics
- Adding API Gateway to our solutions to enable more management and control
- Using Serverless Framework to manage the lifecycle of our serverless projects, and then learning about how to integrate this workflow into a CI/CD pipeline

- Finding out how AWS has enabled a different breed of automation
- How to run ETL processes to move and transform data in AWS
- Building our own chatbots that integrate with other tools
- How to host a serverless single-page web application
- Learning about GraphQL APIs and how they can benefit our frontends

The time now is yours: go build something awesome!

Questions

1. What are good uses of GraphQL?

   A) Web application frontends
   B) Mobile applications
   C) Facade for any AWS service
   D) All of the above

2. How many endpoints does AppSync create for an API?

   A) An endpoint for every data source
   B) An endpoint for every entity or node
   C) As many as you like
   D) Only one

3. What is the resolver template written in?

   A) JSON
   B) YAML
   C) VTL
   D) SQL

4. What is a write operation in GraphQL?

   A) POST
   B) PUT
   C) Mutation

Further reading

- GraphQL with Serverless Framework: `https://github.com/serverless/serverless-graphql`
- Adding GraphQL to your project using Amplify: `https://aws-amplify.github.io/docs/js/api`
- AWS AppSync quick start: `https://docs.aws.amazon.com/appsync/latest/devguide/quickstart.html`
- Resolver mapping template reference: `https://docs.aws.amazon.com/appsync/latest/devguide/resolver-mapping-template-reference-programming-guide.html`

Assessment

Chapter 1: The Evolution of Compute

1. C) Functions
2. D) All of the above
3. A) Minutes or hours
4. C) The amount of available CPU and memory

Chapter 2: Event-Driven Applications

1. D) All of the above
2. C) Enterprise Application Integration
3. A) Message broker
4. A) Event-command

Chapter 3: The Foundations of a Function in AWS

1. C) Functions as a Service (FaaS)
2. A) CPU cores
3. G) All of the above
4. B) Use environment aliases to point to a particular version
5. D) The execution role doesn't allow access to the bucket
6. A) The request concurrency limit has been exceeded

Chapter 4: Adding Amazon API Gateway

1. C) Public
2. A) True
3. C) Amazon Cognito
4. A) Caching D) Throttling requests
5. E) All of the above

Chapter 5: Leveraging AWS Services

1. D) Intelligent tiering
2. D) All of the above
3. B) 1,000 records
4. A) True
5. C) Step Functions

Chapter 6: Going Deeper with Lambda

1. D) Custom runtime
2. B) Lambda layers
3. B) 1,000
4. A) AWS Secrets Manager
5. D) Service
6. C) HTTP 429

Chapter 7: Serverless Framework

1. C) Share the same bounded context
2. D) All of the above
3. A) CloudFormation templates
4. A) True
5. D) Node.js

Chapter 8: CI/CD with the Serverless Framework

1. C) Using stages
2. B) Canary
3. A) Source
4. D) All of the above
5. D) The IAM role running the build doesn't have access to the artifact bucket
6. A) Time To Live (TTL) value on the DNS record

Chapter 9: Data Processing

1. C) Streaming
2. B) False
3. D) Both A and B
4. C) Parquet
5. A) ApplyMapping C) Deduplicate D) ResolveChoice
6. B) The number of parameters a job requires C) The maximum number of DPUs allocated to a job

Chapter 10: AWS Automation

1. D) Resource tagging
2. C) AWS Config
3. D) NOT_COMPLIANT
4. A) To run a custom action on an instance before it progresses to the next state

Chapter 11: Creating Chatbots

1. D) Amazon Lex
2. B) An intent
3. A) ElicitSlot
4. A) True
5. B) Rule-based bot
6. D) OAuth

Chapter 12: Hosting Single-Page Web Applications

1. B) Web servers
2. A) True
3. C) Dynamic content

Chapter 13: GraphQL APIs

1. D) All of the above
2. D) Only one
3. C) VTL
4. C) Mutation

Other Books You May Enjoy

If you enjoyed this book, you may be interested in these other books by Packt:

Azure Serverless Computing Cookbook - Second Edition
Praveen Kumar Sreeram, Jason Marston

ISBN: 978-1-78961-526-5

- Integrate Azure Functions with other Azure services
- Understand cloud application development using Azure Functions
- Employ durable functions for developing reliable and durable serverless applications
- Use SendGrid and Twilio services
- Explore code reusability and refactoring in Azure Functions
- Configure serverless applications in a production environment

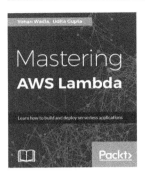

Mastering AWS Lambda
Yohan Wadia, Udita Gupta

ISBN: 978-1-78646-769-0

- Understand the hype, significance, and business benefits of Serverless computing and applications
- Plunge into the Serverless world of AWS Lambda and master its core components and how it works
- Find out how to effectively and efficiently design, develop, and test Lambda functions using Node.js, along with some keen coding insights and best practices
- Explore best practices to effectively monitor and troubleshoot Serverless applications using AWS CloudWatch and other third-party services in the form of Datadog and Loggly
- Quickly design and develop Serverless applications by leveraging AWS Lambda, DynamoDB, and API Gateway using the Serverless Application Framework (SAF) and other AWS services such as Step Functions
- Explore a rich variety of real-world Serverless use cases with Lambda and see how you can apply it to your environments

Leave a review - let other readers know what you think

Please share your thoughts on this book with others by leaving a review on the site that you bought it from. If you purchased the book from Amazon, please leave us an honest review on this book's Amazon page. This is vital so that other potential readers can see and use your unbiased opinion to make purchasing decisions, we can understand what our customers think about our products, and our authors can see your feedback on the title that they have worked with Packt to create. It will only take a few minutes of your time, but is valuable to other potential customers, our authors, and Packt. Thank you!

Index

A

Amazon API Gateway
  about 88
  deployment options 92
  serverless APIs 88, 89, 91, 92
  use cases 95, 96, 97
  WebSockets 93
Amazon CloudFront 338, 339
Amazon Cognito
  reference link 91
  using, for authentication 99, 101, 103
Amazon DynamoDB, with Lambda
  interaction, with SDK 144, 145, 146, 147
  using 138
Amazon DynamoDB
  basics 138
Amazon Inspector 306
Amazon Kinesis Firehose 257
Amazon Kinesis Streams 257
Amazon Lex
  about 310
  used, for building chatbot 310
Amazon Machine Image (AMI) 305
Amazon Managed Streaming for Apache Kafka
    (Amazon MSK) 258
Amazon Resource Name (ARN) 300
Amazon Resource Number (ARN) 68, 162
Amazon S3, with Lambda
  interaction, with SDK 136, 137
Amazon S3
  about 258, 337, 338
  as event source 133, 134, 135
  storage classes, characteristics 133
  using, with Lambda 132
anatomy, Lambda functions
  content 59, 61

context objects 59, 61
    event 59, 61
    handler function 58, 59
Apache Spark 257
API Gateway
  quota management 114, 115
  throttling 114, 115
APIs
  building 107, 108, 110, 111
  deploying 111, 113
  logging 116, 117
  monitoring 116, 117
  securing 98
Application Performance Management (APM) 174
approaches, for building GraphQL APIs
  AWS-managed service, using 348, 350
  Lambda-backed endpoint 347, 348
AppSync 349
Athena
  about 258
  data, querying with S3 285, 287, 288
auditing 305
authentication
  with Cognito 99, 101, 103
Automation as a Service 36
automation, with serverless
  about 35
  Automation as a Service 37
  configuration management 36
  script, on server 35
availability zones (AZs) 47
AWS account
  service limits 47
AWS Certificate Manager (ACM)
  reference link 105
AWS CodeBuild 234, 236
AWS CodeCommit 236, 237

AWS CodePipeline 234
AWS Config
  using, for automatic detection 297
  using, for remediation 297
AWS Free Tier
  reference link 46
AWS Lambda 44
AWS Lambda, use cases
  about 47
  Alexa skill 48
  backend compute 48
  chatbots 48
  data processing 48
  operations and automation 48
  web applications 48
AWS services 233
AWS Step Functions, using as Orchestrator
  about 147
  integration, with services 151
  state machines, with Lambda 148, 149
  Step Functions Local 152
AWS-managed service
  using 348, 349, 350

B

backend services 339
batch data processing workload
  building 258
  data cataloging 261
  data storage, with S3 260
  data transformation 272
  ETL blueprint 259
batch processing 256
blue/green environment switching 230, 231
bot
  brain, crafting 325, 326
  building 316, 317, 318
  connecting, to Slack 326, 327, 329
  testing 318, 320

C

canary deployments 232
certificates 105, 107
chatbot
  about 309

  building, with Amazon Lex 310
ChatOps 321
choice 149
cloud 9
Cloud Native Computing Foundation (CNCF) 29
Cloud9
  reference link 63
CloudEvents
  URL 29
code reuse
  enabling, through layers 160
colocated space 9
colocating process 9
concurrency 172
config-rule-change-triggered 299
containers 12, 13
continuous compliance
  implementing 298, 299, 300, 301
continuous delivery 225
continuous deployment 226, 227
continuous integration 225
controller 179
crawlers 266, 268, 269, 270, 271
Customer Relationship Management (CRM) 30

D

data analytics 284
Data Processing Units (DPUs) 274
data processing
  batch processing 256
  micro-batch data processing 257
  streaming data 257
  types 256
data transformation 272, 284
debugging 214
dependency injection
  benefits 179
deployment patterns
  about 229
  blue/green environment switching 230, 231
  canary deployments 232
  deploying all at once 229
developer-focused workflow model 190, 191, 192
development practices, Lambda
  about 177

ecosystem, using 183
function, structuring 178
optimization 181, 182
reuse 181
Distributed Denial-of-Service (DDoS) 88
DynamoDB Accelerator (DAX) 339
DynamoDB tables
structure 138

E

Elastic Block Store (EBS) 298
embedded security 293
Enterprise Application Integration (EAI) 30, 31
enterprise data centers 8
Enterprise Service Bus (ESB) 31, 32
environment variables
using 169, 170
error handling 173
event sourcing 25
event-command 26, 27
event-driven applications 27
event-first model 28, 29
events 195, 196
execution policies 49
execution role
creating 49, 50
Extraction, Transformation, and Load (ETL) 256

F

failure state 150
first-in-first-out (FIFO) 61
framework
need for 189, 190
fulfillment stage 313, 314, 315
Function as a Service (FaaS) 13
function policies 51
function
about 13, 14, 195
controller 179
ephemeral state 46
fundamentals 44, 45
handler function 179
high availability 47
invoking 45
pricing model 46

service abstraction 180
structuring 178

G

Global Secondary Index (GSI) 139
Glue job
creating 273, 274, 275, 276, 278, 280
running 282, 283, 284
Glue
about 256, 257, 258, 261
custom classifiers 261, 263, 264
databases 264, 265
GraphQL APIs
building 347
GraphQL schema
input 345
mutation 345
object 344
query 345
scalar 344
GraphQL
about 344
core concepts 344, 345, 346

H

handler function 58, 179
Hello World API 202, 203, 205
Hello, world!
in console 76, 77, 78, 80, 81
via CLI 125, 126, 127
with command line 81, 82, 83
with console 118, 119, 120, 122, 123, 124

I

IAM permissions 98
IAM policies 98
Integrated Development Environment (IDE) 63
integration patterns, evolution
about 30
Enterprise Application Integration (EAI) 30
Enterprise Service Bus (ESB) 31
serverless integration 33
integration testing 217
integration tests
writing 218

intents 310

J

JSON Web Token (JWT) 101

K

Key Management Service (KMS) 57

L

Lambda authorizers
  using 104
Lambda functions, invoking
  about 52
  environment variables 56, 57, 58
  event sources 55, 56
  execution environment 56
  types 52, 53, 54
Lambda functions
  anatomy 58
  debugging 71
  monitoring 72, 74, 75
  testing 70, 71
  triggering 140, 141, 142, 143
  unit testing 214, 215
  writing 76
Lambda layers
  about 161
  sharing, across multiple AWS accounts 167
  use cases 168
  using 163, 165, 166, 167
Lambda-backed API
  building 117
Lambda
  Amazon DynamoDB, using with 138
  Amazon S3, using with 132, 133
  bootstrap file, implementing 157
  example 158, 159
  runtime API, implementing 156
  runtime, enabling 156
language model 310
last-in-first-out (LIFO) 61
layers 198
Lex 322
logging 219

M

micro-batch data processing 257
microservices 18, 19
Mocha.js
  used, for creating tests 215, 216
modern applications 25
monolith 16
multiple AWS accounts
  Lambda layer, sharing across 167

N

n-tier 17
nanoservices
  future evolutions 22
  with serverless 19, 20, 21
node package manager (NPM) 199

O

observability 174, 175, 176
Open Systems Interconnection (OSI) model 88
OpenID Connect (OIDC) 100
operationalizing
  about 168
  concurrency 172
  environment variables, using 169
  error handling 173
  observability 174, 175, 177
  secrets management 171

P

parallel execution 149
partition key 139
pass state 150
patterns
  about 224
  continuous delivery 225
  continuous deployment 226, 227
  continuous integration 225
physical data center 8, 9
physical servers 10
pipeline inception 247, 248, 249
pipeline
  building 237
  creating, in production 237, 239, 240, 242, 243,

245, 246
plugins 197
programming model
  about 61
  building 62, 65
  deployment package, deploying 66, 70
  packaging 62, 66
  runtimes 61
  writing 62, 65
Project Management Office (PMO) 10
prompts 312, 313

R

release candidate (RC) 247
reporting 305
reports 305
resources 197
runtime API
  implementing 156
runtimes
  about 61, 62
  phases 62
  reference link 61

S

scheduled tasks
  running 302
secrets management 170, 171
security
  setting up 48
server-based local schedulers
  replacing 302, 303, 305
Serverless Application Model (SAM) 65
serverless development pipelines
  using 224
serverless framework, concepts
  events 195, 196
  exploring 193
  functions 195
  layers 198
  plugins 197
  resources 197
  service 194
serverless framework
  about 20

CLI 201
  dashboard 207, 209
  installing 199, 201
Serverless Framework
  SPAs, building 340
  used, for building Slackbot 321, 322
serverless framework
  used, for creating tests 215, 216
serverless integration 33, 34
serverless offline plugin
  about 210, 211, 212, 213
  reference link 211
Serverless Plugin Canary Deployments 233
serverless project
  managing 193
serverless SPAs
  on AWS 334
serverless stages
  using 228
service abstractions 180
Service-Orientated Architecture (SOA) 18
service
  about 194
  deploying 199, 205, 206, 207
Signature Version 4 (SigV4) 91
Simple Notification Service (SNS) 51, 298
Single-Page Applications (SPAs)
  architecture 334, 335, 336
  building, with Serverless Framework 340
  on AWS 334
Slack app
  registering 323
Slack
  bot, connecting to 326, 327, 329
Slackbot
  building, with Serverless Framework 321, 322
  deploying 323
slots 311, 312
software architectures
  about 15
  microservices 18
  monolith 16
  n-tier 17
  nanoservices with serverless 19, 21
  units 10

software development kit (SDK) 45
sort key 139
stream processing 25
streaming data 257
succeed state 150
supported OSes and libraries
    reference link 56

T

tagging
    example 294, 296
tags 294
task 149
test-driven development (TDD) 214
testing 214
tests
    creating, Mocha.js used 215, 216
    creating, serverless framework used 215, 216

traffic shifting 232

U

unit tests 214
utterances 311

V

Velocity Templating Language (VTL) 349
virtual machines (VMs) 11, 12
Virtual Private Cloud (VPC) 297
Visual Studio Code (VS Code) 64

W

wait state 150
Web Application Firewall (WAF) 89
WebSockets
    about 93
    reference link 94

www.ingramcontent.com/pod-product-compliance
Lightning Source LLC
LaVergne TN
LVHW081513050326
832903LV00025B/1475